# REVIEWS OF RI

*This book is just what w* _____ *...ngly secular and even hostile* _____ *, ... istians are withdrawing more and more from the things of the Spirit, as if the way to win the world was to become like the world. In reality, we need to do the opposite: to be filled afresh with the Spirit and to reach out and touch a dying world in the name and power of Jesus.*

*But how do we do it? Where do we start? How do we avoid making errors of judgment and practice? In this book, you will be guided by two pastors with a combined experience of eighty-five years of ministry, two men with a heart to touch the lost and to engage the culture. Are you ready to step out in the wonderful world of the Spirit? Do it with this book in hand.*

Dr. Michael L. Brown,
Host of the Line of Fire radio broadcast
President of FIRE School of Ministry

---

*There are many books about the prophetic ministry from a theological perspective and likewise there are many books filled with inspiring stories of the life changing power of an accurate prophetic word – This book is unique because it strikes a balance between sound theology and practical spiritual experience. This book speaks to one of the great issues the Church faces in our time – The Why and The How of being a voice to many who are seeking to hear from God in this generation.*

Rich Wilkerson,
Megachurch pastor Miami

---

*What an engaging, challenging, and helpful book about growing our service for Jesus by experimenting with and using Holy Spirit gifts. I wrestled with their suggestion that any follower of Jesus can prophesy even though few have the title of prophet. Trusting their gracious, encouraging approach to this Holy Spirit gift, I find their teaching rings true. If you are up for a spiritual adventure that grows your curiosity and joy, don't just read this book, use it as a manual for personal mission.*

Rev. Dr. Bruce Humphrey,
Retired Head Pastor of a Presbyterian Megachurch

*Deep, sound teaching coupled with lively, relevant experience written specifically and skillfully for our day and age on one of the key functions of the Holy Spirit.*

Gabriel Miyar, Megachurch Pastor, Guadalajara, Mexico

*Reading Reluctantly Supernatural in an Age of Reason is a wonderful reminder that signs and wonders, and the gifts of the Holy Spirit are very much alive in the global church. Mark Cowper-Smith and Bob Maddux have written a riveting book that promises the reader an inside look at the supernatural activity of the Holy Spirit in the lives of those who are Christ followers. In a day of cynics and mockers this book reminds us that the One who dwells within us is greater – greater –greater than the one who is in the world.*

Dr. Wayne Goodall,
Dean, College of Ministry, Northwest University

*This is an excellent book for anyone who is hungry to get past simply going to church and into the tremendous adventure of Holy Spirit led ministry. God has created in us a hunger to see Him invade the impossible and work through us in ways that are beyond our own human efforts. This book will help you explore the wonderful world of what He has made available to all that believe!*

Paul Rapley,
International Healing Evangelist

---

*This is the most comprehensive and informative book I have ever read on the gift of prophecy. The real-life stories will surprise you and the practical application will inspire you to step out and let God use even you in this amazing supernatural gift!*

John Ettore, lead pastor,
Gathering Place Church

---

*The Church around the world and especially in the United States stands at one of the most crucial crossroads in history. We must decide if we will be relevant and have transformational impact or return to the ineffectiveness of the middle ages. Today, people seek real power. They yearn for the true presence of God and are no longer fooled by cheap imitations. God's love and the power of the Holy Spirit are the only things that truly separate us from all the other solutions that end in disappointment. Still, why is the Church opting for an alternate power source to fill the void where the Holy Spirit was once welcomed to flow freely? The book you hold in your hands will answer that question and many more. It wasn't birthed in a marketing campaign or strategy session. It came about as a result of the Holy Spirit placing a heavy burden on the hearts of Mark Cowper-Smith & Bob Maddux to provide you with biblical keys to turn the tide and experience true revival. Read this book cover to cover and encourage those God has placed in your life who share your burden to do the same.*

Jason Frenn, Author, Missionary and Evangelist

*One is never enough. Two may be O.K. but three is even better and also more like God who shows Himself as our Uncreated Triune Creator. "This is the third time I am coming to you" (said a man who knew what he was talking about:) "EVERY FACT IS TO BE CONFIRMED BY THE TESTIMONY OF two or three witnesses." (2Cor. 13:1) In a world deeply hungry for the supernatural, if you want to find a clear path through the spiritual fog that so often clouds a simple quest for the joy and pleasure of trusting God, you need to hear wise words from the mouth of two or three witnesses. Here it is. Two who have long learned from the Lord passed on to you what can help you be more like the Big Three. I loved what I learned from this book.*

Winkie Pratney, Author, Teacher, and Conference Speaker

*Cowper-Smith and Maddux are concerned that the Western Church isn't more Trinitarian. That is to say, where is the activity of the Holy Spirit? Over the past thirty years I have worked in Asia, Africa and South America where healing, deliverance and prophesy by the power of the Spirit is as common as worship bands are in western churches. The authors think they know why the supernatural activity of the Spirit is much less experienced here. In brief, the west has a non- supernatural tradition dating back to the Enlightenment while other cultures were not influenced as much, therefore, more open to the unseen real. They also offer ways for westerners to participate more in that unseen real.*

Dr Ken Blue,
Author of "Authority to Heal" and "Healing Spiritual Abuse"

# Reluctantly Supernatural
## In an Age of Reason

Lepers in the Twilight

Mark Cowper-Smith
Bob Maddux

# Reluctantly Supernatural
## In an Age of Reason

## Lepers in the Twilight

**ISBN- 9781692105419**

# Acknowledgements

The writers wish to acknowledge the contributions of those without whose efforts, this book would not exist.

Firstly, to our wives: Claudia Maddux and Shell Cowper-Smith. They have read and listened to draft after draft of this book with patience and enthusiasm far beyond what any wife should have to endure.

Secondly, to Claudia Maddux and Mary Puplava who scoured our first draft for grammatical errors. It was a great gift of their time for which we are eternally thankful.

Thirdly, we wish to thank our reviewers who gave us the gift of their most precious resources; their time and their wisdom.

Finally, we wish to acknowledge the empowering of the oft neglected third person of the Trinity, the Holy Spirit, who has empowered every gift necessary to write this book. He is the inspiration for all we desire this book to accomplish.

# Table of Contents

Foreword    1

Preface    2

Chapter 1: Lepers in the Twilight    6

Chapter 2: Reluctantly Supernatural    19

Chapter 3: Bob's Brush with the Supernatural    24

**PART ONE:  HOW WE LOST THE SUPERNATURAL**

Chapter 4: Where Did All the Power Go?    29

Chapter 5: Talking Ourselves Out of Our Birthright    39

Chapter 6: The Church's Fear of Spiritual Counterfeits    50

Chapter 7: Getting "Carried Away"    59

**PART TWO:  OUR FAITH IS SUPERNATURAL**

Chapter 8: What Is Being "Born Again" Anyway?    68

Chapter 9: Can We Do Evangelism Like Jesus Did?    74

Chapter 10: Evangelism: Spiritual Experience versus Intellectual Assent?    79

Chapter 11: How Did the Early Church Do Evangelism?    88

Chapter 12: Supernatural Evangelism    100

**PART THREE:  HEARING GOD'S VOICE IS THE KEY**

Chapter 13: Defining and Explaining Revelatory Gifts    112

Chapter 14: More Terms to Define and Explain    123

Chapter 15: Is Prophecy Really for Everyone?    136

Chapter 16: Old Testament vs. New Testament Prophecy    149

# PART FOUR:  HOW TO HEAR AND SPEAK GOD'S WORDS

Chapter 17:  Okay, Show Me How to Do It                      167
Chapter 18:  No more "Ws", Now for the "How's"               182
Chapter 19:  More "How To's"                                 197
Chapter 20:  Being Natural with the Supernatural             209
Chapter 21:  How to Respond to a Prophetic Word              215
Chapter 22:  More on Responding to a Prophetic Word          232

## PART FIVE:  SAFETY TIPS

Chapter 23:  Pitfalls of the Prophetic                       246
Chapter 24:  More Potential Prophetic Problems               258
Chapter 25:  The False Prophet Syndrome                      280
Chapter 26:  Recognizing False Prophets                      284
Chapter 27:  Character Matters, Even for Prophets            298

## PART SIX:  FINAL THOUGHTS

Chapter 28:  What Did We Learn?                              311
Appendix A                                                   315
Appendix B                                                   318
Footnotes:                                                   318
About the Authors                                            319

# Foreword

Our assignment is to bring heaven to earth. But that's an impossible task without the Holy-Spirit-inspired supernatural. In Bob Maddux and Mark Cowper-Smith's book, *Lepers in the Twilight*, they sympathetically challenge the hesitancy many people feel about the supernatural through humor, personal testimonies, sound theology, and practical application. Our intellect is a gift, but on its own it is not enough. For the love of God to be manifested accurately, it must include power. *Lepers in the Twilight* is a comprehensive resource for anyone interested in both growing in the gift of prophecy and also in their relationship with the Holy Spirit. I encourage you to read this book. We owe people a full demonstration of God's goodness.

Bill Johnson

Bethel Church, Redding, CA

Author of *The Way of Life* and *God is Good*

# Preface

*Lepers in the Twilight*? What a strange title for a book. If that's your response, it's normal, but there's an amazing story from the life of an ancient prophet that makes this title as contemporary as any modern movie or hit song. It's all about stepping out into the unknown and seeing something supernatural happen. It seems that the more reason and science tell us there is nothing to the world of the para-normal, the more the arts and media create stories that contradict those assertions. This is because there is something in all of us that longs for these stories to be true.

Do you remember the first time you heard about the miracles that Jesus and His followers did? Maybe you were a child or teenager when you first heard those stories. Or perhaps you became a Christian later in life and discovered the Bible as an adult. Do you remember your first reaction to reading these amazing stories - stories about a supernatural God interacting supernaturally with ordinary people? Do you remember a yearning to experience the sort of "God encounters" the Bible is filled with?

Mark and Bob remember very well the sense of longing the Book of Acts engendered in them. Sadly, we also remember being told that these accounts were nothing more than the ancient history of Jesus' early followers. We were told that the supernatural events common in those days are no longer possible today. We were told that God no longer wants to work that way through us in our age.

Naturally, the longing for a supernatural dimension to our faith waned somewhat, but it never really ceased. Just the idea of such a life birthed a question in us; why would a supernatural God not want the people He indwells to be supernatural as well? If fact, how could we not be supernatural given the fact that His Holy Spirit is living within us?

When we asked these questions of our Bible teachers we were met with a variety of theological answers, none of which were adequate to dispose of our longing for "something more". The sad thing about inadequate answers is that once you accept them you rule out the probability of growth. Growth becomes limited from being a journey of intentional exploration to one of accidental discovery.

As co-authors of this book, neither of us set out on a spiritual journey to answer the question, "Are the supernatural acts of the Holy Spirit really nothing more than history?" Nor did we us set out to resolve the issue of the relevance of the supernatural gifts of the Holy Spirit to our "church age". Both of us discovered the supernatural dimension of the Christian life through an incidental supernatural experience - through experiencing a supernatural spiritual gift. These encounters sparked a desire to understand what we had experienced.

In writing a book about the supernatural dimension of the Christian faith it may seem to you that we are valuing spiritual experience above reason. Nothing could be further from the truth. What we desire is a healthy balance between the two. No lesser authority than the Apostle Paul tells us that the supernatural prophetic word must be judged against the reasonable application of scripture. Without reason and intellectual understanding, a spiritual experience has no lasting value. Our goal is to achieve that lasting value.

This book is the result of our journey toward understanding the role and value that supernatural Holy Spirit experience has in the Christian life in our age. It starts with a confession and a question. The confession is that we, and most of the Christians we have known, grew up with some kind of aversion to the idea of a supernatural dimension to the Christian life. We grew up with a built-in prejudice or, at best, we were merely ignorant of this dimension. The question is; why?

To answer this question, the book begins with an examination of our rapidly changing secular culture and its growing hunger for supernatural experience. We then describe our individual initiatory experiences with the revelatory gifts of the Holy Spirit: the supernatural expressions of God's power through prophecy, words of wisdom and knowledge, and the discerning of spirits.

In our investigation of this matter we look at the foundations for our Western cultural bias against spiritual experience as well as the psychological, emotional, and theological reasons for our aversion to it. Then we examine the Holy Scriptures to explore the texts used to dismiss the supernatural gifts together with those that argue for their continuance. Already it sounds rather dry and theological, but nothing could be farther from the truth.

This is more than a book of theology; it is a book containing stories of our personal experiences with the Holy Spirit, as well as the experiences of others. The purpose of this book is to give you, through sound teaching and real-life examples, all the guidance necessary to begin co-operating with the Holy Spirit in living a supernatural life style.

The Apostle Paul tells us to eagerly desire the gift of prophecy above all other spiritual gifts. For that reason, we are treating the gift of prophecy as the entry level spiritual gift leading to a supernatural life style. Our hope is that once you experience living a life "in the Spirit" you will never go back to "cook-book Christianity". Through experiencing the supernatural gifts of the Holy Spirit, we have both come to understand that there is more to the Christian life than merely the correct application of biblical principles, as important as they are. Receiving the immediate guidance of the Holy Spirit ushers us into a whole new dimension of Christian living.

To see God's supernatural works in our daily lives involves a walk of faith, stepping out into the "twilight" so to speak. We recognize the "twilight" is a place of uncertainty, pitfalls, temptations and counterfeits, all of which need to be discerned and avoided. We do our best to uncover them all. We teach how the gift of prophecy should be pastored, how to identify false prophecy and false prophets, how to respond to a potential prophecy for your own life, and the importance of character over giftedness. For those questions we missed, we would be happy to hear from you on our webpage where we will do our best to help you toward your own growing supernatural life with God.

This is not the only good book available on the subject of prophecy. There are books approaching this spiritual gift from a theological perspective and several that provide a manual to introductory prophetic ministry. What separates this book from many is the balance struck between the correct biblical understanding of present day prophecy ministry and the hands on [pun intended] instruction into how to operate in the prophetic gifts – to discern the "voice" of God and deliver His messages.

This book also benefits from being co-written. Two perspectives are usually better than one, particularly when one of those perspectives is that of a seasoned local church pastor. Between them, Bob and Mark have over 70 years of pastoral experience. As well, Mark has travelled extensively teaching and training local churches how to integrate a successful prophetic ministry into the weekly life of the church. We bring a very balanced and sensible approach to what can easily be a misunderstood and potentially divisive ministry. Good news indeed!

The Bible often uses culinary language to refer to words from God. Our prayer is that this book will be nourishment to your mind, soul and spirit. Bon Appétit!

# Chapter 1:  Lepers in the Twilight

What's it like to be on the outside? We've all been there from time to time. We watch others with their lifetime "total access" go by us and we're excluded. Most of us have had a moment in life where others have shut us out. It's hard to be on the wrong side of those big burly sunglass-wearing security guards that protect life's joys. The privileged few push past us and go on into the excitement and we find ourselves as outsiders. It's lonely, depressing and a big blow to our egos. Such was the fate of four outcasts at the gate of the ancient city of Samaria.

**"And there were four leprous men at the entering in of the gate: and they said one to another, "Why sit we here until we die? If we say, we will enter the city, then the famine is in the city, and we shall die there: and if we sit still here, we die also. Now therefore come, and let us fall unto the host of the Syrians: if they save us alive, we shall live; and if they kill us, we shall but die." 2 Kings 7:3 (KJV)**

Imagine a city shut up. Massive walls and iron bared gates closed to all but those who can legally pass through. You're shut out. And why can't you go in? Some horrible disfiguring disease, some freak of nature, some accident has made you a pariah, an outcast. You're a leper and under the laws of your culture you must not only stay far away from others, but inform them as they approach just why you must move away. "Unclean, unclean," is the mandatory cry that must come from your lips.

Here you are at the capitol of your nation, a city filled with starving people, a rebellious king and the greatest prophet since Moses, but you're excluded. It has been years since this small hillside has been turned into the leading city of the ten breakaway tribes of Israel. This northern kingdom has known idolatry, war and now famine. Sitting outside the walls of the city are four disfigured men coming to a startling conclusion. They are dying.

They're not the only ones dying. A whole city inside the gates is dying, dying in a way that would make a good script for a modern horror film. Within the city mothers are eating their children, rotten worthless food is going for a King's ransom and dried bird excrement has become more valuable than currency.

And where are you in this scenario? You're outside realizing that you will suffer the same fate as those in the city even if somehow, by a miracle of grace, you are invited inside. And what is the cause of this food crisis? Your city is under siege. Your city has been surrounded by invaders that are set on conquest. Your leaders in their military brilliance have kept the enemy out, but your foe is content to let you starve knowing that at some point you must surrender to the inevitable fate that has faced besieged cities throughout history.

Human beings can only go so long without the necessities of life until their social structure unravels, and their courage fades away like their ravished bodies. Your present predicament is no better. You're without food as well. And your chances of getting any are as slim as anyone in the city.

**Sometimes desperation brings us to that place where "It's all or nothing.**

So, what are your options? Sit and complain or wait to die. There is another option. Reluctantly, you can go out to the camp of your enemy and throw yourself on their mercy. Any other alternative means certain, slow and emaciating death. So, after some deliberation these men set out on the journey of a lifetime, a journey that will take them into the unknown and bring life to a dying city.

**"And they rose up in the twilight, to go unto the camp of the Syrians." 2 Kings 7:5 (KJV)**How does one begin such an odyssey? Reluctantly, one step at a time they advance against their fears, hoping that some miracle will magically emerge once they reach their destination.

Desperation sometimes brings us to that place where "It's all or nothing." Many times, it's nothing. This time, it would be all with a big ALL. It would mean abundance for them and those wasting away in the city. You see, these men had another player in their game. A daring prophet who saw deliverance for a starving people and who wasn't afraid to declare it, even in the face of mockery and unbelief. His name was Elisha, a man whose name had become synonymous with miracles.

During Elisha's lifetime, he would do twice as many miracles as his forerunner Elijah, leaving a legacy of power that even rested in his bones and raised the dead. He had declared a future wonder: famine one day and abundance the next. It was sure to happen, and God had chosen this unlikely troop of rejects to be the catalyst for this marvel.

And so, they set off on their walk of hope. What is equally as odd as their venture is the unlikely time they have chosen to begin it: twilight. It's that mystifying time when light either fades to gray or darkness slowly releases its opaque grip on the night. It's that time when little is clear, even as things start to become clear. It's that time when the unknown is almost known, but still must be seen through the eyes of faith. It's out into this dim world that these four straggly specters begin their journey into history.

**Sometimes the miracle we're looking for can only be found in that realm of the unknown.**

They begin their expedition as a walk into another world. It's a lesson for many of us today. A reminder that sometimes the miracle we're looking for can only be found in that realm of the unknown. God has met people there from the time of Moses to the present day. He meets them in that realm, an unusual place that tests our faith. It's a strange zone where fear and hope meet. To borrow a phrase from 50's television, it's sort of a "Twilight Zone." And if today we want to find the "Lord God of Elisha" we must take a walk into that same twilight.

The church in America has much in common with the four forlorn men at the gate of Samaria. More than any generation in recent memory Christians are finding themselves on the outside. We have become a pariah to many in our culture. We are not only outcasts because of our faith, but also because of our lack of faith. Many of us say we believe, but our declarations have far outdistanced our behavior. The moral and ethical failures of our leaders and common members have left open sores on the body of the church as horrific as any leprosy. We have become easy pickings for the "Richard Dawkins" and a troop of atheists who stand in the corridors of the media and declare our faith unreasonable and our beliefs dangerous. We can pound on the gates of the "secular city" all day and still they will remain shut.

Why are we "outsiders?" It just seemed like the other day we were "insiders." The head of the National Association of Evangelicals had access to the Oval Office and rightwing religious leaders wheeled power in the corridors of Congress. But, much has changed in the last decade and for good reason. That access may come and go with the fickle winds of politics, however it's obvious that the current arc of our culture is post Christian. We can complain all day about the bias in the media, but much of what has humiliated us has been of our own doing. We have handed our enemies the fodder for their media canons. Let's not forget that Jesus warned us about the danger of losing our salty savor. Is it possible that part of the reason we're being walked on is because we have lost our saltiness?

**If ever there was a day to be supernatural it's now. We live in a culture that is "set up" for such a time.**

Not only have brilliant men of letters become our antagonists, but television, movies, video games and pop music are increasingly taking aim at a church that is hiding under its rags, starving at its core and crying not to God but to each other about our predicament. This must not be a day of sadness, but a day of hope.

We have an amazing heritage as God's people. We have another player in this game and His arsenal is immense, His gifts unlimited and powerful. We can speak with eloquence to this generation in a way that they've not heard before. We don't have to be an echo of the past, rather a voice — a prophetic voice.

The twilight is that "in between" place somewhere between the clarity of waking and the mystery of dreams. It is a place where the supernatural meets the natural, where they both exist together in one harmonious moment. It is a place where we set aside the false certainties of materialism and risk encountering the God of the supernatural. Above all, it is the place we were intended to live – boldly hearing the voice of our God and confidently obeying His instructions.

Reluctantly or not, we must be willing to take a walk out into the unknown. God is waiting for us. In fact, God has commissioned us to walk there. If ever there was a day to be supernatural it's now. We live in a culture that is "set up" for such a time.

**"'The days are coming,' declares the Sovereign LORD, 'When I will send a famine through the land- not a famine of food or a thirst for water, but a famine of hearing the words of the LORD. Men will stagger from sea to sea and wander from north to east, searching for the word of the LORD, but they will not find it.'"** Amos 8:11–12

Look at the day we're living in. There is a famine in the land - a famine for hearing the words of the Lord. Today the cry of the prophet Amos has become relevant again. But first, let's go back half a century. Almost fifty years ago, a generation known as the Hippie Movement, was "wandering from sea to sea" looking for a "word from the Lord." It's true that they were also looking for a lot of other things: sex, drugs and rock and roll. However, the fact is that underneath the veneer of hedonism, there was a hunger for true spiritual reality. Evidence of this is borne out in truth. When God began to move by His Spirit across the land their radar honed in on it. Within a short time, millions of hippies came to real faith in Christ and the Jesus Movement was born. Our prayer is that history will repeat itself today.

## A Generation Begins Its Walk into the Twilight Zone

January 4, 1967 dawned bright and warm in San Francisco. It was unusual for that time of year. The clear sky and temperate weather appeared to be a good omen. As the sun chased the last bite of chill from the air, Golden Gate Park began to fill up with an unusual group. The "Tribes" were gathering just as it had been advertised. Thousands of stoned and animated youth poured through the Haight Ashbury district and into the area around the stage to be greeted by music from the likes of the Quick Silver Messenger Service, the Grateful Dead and the Jefferson Airplane.

By the end of the day 30,000 people had not only heard the latest in Acid Rock, but also listened to the preachments of Timothy Leary, Jerry Ruben, Richard Alpert and Allen Ginsberg to name a few. It was a blending of philosophies that included new age spiritual teachings and political revolt. It was a milestone marking the emergence of a new era. Even though the platform was filled with Berkeley radicals and non-violent spiritual gurus the theme, clearly echoed in topics ranging from consciousness expansion to women's rights, was prophetic in nature: It declared the rise of a new generation that would transform America.

If you had wandered into the park that day you would have been struck by many things. One standout would have been the prophetic overtones of the music. One of the groups performing at the event was the Quick Silver Messenger Service. During their set, they hammered out one of their regular numbers: Pride of Man. The lyrics had an overriding message that blended anti-war sentiments with clear spiritual and biblical themes. It was a sort of prophecy put to music.

*Thou that dwell on many waters rich in treasure wide in fame*

*Bow unto a God of gold thy pride of might shall be thy shame*
*Oh God the pride of man broken in the dust again*

*And only God can lead the people back into the faith again*

*Thy holy mountain be restored thy mercy on thy people*
*lord[1]*

Here you had rock music that was not only pushing out into a sphere of the mystical through the synthesis of psychedelic and new age spirituality, but it was also a warning of a frightening future. This rock band found themselves in the role of musical sages riding out like horsemen onto a cosmic prairie with an apocalyptic message for America and the world. This generation would not be like their fathers or their forefathers. They would bring their jeremiad in a way that no pulpit in America could bring it. The song, a cover written by Hamilton Camp, a song writer and folkie, was just one of many from the early 60's that used folk music as commentary and a hammer of righteousness against the materialism and warmongering of the "military industrial complex." The song contains this clarion call.

*Shout a warning to the nations that the sword of God is*
*raised*

*On Babylon that mighty city rich in treasure wide in fame*
*It shall cause thy towers to fall and make it be a pyre of*
*flame[1]*

As we think of the events of 9/11/2001, these lyrics have a prophetic overtone. And in a sense so did the Human Be-in. This "Gathering of the Tribes for a Human Be-in", was a sentinel to millions of youth worldwide. It was the forerunner of the huge "Summer of Love" that drew major media attention and put the whole hippie scene on the map. This youth movement that was being formed out of the womb of Haight Ashbury and Greenwich

12

Village was generations old. The Hippies' fascination with spiritual and cosmic thought was only a birthing of a movement that had been carried to this continent in embryonic form years before. It started as a European bohemian culture, which was then nurtured by beatnik musings until it came to full gestation. At the heart of these movements was a connection with the supernatural. How did all this arise and where did it take an entire generation?

Today there's a new movement across our globe. From drug filled raves that draw thousands to be inspired by rave shamans, to the growing interests in paranormal themes in movie and television, we are in an age of supernaturalism. Where will it lead us? Will we see a spiritual awakening like the one that followed the hippie movement, or will we continue into delusion and worldwide deception?

## Tomorrowland Visions and Yesterday's Ecstasies

In recent years, Boom, Belgium has hosted nearly two hundred thousand revelers to its massive annual rave music gathering. That electronic music festival and others like it are part of a growing global movement that celebrates dance, bacchanalia, creative expression and community on a huge scale. It's also being fueled by the massive use of psychoactive drugs like MDMA better known as Ecstasy or Molly. This movement is not without precedent.

The Human Be-In that took place in Golden Gate Park that January of 1967, along with the Woodstock music festival were forerunners of these events. The gathering in San Francisco in the 60's was made even more significant through the gift of huge amounts of LSD that had been donated by Owsley Stanley, the legendary underground chemist and pop culture Johnny Appleseed of the Psychedelic Movement.

Territory that had once been exclusively explored in the plush compounds of Harvard elites like Timothy Leary, and in secret CIA human testing programs, had now become a modern-day

13

land rush where young pioneers of the "purple sage" were staking their claims.

Many of those stoned out that day in Golden Gate Park were seeing visions for the first time. Most were filled with hope, but definitely not the sort that you get reading the Bible. They were visions nonetheless and would become an increasing mark of this movement. Drugs, and the "visions" they engendered, would shape a whole mass of youth and later generations as well as those who followed them into the 21st century.

Like the ancient prophets, this generation would not be content to merely see visions, they had to proclaim what they'd seen from every "house top." Sadly, the visions were often empty and faded as quickly as their drug induced euphoria evaporated. And as hopeful as their proclamations were, many soon dimmed against the greed and indulgence of the 1980s.

Over 2,500 years ago the prophet Joel said that one of the signs of the last days was that young men would see visions. We don't think he meant the kind of visions that come though psychoactive drugs. Nonetheless, one of the things that has marked every generation since the late 60's is their fascination with drugs and the ecstatic experiences that come from them.

Millennials have their own "Woodstock" these days, in fact more than one. Large "Raves" are held in Europe and America where drugs like Molly and other psychoactive substances flow in abundance and the DJs at these meetings have been called Techno Shamans mixing up music that enhances the effect of the drugs being taken by those in attendance.

As concerning as this may appear, there is perhaps a positive side. The generation of the late 60s and 70s delved deeply into LSD and other drugs, but when God visited them hundreds of thousands who had explored the psychedelic prairies of the hippie world soon had visions of Christ. Those "visions" became a reality as many of them followed Jesus with all their hearts.

This is our hope for Millennials as well. We believe that the ecstasy that they experience on their drug highs will soon become empty and instead they will eventually find their place at the great gathering of music and worship that will assemble around God's throne. In their hunt for the supernatural dimension of life many today have found the counterfeit. Our prayer and one of the purposes of this book is to prepare a prophetic minority that can introduce their generation to the genuine supernatural life that God has designed us for and for which we must hunger.

### A Walk in the Twilight Zone

One of the icons of the 60's was the television show, The Twilight Zone. Most of the episodes began with Rod Serling standing in front of a scene from ordinary American life, intoning words that carried the viewer into the exotic world of another dimension. As the program played out its alluring and twisting plot, the viewer was left with a message that things are not always as they appear.

**In this book, we hope to challenge this current generation with the amazing opportunity that is before it.**

Yes, it was a real possibility that there were other worlds and facets to life beyond the ones the viewer was familiar with. Today such shows have now found a permanent place in our culture. That sort of T.V. programming was unique for its time and one of the few that carried any message about "other world" possibilities.

Yes, there were others that dealt with supernatural issues, but they came on in the early hours of Sunday morning and were just the old "churchy" messages that had been heard before. Sadly, they were cloaked in the same old garb of a religious culture that was out of touch with what was really going on in the world and where most of the youth of the 60's lived.

But there was a whole generation of youth fascinated by the issues that Serling raised. Whether it was "beings" from another planet or magical happenings closer to home, they had a special allure. It told them that there was a world of power, a strange world of power just out of reach. It was there if they would but look for it. And certainly, a whole generation did. Now in the new millennium there is not just one program dealing with the supernatural on T.V., but a host of them probing into themes that range from super humans with powers that move nature to cosmic battles between magicians and sorcerers.

Today, in this postmodern world that is over halfway through the second decade of the new millennium, there is not only a fascination with the supernatural, but an obsession with it. In this book, we hope to address the whole realm of the supernatural and challenge this current generation with the amazing opportunity that is before it. We hope they will see that there is a fantastical and powerful world of the supernatural that is the legitimate domain of those who truly know God. These have a mandate to display it to a world that is wandering and wondering in the "twilight.

One thing is for certain, a fascination with the supernatural is alive and well. It is living in the hearts and minds of people like never before. It's clear that the human condition – whether religious or not is that we have been designed to hunger for a supernatural lifestyle.

Such a huge subject... where should we start? Our motto is: "When in doubt, look for the answer in the Bible." The Apostle Paul tells us to "desire spiritual gifts, especially the gift of prophecy." This supernatural gift is valuable because there is no problem or life circumstance that cannot be endured or overcome by simply hearing what God says about it. His word is our comfort.

Hearing a stranger speak the secrets of our hearts to us and then hearing him tell us what God says in response, in the very moment of our need, brings God's presence to us in a way that no other experience can. A genuine and specific prophetic word delivered in love is truly an encounter with a supernatural God.

Our premise, regarding the spiritual gift of prophecy, is that hearing God's "voice" and communicating what He is saying to those around us is a spiritual gift for all of us – everyone gets to play! We believe that God is speaking far more often than we are hearing. The problem is that often we are not aware of how He is communicating to us. Our culture is conditioned to look for special effects; while our God is content to use a "still small voice." How do we learn to hear His "still small voice"? This book will answer that question, and it will also explore how we came to lose our "spiritual ears".

This book is a practical book. Over the last 40 years we have taught this material all over the world, and we have seen the vast majority of participants become confident in their ability to hear the voice of God. We invite you to come along for a walk in the twilight.

Before we do that, how about you get to know a little bit about us. Both of us began "walking in the twilight" by being the recipient of a "word from the Lord." Our lives were radically changed through these experiences.

Here are our stories… but first…

## Some questions to consider:

1. What have you learned from this chapter?

2. Have you noticed an increasing interest in the supernatural within our popular culture? If so, why do you think this interest is increasing?

3. Do you believe that a desire for supernatural experience is a part of our human nature? Why or why not?

4. Can our Christian lives be complete without a supernatural element?

5. Are you ready to explore the supernatural component of your experience with God? If not, why not?

6. Do you believe that God can communicate directly with us today?

# Chapter 2:  Reluctantly Supernatural

## Mark's Story

Reluctantly supernatural. That about sums me up. Have you ever been in a church meeting where things get sort of out of control? I don't mean the usual out of control which involves a 25-minute introduction to taking the offering or a 40-minute altar call. I mean the kind of meeting where weird stuff is happening and someone is telling you "We're having a visitation of the Holy Spirit!!" You look around at the people falling to the floor, laughing uncontrollably, crying without shame, groaning and convulsing and you wonder, "How much of this is real?"

That's me doing the wondering. I suppose that would be OK if I was just a spectator, but often I am the one running the meeting. I am the one responsible for all this. I just can't help wondering, "How much of this is real?" I know much of it is, because I've been the guy experiencing one or all of those strange things at one time or another, but I also know human nature.

Here is a sad truth; people will do almost anything to belong. An older pastor friend of mine was telling me about a meeting at his church in which almost everyone he prayed for "fell under the power of the Holy Spirit." I was impressed until he said, "Most of them were "courtesy falls.'" I asked him what he meant by that and he said, "You know, the person just wants to please you, so they do what they think you want them to do." All very well intentioned, but it makes it almost impossible for me to avoid the question, "how much of this is real?"

I came by this skepticism honestly. I was raised by a lawyer. Usually that would ensure the high-water mark of skepticism, but it gets worse. My father was a child during the great outpouring of the Holy Spirit that came out of Azusa Street at the turn of the last century. He was a boy as the movement was cresting. He was in some of those truly power-filled meetings in which the weird and wonderful were common place.

Sadly, he was also in the meetings after the wave had broken on the beach and started to retreat. He watched as "courtesy falls" became the norm and people acted out a human version of what was once Holy Spirit empowered activity. He listened to one too many prophecies that never came to pass and his fine mind began to reject these meetings as little more than nostalgia.

This was the environment in which I was raised – with a skepticism about anything supernatural. All this is to say, I was raised with a religion without power. I had a built-in aversion to the supernatural gifts of the Holy Spirit. Not knowing why, I bought the party line that the supernatural gifts of the Holy Spirit ceased when the Canon of Scripture was closed. And that theology made perfect sense to me because I certainly wasn't seeing any of these gifts in our church and, so they must have passed away. After all, if they are not happening among a great group of Christians like us, where else would they occur? What a wonderful recipe for ignorance.

All was stable and predictable, and the years passed until my mentor decided to pursue his doctorate at Fuller Theological Seminary. While there he took a course called "Signs and Wonders and Church Growth." The course was taught by a man named John Wimber. He believed that, based on the testimonies of many returned missionaries from the Third World, the supernatural gifts of the Holy Spirit [which supposedly ceased about 1700 years ago] were responsible for much of the evangelism they were experiencing. The gift that most interested him was the gift of healing. He decided to try a very un-seminary like experiment. He invited sick people to come to the class for healing prayer - long story short, it worked.

At this point a little background will be helpful. My mentor was a full on intellectual. I had never seen a show of emotion on his part except perhaps his enthusiasm for BBQed ribs. He was, and is, a no-nonsense stick-to-the-facts kind of guy. We had a nickname for him; "God's Clint Eastwood." He really was the rock-solid guy many of us wish we were. And here he was telling me about these supernatural healings he was watching in his seminary class. More impressive still, he was learning how to pray for the sick. He was actually healing people! Or put more accurately, seeing the Holy Spirit heal people.

My reaction was shock. Had anyone else told me about these sorts of things happening I would have dismissed them as well-meaning souls, sadly deceived. Knowing him as I did, I could not dismiss his stories so easily and when he invited me to come down and see for myself, I could not say no. So off we go; two innocent and sincerely committed Canadian [conservative] Christians venturing into the weird and wonderful world of Southern California.

Culture shock does not begin to describe our first visit to his church.

Again, a little more background will be helpful. My idea of radical revival culture was using an overhead projector to sing a praise chorus rather than a hymn. We show up at the church which turns out to be a huge warehouse. There are 3000 + people milling around and most of them are young surfer types; T shirts, board shorts and sneakers. No one looks like they have a job.

Suddenly, without introduction, a band starts playing and the worship begins. Not like any worship I had ever experienced. Something came over me and I wanted to shout and cheer at the end of every song. I knew this was an unbiblical response, so I controlled myself until the end of the third song when the place went nuts. Everyone was shouting out praise to God and waving their hands and jumping up and down. So, I let go and did the same. It was my first taste of spiritual freedom.

A short mediocre message followed which, as an intellectual, I judged harshly. This was followed by what John Wimber [the fat guy who had been playing the grand piano] called "clinic". I asked my mentor what "clinic" was and he said "watch." It turns out clinic was an exercise in spiritual chaos where everyone was free to pray for everyone else. How unbiblical! Where is the structure, where is the order?

I was thinking of writing all this off as some sort of Californication of real church when a young teenage boy came up to me to tell me that God had a message for me. I thought, "He's just a kid. I don't want to be rude. I will let him deliver his "message from God" and then we can leave." He started to deliver his message and I started to cry! He was speaking the circumstances of my life and the secrets of my heart! I had never experienced anything like this before and I knew without a doubt that he was speaking from God.

My first rational reaction was shock and my second was anger. I found myself extremely angry with God. I said to Him, "I have been working for You for years and I am exhausted. I feel like I have been crawling across a desert dying of thirst in search of a small vial of water and here are these immature teenagers playing in a fountain and splashing the water all over the ground with no regard for how precious it is or how hard it is to find! And they are wasting it!!" I was jealous and self-righteous and angry all at the same time.

I came to terms with my bad attitude, which was just a negative way of expressing a longing for more of God. I returned to Canada a changed man. Thus, began my life with the Holy Spirit.

The point of this story is simple; my faith was transformed by an encounter with the Holy Spirit through the gift of prophecy. Some unworthy [in my eyes] surfer kid spoke things about me that only God could know. This was a drive-by encounter that changed my faith forever. It was a genuine paradigm shift and it got me to thinking, "What if experiences like this are supposed to be the rule rather than the exception?" I want to leave you with the same question.

## Some questions to consider:

1. What have you learned from this chapter?

2. Were you raised with a skepticism about the supernatural dimension of life? If so, how has that affected the quality of your life?

3. Were you raised with a skepticism about the supernatural dimension of your religious faith? If so, how has that affected the quality of your life?

4. Do you think your life can change through just one supernatural experience?

5. Can you recall a supernatural experience in your own life? What affect did it have on you?

6. What affect would it have on your life if supernatural experiences of God were the rule rather than the exception?

# Chapter 3:  Bob's Brush with the Supernatural

**Bob's Story**

In the fall of 1964, after graduating high school the previous spring, I headed off to college in the San Francisco bay area. I soon found myself deeply immersed in the budding counter-culture that was emerging in that region. It wasn't long before I was experimenting with drugs and the "hippie" lifestyle. This soon led to an increasing inquisitiveness about spiritual alternatives. "Trips" on LSD and other hallucinogenic drugs caused me to encounter spiritual dimensions that I had never experienced before. I had attended various churches as I was growing up. But for the most part, I had remained unmoved by the typical "church-ianity" I came across.

One day in late December of 1966 I had an experience on LSD that shook my idealistic world. The supernatural suddenly became a very scary place. I stumbled upon what appeared to be the evil side of this drug-induced domain. You could say that I felt like I had a face to face with the demonic. One thing for sure, I came to believe that this realm was real, however, when I held up my "experience" in this dimension against what I'd found in church, the church came up sorely lacking.

Christians had been witnessing to me, but it all seemed like just words; kind and interesting words, but still, just words. By the fall of 1967, after an odyssey that had led me from Big Sur to the desert town of Joshua Tree California, I found myself back in my home town of Chico in a state of apathy. It felt like after all my "searching", I'd come up empty. It was then that I was invited to attend a meeting in a home near the college campus. I was told that there was a 19-year-old preacher speaking that night. This in itself appeared as a complete anomaly to me. Most of the preachers I'd seen or heard had been old men that were for the most part completely irrelevant to me. I was fascinated and attended the meeting with more than the usual level of curiosity. This night my life was about to change forever.

When I sat down with the other 25 college-age kids that night I was first stuck by the wonderful singing that filled the small apartment. Then something truly unusual happened. They all began to sing in another language. Later I was to learn that this was known as "singing in the Spirit". Not knowing this language, I joined in, singing some made up chant of my own in English. I was immediately overwhelmed by a tremendous peace. This didn't last long. No sooner had I arrived at this new state of mind than I began to sense real nervous stress, almost, as if every nerve in my body was on fire. I sensed something very strange and new to me, something wanted me out of that room! The sense of discomfort was intense, and it took all my will power to remain seated. I was determined not to let on to those around me what I was going through. In the past, I'd practiced various forms of meditation. So, I fell back into the mode of peaceful contemplation, appearing to all around me to be in a state of "bliss." I was confident that my real condition was going unnoticed.

> **I knew immediately that there was a God of power and knowledge that knew all about me, right down to the internal struggles that I was hiding from the world around me.**

It was then that the young, 19-year-old preacher stood up and began to address the students. I'd never seen him before. His name was Mario Murillo. He had short-cropped hair, dark eyes and wisdom beyond his years. The first thing I remember him saying once he was on his feet was this, "There's someone in this room right now and you're very nervous in your body." As simple as that phrase sounds there was something truly profound in it. It was as if unexpectedly this young man had looked inside my soul.

25

It was as if God had lifted the roof off the building and pointed His finger at me and said, "I'm real." There was no way that Mario could have known that this was exactly what I was going through at that moment. Suddenly, I knew that God was there. I knew immediately that there was a God of power and knowledge that knew all about me, right down to the internal struggles that I was hiding from the world around me.

I raised my hand and acknowledged Mario's words. He asked me to sit in a chair in the middle of the room and instructed me that there were spirits in me that needed to come out. He said I needed to surrender to God's will and as I did the spirits came out without a struggle. Mario marveled at how quickly it took place. He told me to repeat a prayer asking Christ into my heart as my Lord. The prayer included words of repentance as I renounced the other religions and philosophies that I had been involved with.

I acknowledged that Jesus was the Truth. I was making a clear distinction between Christ the true light and the false light I had followed before. Mario then prayed for me to be baptized in the Holy Spirit. The power of God touched me, and I was soon praying to God in another language. This seemed to just explode from deep within me and although it was only a few words, within a few weeks it became a clear, distinct and fluid expression of the Spirit's gift. This language, called speaking in tongues was my evidence that I'd experienced the Baptism of the Holy Spirit.

The supernatural power of God, through the prophetic word of knowledge, had broken the spell of deception over my life and brought me almost instantly to an understanding that the God of my youth was a God of power that could outmatch any supernatural power of the evil one. Now almost 50 years later after nearly 49 years in full-time ministry, I'm hungrier than ever for the reality of God's power to flow through my life to touch a world looking for a "God who is there."

## Some questions to consider:

1. What have you learned from this chapter?

2. Do you believe a spiritual battle was going on within Bob when he went to that meeting that changed his life? How do you explain what was happening to him?

3. Have you ever experienced a spiritual battle taking place within you? What was the result?

4. How do you explain what the young preacher did when he described the "nervousness" in someone's body in the room?

5. Have you ever had an experience like that for someone else?

6. Are you open to God using you that way? Why or why not?

# PART ONE:

# HOW WE LOST THE SUPERNATURAL

# Chapter 4:  Where Did All the Power Go?

Let's be honest. Mark is not the only one who has an aversion to the supernatural. At least 95% of the Holy Spirit enthusiasts and spiritual bungee jumpers we know didn't start that way. Maybe as kids they were open to the supernatural world, but school did all it could to take it out of them. The fact is, until the last few decades, our entire Western culture was averse to anything supernatural. An aversion to the supernatural is an inarticulate assumption that most of us have acquired unconsciously.

Without an understanding of human history, we are prone to assume that this bias against the supernatural is natural. Nothing could be further from the facts. Until the last 200 years a belief in the supernatural was the norm. Even today, apart from the Western world, the world has a supernatural worldview. Our Western culture is the exception to the historic rule. Given this fact it would benefit us greatly to understand how our cultural aversion to the supernatural developed.

**An aversion to the supernatural is an inarticulate assumption that most of us have acquired unconsciously.**

It all began with a perfect storm. Humanism met Scientific Method, fell in love, got married and birthed the Enlightenment. [For an expanded discussion of the definitions of these, and more terms, used in this chapter and their interaction to create a Western world view averse to the supernatural please refer to appendix A].

Humanism began the move away from a supernatural faith by replacing God with humans as the legitimate subject of contemplation and study. Prior to Humanism the study of nature was not of intrinsic value. It was a means to a better understanding of the nature of God. This purpose is best described by the Apostle Paul in Romans 1:20, "**For since the creation of the world God's invisible qualities—his eternal power and divine nature—have been clearly seen, being understood from what has been made, so that people are without excuse.**"

Until Humanism, all science and study of nature [including the study of humans] was just another way of coming to understand God. In other words, to understand ourselves we had to first understand God. This follows naturally from our understanding of ourselves as created beings. We exist because we have a Creator and so our purpose and significance cannot be understood in the absence of our creator's intentions for us and the world we live in.

Through Humanism we came to believe that we can best understand ourselves by studying ourselves - apart from God. So far so bad, but it gets worse. Humanism now meets the "scientific method". It was love at first sight and marriage followed.

Their marriage results in a partial definition of reality that believes only what it can prove scientifically. We say a partial definition of reality because in the early days of the scientific method it co-existed alongside of spiritual and/or religious knowledge. It was both possible, and considered legitimate, to believe in both scientific facts [observations about the physical world] and religious experience of God which was largely emotionally experienced e.g. love, peace, belonging, security, and what we consider a personal relationship with God. Sadly, this two-tracked path to knowledge did not last.

Humanism and Scientific Method welcomed into the home of knowledge their new baby. They named it "The Enlightenment."

It is interesting to note that "The Enlightenment" is in the top 10% of words by popularity. The Western world is very enamored with the term because the coining of the term marks the beginning of what we consider to be our modern Western culture.

The Enlightenment has brought us to our present understanding of our world. It tells us that our world can only be understood through our 5 senses as guided by the scientific method. It relegates God to, at best, a first cause event which has politely left the room, never to return. Knowledge of God becomes little more than the understanding of our own fears and our need for explanations of that which has not yet been explained by science [with the promise that eventually science will explain all we need to know].

The Enlightenment gave birth to a host of ism's which have resulted in a morass of confusion which ultimately culminated in our present situation which is best described as a life without deep meaning and purpose. The ism's which define most of our world view in our postmodern age are Determinism and Hedonism.

**Determinism**

Determinism tells us three related things:

First, it tells us that all facts and events [including our human choices, decisions and actions] are the result of natural [think scientific] laws. In other words; humans are nothing more than a collection of cells which interact according to immutable laws of cause and effect such that our feelings and sense of free will is just a matter of chemical reactions.

Second, it tells us that; "Every human event, act and decision is the inevitable consequence of a chain of causation that preceded it. To put it another way, you are nothing more than a series of chemical reactions determined thousands of years ago. You are a prisoner of your DNA and your conditioning. To be truly contemporary; you are nothing more than a very sophisticated organic computer.

Third, through some determinist philosophers, Determinism has been taken to its logical ethical conclusion to tell us that the individual is not responsible for his or her choices because free will is an illusion.

Although these conclusions seem contrary to our sense of self, individuality and freedom of choice, they are entirely logically consistent with Humanism and the Scientific Method. If all we can be certain of are those "facts" which can be scientifically demonstrated and explained, then we can only be understood by investigating our humanity as the interplay of natural physical cause and effect. Crazy as it may seem, our culture has embraced many of the conclusions that come from seeing ourselves as nothing more than blips in a chain of cause and effect.

By way of example, our present understanding of legal and moral responsibility has been greatly affected. As little as 70 years ago criminal law was centered on the understanding that people are capable of making free choices and when they make "wrong" ones, they are responsible for their actions and should be punished. Today this understanding has changed.

The usual defense in many criminal trials centers upon convincing the jury that the accused was "forced" to commit the crime due to his underprivileged past. When humans see their choices as nothing more than cause and effect reactions, moral accountability becomes impossible. So, does the concept of good and evil.

When one's actions are predetermined, they cannot be considered moral, because no choice is involved in the action. Neither good nor evil are true; they are merely the expression of the current social conventions [which deteriorate rather quickly once good and evil become relative].

Another example involves the purpose of human life. Prior to The Enlightenment the purpose of human life was commonly understood to be the pursuit of God. This was replaced by Humanism by which man's proper purpose became the pursuit of self-understanding [apart from God]. The Scientific Method added the rules by which the process of self-understanding must

32

proceed. Only physically proven "facts" can be allowed, hence the new definition of a human as a sophisticated mechanism. So, what becomes the purpose of human life if only the 5 senses can be trusted to bring self-understanding? In a word - "Hedonism."

## Hedonism

**Our problem as Western Christians is that we have been influenced far more by our culture than by the Bible with respect to the place of the supernatural in our Christian lives.**

Hedonism tells us that pleasing our 5 senses is the highest good that humanity can attain. As repulsive as that may sound, it is completely consistent with Determinism. If we are defined by our chemical reactions, then let's have the most pleasant chemical reactions we can find as often as possible. If it feels good –do it! One more relevant ism to visit... Materialism.

## Materialism

Materialism is Determinism's practical cousin. Materialism is to things what Hedonism is to feelings. Again, the logic works. If humans are really nothing more than physical matter, then physical matter is the be-all and end-all of human purpose. The person who dies with the most toys wins! If it looks good, buy it! If it feels good, do it!

We know this may seem like an unnecessary rabbit trail, but these last two isms pretty much describe our current culture. In our opinion, except for a minority of genuine Christians and some kooky New Age gurus, our culture pretty much lives by these two goals; 1. As long as it doesn't hurt anyone, if it feels good, do it, and 2. The route to happiness is via acquiring bigger and better stuff.

## The Media has Superseded the Bible

We used the phrase "minority of genuine Christians" to describe the exception to the rule of Hedonism and Materialism very carefully and after much thought. Our problem as Western Christians is that we have been influenced far more by our culture than by the Bible with respect to the place of the supernatural in our Christian lives. Genuine Christians, on the other hand, are influenced more by the Bible than their culture. In our experience, genuine Christians are in the minority. To be fair, we came by it honestly.

Science, Materialism and Hedonism really were the dominant cultural values of the last 200 years. It is very hard to analyze one's own culture when it is the only culture you have ever known. The power of a pervasive cultural value to shape our understanding of reality cannot be overestimated. We are a people highly influenced by influence. Let's look at the influence of our popular culture on the average Christian in America.

A few years ago, Mark decided to compare the time spent by American Christians absorbing the truths of the Bible vs. our popular culture. The news was not good. The data has been updated to 2016 and the news is worse than it was only a few years ago. The decline in time spent reading the Bible has been a victim of the rapid expansion of the internet through smart phones and similar devices. Social media is also a major factor.

To understand the surveys, we need to start with the duration of Bible reading when our subject picks up the Bible to read it. For a reference to the surveys being quoted please refer to Appendix 2. Here is the breakdown comparing the percentage of Americans reading their Bibles to the time they spend per reading session:

| Minutes of Reading | % of People Reading the Bible |
|---|---|
| 0 to 14 minutes | 13% |
| 15-29 minutes | 24% |
| 30-44 minutes | 30% |
| 45-59 minutes | 6% |
| 60 + minutes | 27% |

At first glance, these seem like encouraging statistics. We "weighted" the numbers and came up with a "weighted average." It appears that the majority of times we read our Bibles it is for at least 37.67 minutes. That sounds like a very real commitment to Bible reading, but of course the real issue concerns how often we spend reading for 37.67 minutes. If we read daily, then that 38 minutes is very impressive. On the other hand, if the 38 minutes only occurs once or twice per year, we have a serious lack of input from God's word. We need to check the statistics to see how often Americans sit down to read their Bibles. Let's do that and at the same time compare the time spend in God's Word with the time we spend absorbing the world's media.

Media includes; TV, web surfing, Smart phone, Face book, Twitter, Instagram, iPad, and radio. We will start with adults. The statistics will show the percentage of people reading for various decreasing frequencies, the minutes per reading, the minutes of media consumption and the ratio of Bible input to media consumption.

| Frequency | Minutes/ Bible | Minutes/ Media | Ratio |
|---|---|---|---|
| Daily - 14% | 37.67 | 639 | 1: 16.96 |
| 4 x week - 16% | 150.68 | 4459 | 1: 29.6 |
| 1 x week - 6% | 37.67 | 4459 | 1: 118.37 |
| 1 x month - 6% | 37.67 | 17,838 | 1: 473.5 |
| 3-4 x a year - 7% | 150.68 | 214,056 | 1: 2841.2 |
| 1-2 x a year - 9% | 75.34 | 214,056 | 1: 5682.4 |
| Never – 27% | 0 | 214,056 | 1: 214,056 |

For the small proportion of American Christians who read their Bible daily, the ratio of God's influence compared to the influence of the world is 1 to 16.96! This means that the world has almost 17 times more input than God into the thinking of our most committed Christians. For more than half the American Christians the ratio of the world's input versus God's input ranges from 473.5 to 214,056 to 1.

Do you find this disturbing? Wait, it gets worse! The situation for our teens is much worse:

| Frequency | Minutes / Bible | Minutes/ Media | Ratio |
|---|---|---|---|
| Daily - 3% | 37.67 | 639 | 1: 16.96 |
| 4 x week - 11% | 150.68 | 4459 | 1: 29.6 |
| 1 x week - 11% | 37.67 | 4459 | 1: 118.37 |
| 3-4 x a year - 44% | 150.68 | 214,056 | 1: 2841.2 |
| Never – 31% | 0 | 214,056 | 1: 214,056 |

The statistics for our teenagers are very troubling because the percentage of daily Bible readers is much smaller, and the percentage of negligible Bible readers is much higher. Our teens are also the major users of "smart" technology, [arguably not so smart for those who profess a desire to know God].

Here is the question: if we Christians are not getting our values from the Bible, where are we getting them from? The answer is: the world.

Perhaps the following graph will help you to visualize what is happening to our thoughts. Series 1 represents the input from the world and Series 2 represents input from God's thoughts [His Word]. Remember this graph indicates the ratio for the radical 14% of Christians who read their Bible for an optimistic maximum of 38 minutes per day. For the rest of our brothers and sisters we cannot do a meaningful graph because the input from God would not be visible – get it?

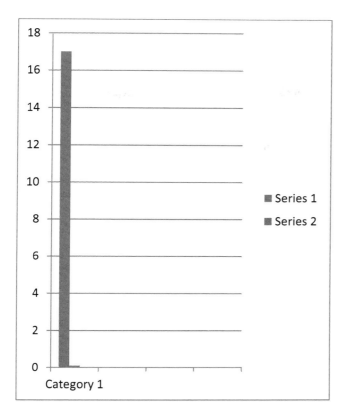

The expression that comes to mind is "garbage in, garbage out." How can God's truth compete with the "isms" of our Godless culture when we are being marinated with a constant barrage of ungodly values and assumptions? The present state of the American Church suggests the answer is; it can't.

## Some questions to consider:

1. What have you learned from this chapter?

2. After reading this chapter can you explain how our Western culture moved away from God?

3. Do you recognize in your own life how our scientific and humanistic values have affected your belief regarding the supernatural nature of your Christian faith? Explain.

4. Do you believe that God intervenes in our lives to override natural laws from time to time?

5. Does your Bible reading increase only when you are faced with some sort of crisis?

6. Where does your search for truth begin; with Google or with the Bible?

7. How often do you read the Bible and for how long when you do?

# Chapter 5:  Talking Ourselves Out of Our Birthright

One of the results of a failure to dwell on God's Word is that the supernatural nature of our faith becomes neglected – out of sight, out of mind. A significant portion of the American Church has dismissed the supernatural from its Biblical vocabulary. We say this not out of criticism, but simply by way of observation. Much of the Western church has replaced the supernatural work of God with human excellence and intellectualism. Sadly, we have even developed doctrines to dismiss God's supernatural work from our experience. Another ism, "Dispensationalism", facilitated the conclusion that God's supernatural work within the church became unnecessary once the Canon of Scripture was closed approximately 1700 years ago.

**Much of the Western church has replaced the supernatural work of God with human excellence and intellectualism.**

It is an interesting argument: we no longer need the supernatural power of God active in our lives because now we have a book about it. That is like going to a restaurant and telling the waiter, "I am not going to order any food to eat because I don't need to eat food because now I have a menu with photos of food in it and I can eat the menu!"

## Dispensationalism

Let's take a quick look at Dispensationalism. It tells us God's truth is revealed through a system of historical progression, as revealed in the Bible, consisting of a series of stages in God's self-revelation and plan of salvation.

On the face of it, the idea that God works through different stages of history to reveal Himself makes sense. There is little controversy surrounding the distinction between Israel's life under The Law and the Church's life under Grace [the period wherein God's law was written on stone tablets vs. when He writes it on our hearts through the Holy Spirit]. Dispensationalism itself is not the reason for the church abandoning a supernatural lifestyle. The problem comes with one of the conclusions that Dispensationalism facilitated; that being Cessationism.

## Cessationism

In Christianity, Cessationism is the doctrine that spiritual gifts such as speaking in tongues, prophecy and healing ceased with the original twelve apostles and/or once the canon of the Bible was complete.

In general terms, the idea is that God works through distinct periods of human history to fulfill His plan [Dispensationalism] and that the period of supernatural spiritual gifts ended with the first apostles and the completion of the Canon of Scripture, never to be seen again.

An idea this contrary to the history of Israel and the activity of the Holy Spirit in the life of Jesus, the apostles and the early church, must have a proof text. Without a Biblical justification, this idea is preposterous. Why would a supernatural God cease to be supernatural in and through His people? The chief proof text offered to explain away the supernatural in the life of "church age" Christians is found in 1 Corinthians 13:8–13.

After providing us with the "go to" passage for every Christian wedding ever celebrated, Paul goes on to contrast the eternal reality of love vs. the temporal gifts of prophecy, tongues and knowledge. He says, **"Love never fails. But where there are prophecies, they will cease; where there are tongues, they will be stilled; where there is knowledge, it will pass away. For we know in part and we prophesy in part, but when** *completeness* **comes, what is in part disappears. When I was a child, I talked like a child, I thought like a child, I reasoned like a child. When I became a man, I put the ways of childhood**

40

behind me. **For now, we see only a reflection as in a mirror; then we shall see face to face. Now I know in part; then I shall know fully, even as I am fully known. And now these three remain: faith, hope and love. But the greatest of these is love."** 1 Cor. 13:8-13

Cessationism argues that the phrase "when completion comes" is referring to the close of the Canon of Scripture. In other words, once the Bible is completed, all the supernatural sign gifts are now unnecessary. At the risk of redundancy, this argument is suggesting that once we have a book to describe God's supernatural gifts, we no longer need the experience of these gifts.

> **Cessationism is suggesting that once we have a book to describe God's supernatural gifts we no longer need the experience of these gifts.**

This suggests that becoming a Christian is nothing more than a matter of getting one's facts straight as far as correct ideas about God are concerned. As we will see in a later chapter, becoming a Christian is much more than intellectual assent to a group of propositions about God and man. Becoming a Christian is a supernatural event which, we will see, is impossible without the supernatural power of the Holy Spirit acting in the process.

For now, let's return to the passage. The word translated as "completion" in this passage is the Greek word "teleios" which is defined as and used for the following:

1. brought to its end, finished
2. wanting nothing necessary to completeness
3. perfect
4. that which is perfect: a. consummate human integrity and virtue, b. of men – fully grown, adult, of full age, mature.

Church theologians have come up with four interpretations for the word as used in this passage:

1. Paul is referring to the return of Christ [the second coming].

2. Paul is referring to the death of the Christian [when he will be released from the struggle against sin].

3. Paul is referring to the completed work of the establishment of the Church.

4. Paul is referring to the completion of the canon of the New Testament scriptures.

It is worth noting that the 4th interpretation, the Cessationist interpretation, is a very new interpretation. This idea never occurred to the greatest theologians in church history. It arose as a proof text for a lack of the experience of the power of the Holy Spirit in the recent Western church.

Returning to the passage, we need to ask ourselves which interpretation makes the most sense in the context of the passage and in the context of the chapters before and after the passage. Before we do that, we need to remind ourselves of perhaps the most important rule to keep in mind when trying to determine what a passage means for us today.

The rule is both simple and sensible: Whatever the phrase or passage means to us today, it cannot mean something it could not have meant when it was written. **Our goal is always to determine what it meant to the person who wrote it and what it meant to those to whom he was writing**. This is profound common sense.

When the writer [Paul] wrote these words, he had in mind what he wanted to say. He received divine inspiration and he had that meaning in mind when he put pen to paper. He was trying to communicate to a known group of people, at a known time and place. His primary goal was to communicate to people who shared his time and culture.

Good Bible interpretation tries to answer the following questions: 1. What did the writer understand he was saying? and 2. What did the hearers or readers understand the writer was saying? Another way of saying it is: the passage cannot mean to us today what it did not mean to them in their day.

With this rule in mind, let's look at the passage through the Cessationist's lens. In order for the then reader to reach the conclusion that Paul is suggesting that the spiritual gifts of power [which the Corinthian church is experiencing to an overwhelming degree] are going to cease 200 years in the future, he must believe that the letter he is holding in his hands will be determined to be on the same level of divine authority and inspiration as the Old Testament. Not only that, but he must believe that Paul is operating on the same level of authority as all the Old Testament prophets including Moses himself.

It is more than evident from most of Paul's letters that much of the time, the people he was writing to never came close to affording him this degree of respect.

**Whatever the bible passage means to us today, it cannot mean something it could not have meant when it was written.**

Can you really see this first century reader saying to himself, "Oh, I know what Paul is talking about when he refers to "perfection" is coming. Two hundred years from now this letter and a bunch of others are going to be argued about by theologians [which they didn't have then] and a vote will be taken and some of the letters will be elevated to divine decree and others will be rejected and once that work is done we will never need the power of God again. No problem, if people get sick 200 years from now, they won't need the healing gift, they can just read about the healings we are experiencing today and take comfort from the fact that, at least, it used to happen."

We have very good imaginations, but we cannot contort them to come up with this scenario.

Now let's return to the passage. The question arises: when Paul goes on to describe this coming perfection as a time when "... **now we see but a poor reflection as in a mirror; then we shall see face to face. Now I know in part; then I shall know fully, even as I am fully known,**" 1 Cor. 13:12, what is he most likely referring to?

To answer this question, it is critical to note he has *personalized* this perfection. He has made it *relational*; "face to face" and "knowing fully, even as I am "fully known." The most common and sensible interpretation of "completion" is the return of Jesus Christ. It is only then that we will see God face to face and know Him fully just as He knows us fully now.

Right now, I suppose some reader may be saying to himself; "This is an interesting argument they are making, but who are they to say these things?" Fair question, so let us quote someone with a truck load of theological qualifications: Dr. Gordon Fee in his Eerdmans commentary on the book of First Corinthians concluded his comments on the foregoing passage thusly:

"What is more difficult is the way the emphasis on the 'present only' aspect of the gifts has been treated. Most have simply yielded to the historical reality and have tried to make a virtue out of that reality, that for the most part these extraordinary gifts have already ceased for so many. The irony, of course, is that our present view [Cessationism – author's note] is almost the precise opposite of that of the Corinthians, who thought of these things [the supernatural gifts -author's note] as eternal and therefore needed to have that view corrected. One wonders how Paul would have responded to present day cerebral Christianity, which generally has implied that we can get along quite well without the Spirit in the present age, now that the church has achieved its maturity in orthodoxy. It seems likely that he would not be pleased to see this text used to support such a view of things."[2]

Our final argument, for the purpose of this discussion of Cessationism, concerns the context of this "proof text" within the rest of the book of 1 Corinthians. This chapter is sandwiched between two other chapters dealing with the supernatural gifts within the life of the local church. In these chapters Paul makes it more than clear that his reader is to "eagerly desire" spiritual gifts, especially the gift of prophecy. Much time is taken to explain the correct use of these gifts. At no place does he suggest that his teaching is only for some present time which will end when the very letter he is writing will be canonized, along with other letters he has not yet written, into a New Testament carrying the same authority as the holy scriptures he grew up reading. One has to assume that if Paul envisioned a time when the supernatural gifts would cease, he would have said so. To not say so would be intentionally misleading to his readers and Paul is not that kind of careless writer or leader.

Gordon Fee's statement suggests that the reason for the Cessationist argument is the historical fact that the church, at the time Cessationism was born, was not experiencing anything close to the signs and wonders evident in the early church. Cessationism is understandable and almost forgive-able because we tend to theologize from our experience. When something is not occurring as a routine matter we look for an explanation and rarely do we look at our own failure first.

It is a rare thing to encounter a spouse during marriage counseling who says, "This marriage problem is mostly my fault, I need to change my understanding of marriage and take responsibility to change." If this were the case, marriage counseling would always be easy and effective.

At the risk of redundancy, the Cessationist argument came about during a time when the supernatural was all but absent from the life of the Western church. It is a convenient exculpatory explanation which relieves us of the responsibility to look inward for an explanation.

As well, we should keep in mind that the "doctrine" of Cessationism was created in the historic context of the full bloom of the Scientific Method. The faith being exercised in the scientific method was far greater then than it is today. It was truly believed by the then culture [and by much of the church] that science would answer all our relevant questions about the purpose of human life. Because of this faith in science, and its application to medicine, it was less and less necessary to resort to faith for healing through prayer. During the rise of science, those who clung to their simple faith in a supernaturally active God [ready and willing to transcend the laws of nature] were considered simple and uneducated. The social pressure to abandon a supernaturally active God was extreme. The creation of Cessationism was not surprising under the circumstances.

**The Power of the Status Quo**

There is another factor to consider: human nature has a bias towards the status quo. Studies indicate that only a small percentage of people actually like change. A far greater number fear it and most tolerate it when they have to. When the church is weak in faith and has been living without experiencing the supernatural gifts of God, it has a strong tendency to stay in that state. We seek justification for staying stuck.

Back in the 1980s Mark was part of a movement of the Holy Spirit that had worldwide influence. Because of its visibility, it became controversial. One well known opponent of the supernatural gifts of the Holy Spirit said that this move of the Holy Spirit cannot be genuine because if God had intended to pour out His Spirit in this way, it would have started at his church.

Amazing arrogance, yet we all tend to think this way. If it were real, it would be happening through us. Since we are not experiencing it, it can't be real. This attitude never considers that perhaps these Holy Spirit experiences come to those who actually hunger and ask for them rather than remain passive and protect the status quo.

Like it or not, **God rarely imposes Himself on people who do not want Him. This applies to conversion, but it also applies to His works of power after conversion.** God forces no one to accept the gift of salvation and He forces no one to seek after His gifts of power. He tells us to "eagerly desire" after His gifts of the Holy Spirit, but He will not force us to do so. He leaves us free to choose to live a less powerful life. What an amazing God who respects our free will so much as to allow us to live a subnormal Christian life, if that is what we truly want.

Mark had a shocking experience of this some years ago. In his words,

*"During the outpouring of the Holy Spirit we referred to earlier, I took many of the leaders of our church out to a John Wimber conference at the coast. These men were all good friends and committed Christians.*

*I was sitting beside one of them I had known since childhood. The time for the application of the teaching on Spiritual Gifts came and the Holy Spirit began to manifest His presence. People were crying and laughing spontaneously, falling to the floor, crying out, shaking, and being healed. I was thrilled! I turned to my friend and said, "Isn't this great?!?" He looked at me with real fear in his eyes and said, "I have to leave now, I can't stay with this going on all around me!"*

**Human nature has a bias towards the status quo.**

*I said, "John, this is God at work!" He said, "Yes, I know it is, but I can't stand it!" He left and never entered a work that he truly believed was God. His loss was all because it was too strange and*

*uncomfortable - all because he had never seen it before. Kingdom of God "0", Status Quo "1."*

*You can have change without growth, but you cannot have growth without change. For most of us change is not welcome when it comes with discomfort [and it usually does].*

*During the same conference, I was sitting beside our pastor who I had also asked/strong armed to come. Ministry time came with the now expected manifestations and again I was thrilled. I turned to say something to our pastor and he was crying. It wasn't tears of joy! I asked him what was wrong, and he said, "I am your pastor. I have to lead you. I know this is God, but I don't know anything about any of this. How am I going to lead the church into this? I have no idea how to do this. This is like a new world to me and I know nothing about it!"*

*He felt totally inadequate and ill equipped. The fact is; he was ill equipped. All of us were. So was Moses when the supernatural confronted him. This was my first experience with the power of the status quo to resist God's work in our lives. Since then I have never underestimated its power and I have never been disappointed. Most people resist change even when they know intellectually that it is going to be good for them. Ditto, even when the change is God at work."*

There are a few more factors at work against the Western church opening itself to the supernatural lifestyle God desires for us. Let's look at them in the next chapter. But first...

## Some questions to consider:

1. What have you learned from this chapter?

2. The idea that God would discontinue His gifts of power through His people because the Bible has been completed is a very poor

reason for dismissing His supernatural gifts. Why do you think the Western church embraced Cessationism?

3. What reasons, if any, have you been given for not seeking after the supernatural gifts like healing, prophecy, demonic deliverance and tongues?

4. Paul tells us to eagerly desire spiritual gifts, especially the gift of prophecy. Do you eagerly desire these gifts? Why, or why not?

5. Are you afraid of the supernatural in your Christian life? Why, or why not?

6. How have you experienced the power of the Status Quo in your life?

# Chapter 6: The Church's Fear of Spiritual Counterfeits

We have made the case that Humanism and the scientific method have resulted in a strong bias against the supernatural, but a question may have occurred to you. If this cultural bias exists, why did we see the rise of New Age Spirituality in our popular culture? More people in the Western world have embraced a non-Christian spiritual worldview today than ever before. If we are so anti-supernatural, why the strong move toward crystals, pyramids, power centers, gurus, eastern mysticism and the like?

If you were asking this question - good for you. We believe the answer is; the golden age of science has passed. Science has not fulfilled its promise to explain our purpose. It has failed to deliver on the issue of meaning in our lives. Science has been very helpful on the question of "how", but it has failed on the question of "what" and "why".

**Science has not fulfilled its promise to explain our purpose and Hedonism and Materialism have failed to deliver on the issue of the meaning and purpose of human life.**

Hedonism and Materialism have failed to deliver on the issue of the meaning and purpose of human life. The greatest hedonist Mark knew committed suicide last year. He was not sick or in pain and he had lots of money so why commit suicide? He lived for things and pleasure and he just plain ran out of pleasure. He gave his life to nothing of significance and nothing of significance returned the favor. There was nothing of significance for him to live for.

More than ever before our Western society is looking for spiritual answers to the emptiness of life without the spiritual component. There is also a hunger for spiritual experiences of power. Sadly, this void is being filled by the dark side. Have you noticed how many popular TV shows have arisen that deal with the supernatural? Witchcraft, evil supernatural beings, vampires, werewolves, demon possession, mediums, white witches, warlocks, dungeons and dragons and the list goes on and on. Our young people are infatuated with just the idea of supernatural power, how much more so the reality of it?

**Much of the Western church is still trying to give intellectual answers to questions that are principally spiritual.**

It is easy for the Church to criticize this phenomenon because of the ungodly sources our young people are feasting upon, but criticism without understanding leaves us powerless to fix the problem.

### What if our human infatuation with the supernatural is God given?

What if our hunger for this reality in our lives is really designed to be a hunger for Him? What if we were created to operate as powerful naturally supernatural beings? What if Paul is simply suggesting that we act as normal Christians when he tells us to desire spiritual gifts? We think the answer is yes to all these questions.

The problem the Western church faces on this issue is the problem of being behind the culture. The Western church is still living under the influence of the golden age of science which our popular culture is rapidly abandoning. Much of the Western church is still trying to give intellectual answers to questions that are principally spiritual. There is a very sad irony here. At a time when the church could lead in filling the supernatural gap, it is falling back on either intellectualism [which attempts to deny the place of the supernatural in our lives] or it makes the mistake of throwing the baby out with the bath water. What do we mean by "throwing the baby out with the bath water?"

One of the most common dismissals we have experienced as spiritual-gifts-practicing Christians is that these gifts we are operating in are actually demonic spiritual activity. The idea is that our culture is full of New Age demons and when we, as Christians, begin to open ourselves to the supernatural world, we become duped by counterfeits. It is the same criticism that Jesus endured from the Pharisees – "It is by the power of Beelzebub that you do these miracles." The problem with this criticism is that it fails to take into account the definition of a counterfeit.

"Counterfeit: made in exact imitation of something valuable or important with the intention to deceive or defraud." The only reason counterfeits are effective is because they imitate something real and valuable. Mark has been to Tijuana many times and had many sidewalk sales people try to sell him a "knock off" Rolex watch. No one has yet to try to sell him a "knock off" Timex. Logic suggests that if there are counterfeits present, the genuine and real must be present as well. The sad irony is that the church is the factory authorized dealer for God's supernatural spiritual gifts, but it refuses to carry the product, because it is afraid of the counterfeits. A bit self-defeating don't you think?

## The Reaction to Counterfeit Spiritual Power by the Early Church

The reaction to counterfeit spiritual power by the early church is helpful as we wrestle with this issue today. The confrontation between Simon Peter and Simon the sorcerer has much to say to us. Let's read it.

**"Now for some time a man named Simon had practiced sorcery in the city and amazed all the people of Samaria. He boasted that he was someone great, and all the people, both high and low, gave him their attention and exclaimed, 'This**

52

man is rightly called the Great Power of God.' They followed him because he had amazed them for a long time with his sorcery. But when they believed Philip as he proclaimed the good news of the kingdom of God and the name of Jesus Christ, they were baptized, both men and women. Simon himself believed and was baptized. And he followed Philip everywhere, astonished by the great signs and miracles he saw. When the apostles in Jerusalem heard that Samaria had accepted the word of God, they sent Peter and John to Samaria. When they arrived, they prayed for the new believers there that they might receive the Holy Spirit, because the Holy Spirit had not yet come on any of them; they had simply been baptized in the name of the Lord Jesus. Then Peter and John placed their hands on them, and they received the Holy Spirit. When Simon saw that the Spirit was given at the laying on of the apostles' hands, he offered them money and said, 'Give me also this ability so that everyone on whom I lay my hands may receive the Holy Spirit.' Peter answered: 'May your money perish with you, because you thought you could buy the gift of God with money! You have no part or share in this ministry, because your heart is not right before God. Repent of this wickedness and pray to the Lord in the hope that He may forgive you for having such a thought in your heart. For I see that you are full of bitterness and captive to sin.' Then Simon answered, 'Pray to the Lord for me so that nothing you have said may happen to me.'" Acts 8:9–24

This passage sets forth the first confrontation within the church between the power of God and the power of Satan. Let's look at some of the issues this passage raises.

The first issue we need to address is the *fact* of the existence of spiritual power apart from that which God gives His children through His Holy Spirit. Simon moved in spiritual power long before he decided to accept Jesus as Lord. Satan moved in spiritual power long after he stopped accepting Jesus as Lord. Spiritual power is part of creation.

Satan was created by God and was endowed with great spiritual power. Humans were created by God and endowed with less spiritual power. Angels are somewhere in the middle. All this says nothing more than that **all spiritual power comes from God**. What is interesting to note in addition is that God did not take Satan's spiritual power from him when he rebelled against God. Neither did God take away their spiritual power from the fallen angels. Nor did He take away from humans their [very limited] spiritual power when they rebelled against Him?

Perhaps this is an example of the fact that God leaves us truly free to use whatever power we were designed to have, whether we choose to serve Him or not. His respect for our individuality and personhood is profound.

**The purpose of demonic spiritual power for the human practitioner is always to accumulate glory for the practitioner.**

The next point we need to recognize is that because all spiritual power comes from God, there is no difference between the *nature* of the power Satan uses and the *nature* of the power of the Holy Spirit. Therefore, spiritual counterfeits exist. The power we see in witchcraft and the occult resembles what the Holy Spirit does through us because it has the same nature and source –all spiritual power is derivative – it all comes from God.

Therefore, God gave us the spiritual gift of the Discerning of Spirits. The display of spiritual power will look similar if not identical, but the entity manifesting the spiritual power is either God through His Holy Spirit or it is demonic, or at its least potency, it is human. The similarity is what allowed Simon to recognize Phillip's display of power as real but greater than his.

54

This leaves us in a difficult position. What is to stop us from endorsing the misuse of spiritual power by an ungodly entity mimicking a work of God? What is the difference and how can we tell the difference? The passage gives us some great guidelines:

**1. Who Gets the Glory?** Simon used his spiritual power to make himself great in the eyes of people. He boasted that he was "someone great" and he allowed the people to call him "The Great Power of God." Contrast this with Paul's reaction when the people tried to call him a god. Paul corrected them immediately and made it clear he was nothing but a man who was nothing more than a servant of God. All the glory and attention were given to the true source of the power he was displaying.

The purpose of demonic spiritual power for the human practitioner is always to accumulate glory for the practitioner. The purpose of spiritual power for Christians is always to accumulate glory for God. The purpose of spiritual power for Satan is always to enslave people and draw them away from God. He begins by offering spiritual power which he promises will "bless" the practitioner with wealth, health and fame. This comes true for a short while and then destruction follows.

The purpose of God's power is always to set people free from all the destruction that comes from rejecting God's plan for them. This includes freedom from addictions, bondage to pride, control, manipulation, perversions, greed, etc. and, freedom from Satanic power and oppression.

**2. Show Me the Money!** There is a very ungodly relationship between spiritual power and money. It is not clear from the passage, but it appears that Simon was probably living off his sorcery. Without question Simon associated money with spiritual power. When he saw how the power of the Holy Spirit could be transferred by the laying on of hands his first reaction was to try to buy it with money. Peter calls this "wickedness" and prophesies that Simon's money shall perish with him – perhaps a prophecy of death?

Mark had a friend, a world class prophet, who told him of how he was holding meetings in Hong Kong and how many of the Christians there told him they would pay him many thousands of U.S. dollars to prophesy success in selling their houses, etc. He told Mark he could have paid all his living expenses for the year just from the "bribes" he was offered while he was there. He rebuked them and took none of it. Nothing corrupts the power of the Holy Spirit like money... which raises the issue of TV preachers... perhaps another book.

**3. Where is Your Heart?** Peter tells Simon, **"You have no part or share in this ministry, because your heart is not right before God"** Acts 8:21. What Peter is saying is that the safe use of the power of the Holy Spirit depends on a "right heart" before God. It is what James calls an "undivided heart." Moving in the power of the Holy Spirit is intoxicating. There really is nothing like it. To feel the power of God moving through you is absolutely wonderful. It is the feeling of being truly alive. It is like a drug. The only way to survive with our souls intact is to be sold out to Jesus and centered in the truth that our greatest reward is not the power but the person – Jesus.

**4. Surviving the Power?** Peter tells Simon through a word of knowledge that Simon is a "captive to sin." Peter tells Simon this *after* Simon has professed faith in Jesus. There is a very important lesson here for us. You can believe in Jesus and still be seduced by the powers of darkness. Machiavelli said that power corrupts, and absolute power corrupts absolutely. He was talking about political power, but the same holds true for spiritual power. The more spiritual power God allows to flow through us the more centered in him we must be.

Here is a self-test to help you determine whether you are in trouble with this issue; as you "eagerly desire" spiritual gifts do you ever find yourself desiring them more than intimacy with

God? If so, time to repent. Which brings us to our penultimate point.

**5. Repentance is Our Protection** Peter tells Simon to "repent." This is always the solution to going off track. Simon had many things to repent of; greed and pride being the main things. It is very sad that we think of repentance as some sort of exercise in self-hate. Repentance is one of the most enjoyable experiences a Christian can have because it is always followed by a greater intimacy with our Father.

Repentance is not self-hate, it is self-knowledge followed by self-correction, followed by a greater understanding of the goodness of God, which leads to greater joy. Repentance is a form of spiritual breathing – bad air out, good air in.

**6. Occult Power is Off Limits** Finally, we believe it goes without saying, but all occult power is off limits for Christians. If you have been involved in magic and occult activity or Satanism of any sort you need to repent of it and renounce its power in your life. You may also need deliverance prayer, if you find any residual effect of these activities in your life.

## Some questions to consider:

1. What have you learned from this chapter?

2. Earlier in this chapter we asked the following questions: "What if our human infatuation with the supernatural is God given? What if our hunger for this reality in our lives is really designed to be a hunger for Him? What if we were created to operate as powerful supernaturally natural beings? What if Paul is simply suggesting that we act as normal Christians when he tells us to desire spiritual gifts?" If the answer to these questions is "yes", how would this change your life?

3. Why do you think so many Christians are more afraid of being duped by a counterfeit spiritual gift than missing a genuine one?

4. Spiritual power is morally neutral. All spiritual power comes from God. The difference between the spiritual power being used by Christians vs. that used by demons is the purpose and intention for which it is used. How do you tell the difference?

# Chapter 7: Getting "Carried Away"

There is one more significant reason why most Western Christians have an aversion to the supernatural power of God. We believe it is the most prevalent reason. We have suggested that much of the time when God touches us through His Holy Spirit, it impacts us emotionally. This should not be a surprise to us because we received our emotional nature from Him. We are made in His image and He is an emotional being. He describes Himself at times as; jealous, angry, sorrowful, joyous, grieved, rejected, peaceful, etc. Our emotions are a mirror image of His or, in the case of our sinful emotions, a perversion of His. In either case, He is an emotional God.

Jesus told His followers that the truth He was imparting to them was so that their joy would be complete. C.S. Lewis once said that, "Joy is the serious business of Heaven."[3] Paul tells us to weep with those who weep and rejoice with those who rejoice. A rich emotional life is to be a characteristic of the Christian. And most of us can agree with this if we are not emotional about God or, if we have occasional warm feelings about God, it is fine if we don't get "carried away."

What an interesting phrase, "carried away." It suggests that we are in one place and end up in another and the connotation is that the second place is not as good as the first. It also suggests that rather than take ourselves there, someone or something else is carrying us. There is surely uncertainty in this image and a measure of not being in charge or in control.

These two realities, being uncertain and not in control, are very threatening realities for us humans. We wonder if this is exactly what God had in mind for our interaction with His Spirit? Maybe we are supposed to be uncertain about where this experience is going and where we will end up? Maybe interacting intimately with His Spirit is an exercise in trust. Maybe this is how He wants it to be. Maybe we really do start in one place and end up in another and maybe getting there is not up to us, maybe we really are "carried away."

Speaking of being "carried away" this is how we see the Spirit operating in John 3 as Jesus speaks with Nicodemus: **"The wind blows wherever it pleases. You hear its sound, but you cannot tell where it comes from or where it is going.** *So, it is with everyone born of the Spirit"* John 3:8.

### What does it mean to be "in the Holy Spirit?"

Some time ago Mark got stuck on the harmless little phrase "in the Spirit" as it appears in the lives of Jesus and the writers of the New Testament. They seemed to throw the term around without ever defining it. To them it seemed self-explanatory. So, he decided to look up all the places where the term is found and do a word-study on the word "in." We know, it sounds pointless, studying the word "in", but what he found surprised him and gave us an understanding of the Holy Spirit that brought clarity both to our own experiences and to our understanding of scripture. Let's take a closer look.

The phrase, "in the Holy Spirit" appears several times in the New Testament. Here are most of those verses that refer to someone being or doing something in the Holy Spirit:

1] **Luke 10:21: Jesus "rejoiced in the Holy Spirit."**

2] **Jude 1:20: "... pray in the Holy Spirit."**

3] **Rev. 1:10: "On the Lord's day I was in the Spirit and I heard behind me a loud voice ..."**

**4] Rom. 14:17: "… the Kingdom of God is about peace righteousness and joy in the Holy Spirit."**

**5] John 4:23: "But the hour is coming, and is now here, when the true worshipers will worship the Father in spirit and truth, for the Father seeks such as these to worship him. God is spirit, and those who worship him must worship in spirit and truth."**

In each of these passages something is happening; rejoicing, prayer, a vision, the experience of peace, the experience of knowing our righteousness and finally worship. Something is happening through people and to people and it is somehow "in" the Holy Spirit.

The key to what "in the Holy Spirit" means lies in the word "in." In each verse we've listed, the same Greek word for "in "is used. Here is how this word may be translated; "in, on, at, near, by, before, among, with, within, and into."

Here are the three definitions that best describe an activity or experience happening "in" the Holy Spirit;

    1. a marker of a state or condition e.g. "in torment",

    2. a marker of close personal association, e.g. "one with", "in union with" "joined closely to"

    3. a marker of the means by which one event makes another event possible, e.g. "by means of" or "through."

If we put all these definitions together, we get this definition of the phrase "*in the Holy Spirit*": "a state or condition of close personal association or union or joining with the Holy Spirit by which another state or condition, event or activity, is made possible."

By way of example, what is made possible in John 4:23-24 is worship. What this means is that worship "in the Holy Spirit" is a condition or state which happens to us through the power and

61

enabling of the Holy Spirit. It is not something that we can make happen. It comes about by union with or joining closely to the Holy Spirit. It is a different state or condition from that which we were in before we entered into "worship in the Holy Spirit."

The same thing is happening to Jesus when He was filled with joy in the Holy Spirit. It means that something happened to him through the Holy Spirit which was different from what He was experiencing before the Holy Spirit brought the joy. Similarly, praying in the Holy Spirit is a different state from what may be prayed apart from the Holy Spirit.

**In all these events, there is an increase in the "personal closeness or association" with the Holy Spirit. There is an increase in intimacy and an increase in communication between us and Him.** And finally, He [by His power] makes something happen which could not happen without His intervention [with spiritual power].

> **When we are "in the Spirit" we are moved from one state of being to another which result in a union with Him which is not theoretical but experiential.**

We really are carried away in the godly sense of the word. We are moved from one state of being to another which result in a union with Him, which is not theoretical, but experiential. And finally, some activity or experience is made possible by the power of the Holy Spirit which could not have been possible without His power. In every case such an experience leaves us with a greater understanding of the nature of God, not because we read it or heard it in a sermon, but because we experienced it/Him.

Mark's first such experience marked the beginning of his spiritual gift of teaching. Mark's story:

*"I was an evangelical intellectual. My Christian formation after making Jesus my Lord at the age of 28 was through the influence of Inter-Varsity Christian Fellowship, an intellectual lot in the best*

62

*sense of the word. I had no interest in, or understanding of, the Holy Spirit, beyond that He was the spooky part of the Trinity.*

*The local IV leadership had recognized a nascent teaching gift in me and had taken a chance on a very rough diamond – very rough. Today I doubt I would take a chance on me as I was then. They had already used me to teach kids at summer camps and now they were ready to loose me upon college students. They must have been very hard up for a speaker.*

*The retreat took place at a very beautiful place in the shadow of the Rocky Mountains. The weekend went well, without surprises, until Sunday morning. After breakfast, I returned to my room to prepare myself to teach. I was quietly giving thanks to the Lord and asking Him to speak through me when I was overcome by His goodness. That is the only way I can describe it. I felt His love so powerfully that I just had to weep. This was at 9:00 am.*

*It felt so good I just went with it. I cried for 30 minutes then I thought, "Church starts in 30 minutes, I need to stop this now and pull myself together." I began to "control myself", but then I had this thought, "Wait a minute. This is God doing this to me. Do I have the right to stop this?" In tears, I wrestled with this question for a few minutes and then decided, "Lord, I don't know what you are doing but I am certain it is You so go ahead as long as You want." So, on I wept.*

*At 9:45 am I checked my watch and went through the same issue; do I "control myself" and shut this down or do I let it go? I again chose to let it go and on it went. At 9:55 am my friend opened my door to tell me it was time for church. He saw the mess I was in and I saw genuine shock on his face. He said, "What's going on, church starts in 5 minutes and you have to speak, what's wrong? Are you going to be able to speak?"*

*To be completely honest, I was not sure I could get up and teach. I pulled myself together and said to God, "I don't know what You want from me. I know I am supposed to teach, but I also know this is real and this is You. I am going to go down and try to teach, but*

63

*whatever You want to do, I will do. If You want me to get up in front of those kids and cry I will do that."*

*I survived the worship without breaking down. I was barely holding it together when I got up to speak. The message began without incident. About a third of the way through the message, I hit the part about how much God loves us, and I began to speak about His all-powerful, overwhelming love. I started to cry, but I kept teaching as best I could through the tears. Soon several of the kids started to cry. Soon the whole room was crying. It was not what I had any intention of causing. It just happened. We cried for about half an hour and then it stopped. No one moved. We just sat in silence. I had never experienced anything like that. I had no words to describe it, but I knew it was God.*

**God is emotional, and God is powerful. God expects us to be emotional in our response to His emotions and He expects us to move in His power.**

*That afternoon I returned to the city and my band was scheduled to play a concert for a Christian charity. After the show, a girl I did not recognize came up to me and said, "I was there when it happened!" I said, "I'm sorry, but I don't know what you are talking about." She said, "This morning at the retreat, when you spoke, I was there when it happened, and it was the most wonderful thing I have ever experienced! What was it?" I said, "I don't know, but it was God." She said, "I know."*

*I have never forgotten the way she described that experience as "it." Neither of us had the words to describe what we experienced, but we both knew it was God. It was not until years later that I understood that it was the Holy Spirit that we were "in."*

*That experience was the beginning of what many call the "anointing" of the spiritual gift of teaching. Tears are now a part of my life. Although it doesn't happen every time I speak, it happens more often than Mark the ex-lawyer and intellectual would like.*

*Fortunately, Mark the Christian lets it happen and never tries to stop it. I think that is because he fears that if he had "gotten control of himself" that Sunday morning at the retreat, that experience would likely not have happened, and he and they would have missed what for him was a life-changing encounter with God."*

God is emotional, and God is powerful. God expects us to be emotional in our response to His emotions and He expects us to move in His power. It is fine for us to be "out of control" as long as we allow Him to be the one who is in control. Do you really want to get to Heaven to find out that you missed so much of God's power in your life because you were so worried about how you would appear if you got "carried away?"

Allow Mark to leave you with just one more story.

*"Many years ago, while in the first bloom of our new experience of the supernatural power of God, our city was hosting an annual psychic fair. Psychics and mediums, witches and warlocks, gurus and mystics all came together to spend three days advertising their powers. It was no small fair. It filled one of our city's largest convention halls. Like the rest of the churches in the city we had a very negative reaction [who wouldn't?] We believed our job was to pray against this fair and to hopefully confound its power to mislead those who attended.*

*Interestingly some of our church's more prophetic women had an idea to take our role much further. They came to the leadership and said, "We want to rent space at the fair and have a "prophecy booth." We want to offer prophecy from God for free to whoever wants it. We will make sure everyone knows we are doing it by the power of the Holy Spirit and in Jesus' name. Will our church support it?"*

*We thought it was a great idea, so we did it. The women took shifts at the booth and prophesied over many people. In the three days of the fair 24 people accepted Jesus as their Lord and Savior! All had been accurately prophesied over, the secrets of their hearts had been spoken by a complete stranger, and their minds had been freed to hear the gospel! As well, many of the psychics responded positively to our presence at the fair! They actually thought it was unusual and very cool that a church was interested in the supernatural!! Can anyone say, "irony?"*"

Finally, the moment you have been waiting for; the conclusion:

For all of the foregoing reasons, for many Western Christians this is where we live; the supernatural dimension of our faith has become an embarrassment to us. We live apologizing for and avoiding it, yet we are designed by God to move in His spiritual power. We should seek to move in supernatural spiritual power. To fail to do so is to miss out on our birthright. Do not fear God's power, it is always for your best.

All the foregoing is just to keep you safe and close to Him as you move with Him in His power. Maybe it is time for you to get carried away...

## Some questions to consider:

1. What have you learned from this chapter?

2. We know Christians who will jump up and down, scream with joy, and raise their hands high in the air at football games, but never lift their hands out of their pockets during worship at church. Why the difference?

3. Do you have a fear of getting carried away by the Holy Spirit? If so, what are you afraid of?

4. Do you think there might be some experiences with God that only come if you risk getting carried away? If so, what is holding you     back?
5. What percentage of your faith with God is theological and what percentage is experiential? What do you think the percentages should be?
6. Are you embarrassed by the supernatural acts of God?

# PART TWO:

# OUR FAITH IS SUPERNATURAL

# Chapter 8: What Is Being "Born Again" Anyway?

A psychologist once said that each area of human endeavor develops its own specialized jargon in order to lend exclusivity to its practitioners. You know what we are talking about. You are at a party and you ask this obviously nerdy guy what he does for a living. He tells you he designs the interface between the CPU and the RAM so that the VC will run the new GC on the flash drive through the USB port rather than from a SIM card. Your eyes glass over and you realize this guy may be a nerd, but he knows more than you will ever know about that mysterious box on your desk. He smiles smugly as you retreat.

We all do it, but it is really annoying. Not just socially annoying, but annoying as in getting in the way of true communication. Take the phrase "born again" that we throw around as if we know what we are talking about. What do we mean by "born again?" For most of us, the answer, which brings a halt to our actually thinking about the phrase, is nothing more than "accepting Jesus as my personal Savior." Here is another potentially confusing phrase. Who does the accepting, Him or me? Is the option open to me to accept Him as my impersonal Savior?

We think you get what we are driving at. We throw around a lot of Christianeze assuming we all agree on what the words mean. Much of the time the person using the phrase really doesn't know what they think the phrase means. Mark knows. He has an irritating habit of asking people what they mean by these kinds of phrases and much of the time they have a hard time defining their terms. So, let's take a few minutes and ask ourselves what we mean by being "born again."

It must be an important term because Jesus tells us we need to have it happen to us. In fact, He says we MUST be born again. He is not the only one who uses the analogy of new birth. John helps define the term by saying, **"Yet to all who did receive him, to those who believed in his name, He gave the right to become children of God—children born not of natural descent, nor of human decision or a husband's will, but born of God"** John 1:12–13.

## What does "born again" mean?

This verse has been repeated so often that for most of us it has lost its shock value. The fact is, this is a very shocking verse. It is actually saying that something can happen to us which turns us into God's children! Think about it for a minute. It is not saying that we can become God's servants or even His employees. It is saying that we become His actual, really, no kidding, children! John could have used the phrase "sons of God" to describe the change the new birth brings, but he chose to describe us as God's "children."

John is emphasizing the fact that through this new birth we are becoming God's children in a way that results in a radical change of our quintessential nature. John expands on this new birth and puts it this way, **"No one who is born of God will continue to sin, because God's *seed* remains in them; they cannot go on sinning, because they have been born of God"** 1 John 3:9.

> John is emphasizing the fact that through this new birth we are becoming God's children in a way that results in a radical change of our quintessential nature.

The word we translate as "seed" in this verse is the Greek word "sperma", from which we derive our word "sperm". Both words accurately describe a reproduction of the essential nature of the father into the child. Without any risk of exaggeration, what is happening in the conversion experience can be described as a miracle. Becoming "born again" as a child of God means having His quintessential spiritual nature injected into our personhood with the result that we become reborn into His very nature! This is what Paul is talking about when he tells us that once we become a Christian "all things become new". We are truly a "new creation". His nature has come to live within us. As we cooperate with His nature within us, we are being transformed into His likeness.

This is a supernatural event! It is completely without precedent in all of God's creation. It is humanly impossible! It is a deed of supernatural power. It is also kind of spooky. It's sort of like those B grade science fiction movies. An alien life form enters you and slowly turns you into one of "them". It's sort of like getting "carried away" ... Thankfully it is Jesus who is doing the carrying and it is His nature that is being produced in us.

## How Do We Become "born again"?

So far, we have looked at the "what" of conversion but not the "how." Let's look at the how to see if it too is a supernatural process.

The intellectualism presently in charge of much of Western Christianity has resulted in a rather skewed explanation of the process of becoming a Christian. It is often explained as simply an intellectual process wherein the truth of God's goodness and His plan to save us from our sins is presented with logic and reason such that the hearer decides to accept the arguments. From the point of acceptance of these truths, he is now a Christian. It is sort of like hearing about the benefits of joining a club, checking out the rules and upfront costs and determining that the privileges of membership are worth the costs and the rules - all very clean and reasonable.

By the way, this explains much of our fascination with technique in doing evangelism. Formulas abound, and so do seminars and consultants telling us about multimedia systems, graphics, market studies, etc. Isn't it strange how we will put our faith in marketing techniques when it comes to things of the Spirit?

Notice from the previous discussion that the entire onus of deciding to believe the truth is on the hearer. We assume that he or she is possessed of a free will, ready and willing to accept the truth if it is adequately presented. But what if that is not the case? What if our pre-Christian is immune to the truth? To use a computer analogy, what if the human operating system has been corrupted by a virus and simply can't respond to the truth? What if the issue is not unwillingness, but rather inability? That would change everything.

This is in fact the case.

**"For Christ did not send me to baptize but to proclaim the gospel, and not with eloquent wisdom, so that the cross of Christ might not be emptied of its power. For the message about the cross is foolishness to those who are perishing, but to us who are being saved it is the power of God ... For since, in the wisdom of God, the world did not know God through wisdom, God decided, through the foolishness of our proclamation, to save those who believe ... But God chose what is foolish in the world to shame the wise; God chose what is weak in the world to shame the strong; God chose what is low and despised in the world, things that are not, to reduce to nothing things that are, so that no one might boast in the presence of God."** 1 Cor. 1:17–27

**"And I came to you in weakness and in fear and in much trembling. My speech and my proclamation were not with plausible words of wisdom, but with a demonstration of the Spirit and of power, so that your faith might rest not on human wisdom but on the power of God."** 1 Cor. 2:3

What these verses and others in the Bible are telling us is that our faith is foolishness to the world. This is not news to anyone who has tried to tell people about Jesus. What these verses are saying that may be news is that this is by design! It is not an unfortunate accident of misunderstanding. It is not as if God wrote a very clear message, but the word processor mixed up the words.

God has no intention of having His truth dependent upon human ability to be understood. If this were the case our being saved from our sins would be the result of our clever ability to reason.

We would be our own authority on what is true; apart from Him. God does not want His truth and our faith dependent upon anything human, but upon His power. He has allowed that His truth will seem foolish to those who are spiritually blind so that they must be totally dependent on *His* power to know *His* truth.

Because God does not want our understanding of His truth to be a result of our ability to reason, He has allowed Satan a hand in seeing to it that His message is foolishness to the world. **"In their case the god of this world has blinded the minds of the unbelievers, so that they *cannot* see the light of the gospel of the glory of Christ, who is the image of God"** 2 Cor. 4:4. What we are seeing here is an *inability* to perceive truth rather than a *refusal* to believe it.

The unfortunate result is that we are stuck with trying to tell people a message that, to their natural minds, makes no sense. Humbling, isn't it?

> **We are stuck with trying to tell people a message that, to their natural minds, makes no sense at all.**

When we combine Paul's emphasis on a conversion process, which rests on God's power rather than on our delivery, with the understanding that Satan has literally rendered our hearers blind to the truth, we come to see conversion as a truly supernatural event. So much so that Paul relies on a "demonstration of the Spirit and of power."

Given the context of this statement, which we will examine in a later chapter, we will see that the demonstrations of the Spirit and of power which Paul is referring to are in fact the operation of these supernatural spiritual gifts that many of us would rather do without.

To sum up; both the event of the new birth and the means of the new birth are supernaturally facilitated. Following Paul's reasoning; our lives should be demonstrations of a life lived supernaturally. We should be naturally supernatural and supernaturally natural. There should be actions we demonstrate to which the world can respond and say, "That was not human ability. That was supernatural." And we should do them in a way that causes the world to say, "That is amazing! He seems like such an ordinary guy. Wow, his God is amazing!"

At the risk of being considered mean-spirited let us risk saying this; the reason that the Western church is so ineffective in telling people about Jesus these days is not that we are silent. It is that far too often what we are saying and doing has been washed very carefully to remove all the spots that might be seen as foolish and/or supernatural. What is left is very acceptable, very explainable, very natural and very powerless. It is also very boring!

## Some questions to consider:

1. What have you learned from this chapter?

2. In your own words how would you explain the supernatural aspect of becoming a Christian?

3. When you imagine leading someone to Jesus, do you focus on the forgiveness of their sins or on the transformation God has planned for them and Jesus has paid for?

4. 2 Cor. 4:4 tells us that Satan has blinded the spiritual eyes of the lost so that they *cannot* see the truth of the gospel. If this is true, what is it going to take to free them from that blindness?

5. Paul implies that we need "demonstrations of the power of the Holy Spirit" to engender faith in those we witness to. What do you think such demonstrations look like?

# Chapter 9: Can We Do Evangelism Like Jesus Did?

Since our earliest years as a Christians we have been taught some version of the following means of evangelism: through an intense focus on acquiring the character of Jesus I become so wonderful that people spontaneously tell me they wish they were more like me. The ultimate version has them telling me they want what I have [and I'm not talking about my car or my wife].

The idea is that they recognize the wonderful loving character of Jesus in me and then I get to say, "You can be like Jesus too, you just need to believe in Him!" I then take them through the sinner's prayer and soon, they too are working to acquire the manifest love of Jesus, so they too can hear those magic words, "I want to be more like you!" So far it hasn't happened to us. We suppose that says much about us, but it might provoke another question, that being "How did Jesus [the guy we are trying to be like] do evangelism? Did it work this way for Him?"

In our hearts, we want the answer to be "of course" because He **is** wonderful. We reason, "How could anyone meet Him and not recognize His perfect moral character and His overwhelming holiness and love?" We assume that everyone who met Him was confronted with His goodness, but is this what actually happened?

To answer this question let's look at how those close to Jesus reacted to Him. But first, let's be absolutely certain about one thing; Jesus is the only one who truly justifies the question, "How can I be more like you?" The writer of the book of Hebrews makes this abundantly clear:

**"The Son is the radiance of God's glory and the *exact representation of his being* ..."** Heb. 1:3

Given this truth, everyone who meets Jesus, if only for a few moments, should recognize His holiness through His character and loving nature. Is this the case?

Imagine having a friend who was completely holy - never a bad thought and certainly never a bad deed. It must have been like that for John the Baptist. He was Jesus' cousin and they were born a few months apart. They probably played together and sat together at the kid's table during all the in-law dinners. Not only that, they probably went to parochial school together. Maybe they were trained by the same Rabbi. No question - they were close.

John the Baptist was no ordinary kid either. From his earliest years he had a life mission. It was very simple. All he was living for was to recognize the Messiah and announce Him to the world. We think John knew this fairly early on in his life. In other words, for most of his life he was on the lookout for "the Holy One from God." He knew what he was looking for – someone holy like him, only more so. So here is the amazing thing - John grew up across the table from perfect holiness and never recognized it! His cousin was sinless and John, who was working on his PhD in holiness, completely missed it!

John himself describes it this way, **"Then John gave this testimony: 'I saw the Spirit come down from heaven as a dove and remain on Him. *I would not have known Him*, except the One who sent me to baptize with water told me, "The man on whom you see the Spirit come down and remain is He who will baptize with the Holy Spirit." I have seen, and I testify that this is the Son of God.'"** John 1:32–34.

John himself says, "I would not have known Him." Now this is inexplicable! A godly man who spends his life looking for the truly Holy One cannot see Him from across the dinner table! John was not the only one who missed identifying godly character when he saw it.

**"Now some Pharisees who had been sent questioned him [John], 'Why then do you baptize if you are not the Christ, nor**

> **God's humility means that within the trinity none of the three want the glory due their nature.**

*Elijah, nor the Prophet?' 'I baptize with water,' John replied, 'but among you stands one you do not know.'"* John 1:24–26

Here is another shocker; these are the Pharisees we are talking about. They spend every waking minute debating what is and isn't holy. They write books about it and sit at the city gates holding public seminars about holiness. They are the judges who sit on the bench in the court of holiness! Not only that, they educated Jesus. Some of them saw Him every day! Jesus grew up under their religious leadership! So how could these experts in holiness miss perfect holiness when it was literally staring them in the face?

## Humility

There are many possible answers to this question, some of which are discussed in Mark's book, "Is God Religious?"[7], but for now let us deal with what we think is the most relevant answer. It has to do with humility. The Bible tells us that God is humble. Amazing, isn't it? The Creator of the universe is humble! How can that be? Our God is unique in that He is three persons in such unity that they are one God. His humility means that within the trinity none of the three want the glory due their nature.

Have you ever noticed how each of the three is always diverting the glory and attention toward one of the other two? The Father says, "This is my son listen to him!" Jesus says, "I only speak what I hear the Father saying." Then He says, "It will be good for you that I leave and go to my Father because then you will have the Holy Spirit and He will guide you into all the truth you need." The Holy Spirit says, "My job is to reveal the glory of Jesus." We think of the trinity as "love in love with love."

We believe that it is in the nature of Jesus to live for the glory of His Father and this means intentionally not bringing attention to himself. We also believe that it was the Father's intent not to reveal the glory of the divine nature of Jesus all of the time to all of the people. To do so would have overwhelmed their wills with respect to the issue of making Jesus their Lord. We

**Jesus is both all God can be in a man and all a man can be in God.**

believe He does the same today. As we have already stated, God is extremely hesitant to force himself on anyone. He wants our reactions to Him to be from a completely free heart.

Humility is also absolutely necessary to the fact that Jesus is both God and man. We often stress the divinity of Jesus at the risk of missing the full importance of His humanity. Jesus is both all God can be in a man and all a man can be in God. This becomes vital to understand when we come to the question of how God intends evangelism to work in our lives.

When Jesus chose to come to earth to live as a man, it was not some sort of bogus tokenism. He was not pretending to be limited by his humanity, He *was* limited by His humanity. He became reliant upon the work of the Holy Spirit through Him, just as we are. And this is the wonderful part of the equation; He lived a life of reliance upon the power of the Holy Spirit to do all the supernatural things that He did. This is an expression of His humility, but it is also His lesson to us as to how we are to live the Christian life.

When He said, "Just as I was sent, so send I you", He is telling us that our lives are to be equally dependent upon the power of the Holy Spirit. The wonderful news is that this means we are to expect to live supernatural lives as He did. And we should expect to do evangelism like He did it.

We have read through the four Gospels and the book of Acts many times and to the best of our recollection we are not aware of any person coming up to Jesus and saying, "You are such a wonderful person, I want to be more like you. How can I do that?" Jesus' method of evangelism was supernatural. Let's test this against the biblical record. Let's use the first several chapters of the gospel of John.

## Some questions to consider:

1. What have you learned from this chapter?

2. Does it surprise you to realize that those closest to Jesus did not recognize His divinity as He grew up? Why do you think that was the case?

3. What is your definition of humility?

4. When you think of Jesus do you usually focus on His divinity or His humanity? What do you miss when you fail to examine His humanity?

# Chapter 10: Evangelism: Spiritual Experience versus Intellectual Assent?

Please allow us to summarize the last chapter. We are tempted to think that because of Jesus' divinity [His sinlessness and His inherent holiness] people put their faith in Him upon seeing these obvious characteristics. This is not the case. Consistently, everyone from His own cousin to the masses of Jews to the Roman ruling class put their faith in Him because of a *supernatural encounter* with the Holy Spirit operating through Him. Jesus' holiness was true holiness; that is to say that it was based in humility and in fact, rather than drawing attention to Himself, it drew attention to His father and the work of the Holy Spirit.

In the first seven chapters of the book of John we see a consistent pattern of belief through a demonstration of the supernatural. Apart from such a demonstration the world does not recognize Jesus. John makes this very clear early on in his book.

**"He was in the world, and the world came into being through him; yet the world did not know him."** John 1:10

We may be tempted to think that John was just talking about the generation to which Jesus first came, but the problem, as we have seen, lies in our human blindness to the truth of Jesus. It is a problem of the human condition for all time and in all places.

We have already dealt with John's blindness to Jesus' divinity as well as that of the Pharisees. Let's move forward in the Gospel of John to see how regular people came to faith. Let's start with one of the first disciples, Nathaniel.
**"When Jesus saw Nathaniel coming toward him, He said of him, 'Here is truly an Israelite in whom there is no deceit!' Nathaniel asked him, 'Where did you get to know me?' Jesus answered, '*I saw you under the fig tree before Philip called***

*you.' Nathaniel replied, 'Rabbi, you are the Son of God! You are the King of Israel!'"* John 1:47–49

Here is the case of a skeptical man who comes to faith just because Jesus is able to tell him about his character and where he was and what he was doing before Phillip called him. This is not something Jesus, in His humanity, could know. It is something the Holy Spirit reveals to Jesus through the spiritual gift of a word of knowledge. Rather dramatic reaction isn't it – a man has an experience which is obviously supernatural, and he comes to faith instantly, attributing divinity to Jesus.

Nathaniel's reaction is much like that of the people of Lystra when Paul performed a miraculous healing in the middle of preaching about Jesus [Acts 14:8–12]. They recognized a supernatural deed and attributed divinity to the person through whom the power flowed. Paul had to convince them that he was just the conduit not the cause.

Now let's accompany the disciples to a wine tasting wedding.

**2:11 Jesus did this, the first of his signs, in Cana of Galilee, and revealed his glory; and his *disciples believed* in him.** Jesus' disciples believed in Him because He turns water into wine at a wedding. Another brush with the supernatural engenders belief.

Now let's see how the common people react to a brush with the supernatural.

2:23 **"When He was in Jerusalem during the Passover festival, many believed in his name because they saw the signs that He was doing."** The common people come to belief because of seeing the supernatural power of the Holy Spirit displayed through Jesus. It is interesting that the Bible uses the word "signs" to describe these supernatural deeds. A sign is almost always a message and usually an important one, even life-saving at times. The purpose of these signs was to bring evidence of the divinity of Jesus in order to make belief in Him easier or, in some cases, possible.

It is possible to reach the conclusion that the common people are just too simple to come to faith without a brush with the supernatural, so let's see how a member of the educated religious elite comes to faith. We tend to think that the religious leaders were somehow immune to believing in Jesus because most of the time they simply attributed Jesus' supernatural deeds to Satan, but there were some who recognized His deeds as the deeds of God. Nicodemas is one of these.

3:2 **He came to Jesus by night and said to him, "Rabbi, we know that you are a teacher who has come from God; for *no one can do these signs that you do apart from the presence of God.*"** Score another victory for supernatural evangelism.

Our theme continues: 4:1+ The story of Jesus' encounter with the Samaritan woman at the well is one of the most touching of the Bible. Here is a woman who is a social outcast. She has to draw water in the heat of the day because she is not accepted by the rest of the women of her town. She came by her outcast status honestly; she has slept with at least 5 men, some of whom may have been some other townswoman's husband. At the very least, she was a threat to the married women of the town.

Jesus violated serious religious norms by simply asking this woman for a drink of water, followed by having a prolonged conversation with her. In the course of this conversation he tells her that she has had 5 "husbands" and the man she is now living with is not her husband. Her reaction to this word of knowledge spoken by a total stranger is to recognize that Jesus must, at the very least, be a prophet of God and perhaps the promised "Christ." Acting on her growing belief she goes back to her neighbors and says to them, **"Come see a man who told me everything I ever did. Could this be the Christ?"** 4:29

It is worth noting that Jesus did not tell her everything she ever did. He told her everything she ever did wrong. At this point in her life she had come to define herself by her sin [and so had everyone else except Jesus]. Jesus, on the other hand, defined her as a person worth knowing and loving enough to speak the words she most needed to hear in order to come to belief in Him.

As a result of her testimony the woman's neighbors come and hear Jesus for themselves and many come to faith. **"Many Samaritans from that city believed in him because of the woman's testimony, 'He told me everything I have ever done.'"** 4:39 Even a second hand prophetic word of knowledge can provide a supernatural experience significant enough to bring Samaritans [who hated Jews and vice versa] to belief in a Jewish Christ.

So far, we have seen blue collar fishermen, the common people of Jerusalem, an educated religious leader, an outcast Samaritan "fallen woman", and many Samaritan townspeople come to belief in Jesus through supernatural encounters empowered by spiritual gifts of the Holy Spirit. Now we come to the case of a person completely removed from the Jewish religious culture. How will a sophisticated official of Rome react to a supernatural encounter with Jesus?

**"Then He came again to Cana in Galilee where He had changed the water into wine. Now there was a royal official whose son lay ill in Capernaum. When he heard that Jesus had come from Judea to Galilee, he went and begged him to come down and heal his son, for he was at the point of death. Then Jesus said to him, *'Unless you see signs and wonders you will not believe.'* The official said to him, 'Sir, come down before my little boy dies.' Jesus said to him, 'Go; your son will live.' The man believed the word that Jesus spoke to him and started on his way. As he was going on, his slaves met him and told him that his child was alive. So, he asked them the hour when he began to recover, and they said to him, 'Yesterday at one in the afternoon the fever left him.' The father realized that this was the hour when Jesus had said to him, 'Your son will live.' So, he himself believed, along with his whole household.** 4:46–53

In this story, there are several facts worth commenting upon. The first is that Jesus recognizes what is necessary for this man to come to belief; he needs to see signs and wonders. This is not a judgment against this man's lack of faith. This man is not a Jew. He has not been raised with an understanding of the promised Messiah. He has no foundation upon which to base a faith in Jesus. Jesus is nothing more to him than one more non-Roman citizen he rules over. The fact is; if he does not have a supernatural experience, he will have no experience upon which to base a belief in Jesus.

At the risk of getting preachy, this is the case for many of our neighbors. Most of them know Jesus as little more than a cuss word. Telling them that we are speaking truth they need to know is pointless because truth in our postmodern culture is entirely relative. We all have our own personal "truth." For many of our friends, neighbors, and co-workers, a spiritual encounter is necessary to awaken spiritual hunger.

The second fact worth commenting upon is that belief for this man was a two-step process rather than a singular event. Notice that after Jesus told him to go and that his son would live, the man believed the *word* that Jesus spoke and acted on it – he went on his way.

The man did not believe in Jesus, he merely believed the *word* Jesus had spoken. It is possible to believe a word spoken supernaturally without it leading to faith in the source of the supernatural word. Although he does not yet believe in Jesus, he has already begun to obey Him – just on the strength of Jesus command.

**For many of our friends, neighbors, and co-workers, a spiritual encounter is necessary to awaken spiritual hunger.**

The third fact to note is that the Roman official comes to faith in Jesus when he realizes that the "word" spoken by Jesus was, in fact, supernatural. He came to faith when he realized that the healing of his son was contemporaneous with the word Jesus spoke. The supernatural healing was a confirmation of a prophetic word experienced before he found out about the healing.

In our experience, it often works this way; a prophetic word is spoken and then a healing takes place. The sick person cannot discount the healing as "natural" because it has been prophesied in advance. Mark has an interesting and contemporary example:

*A few years ago, a woman invited her cousin to our church. Her cousin was a Christian with no experience in the supernatural gifts of the Holy Spirit. After the worship, our senior pastor got up and gave a word of knowledge that there was someone in the room who had a serious foot infection that had not been healed by medical treatment. He even told them how long they had had the infection. He invited the sick person to stand up and receive healing prayer. No one stood up.*

**The common people make the logical connection between the supernatural deeds they are seeing and the supernatural nature of who is doing the deeds.**

*The woman who brought her cousin told her cousin to stand up saying, "You are the person he is talking about – stand up!" Reluctantly she stood and received prayer. Her foot was instantly healed! She was so excited she went back to her work on Monday and told her whole office including her boss.*

*Her boss, who was also a non-spiritual-gifts Christian, was so impressed he asked if he could come with her the following Sunday to check out this unusual church. He came and they sat in the front row. I had no idea who either of them were. Often, after the worship we have a time of prayer for the sick, as well as for any other needs. I was looking at the people standing at the front, waiting for God to show me who to pray for. I saw this newcomer sitting in the front row. He was not standing for prayer, but immediately I received a message from God for him.*

*I went over and asked him if he would mind if I gave him what I thought was a word from the Lord for him. He said sure. I gave it and he was in shock. He said, "How did you know these things about me?" I said, "God told me." He said, "Could I learn to do that?" I said "sure." He said "how?" I said, "Come with me when I go to do these prophetic training conferences and you will catch it." He came with me on several trips and catch it he did!*

In a later chapter, we will hear about his adventure into the world of supernatural healing, prophecy and evangelism. Believe me, it is worth the wait!

Two more incidents from the life of Jesus and we are done. First let's look at one of His most famous miracles, the one about the loaves and the fishes.

**"Then Jesus took the loaves, and when He had given thanks, He distributed them to those who were seated; so also, the fish, as much as they wanted. When they were satisfied He told his disciples, 'Gather up the fragments left over, so that nothing may be lost.' So, they gathered them up, and from the fragments of the five barley loaves, left by those who had eaten, they filled twelve baskets. *When the people saw the sign that He had done*, they began to say, 'This is indeed the prophet who is to come into the world.'"** 6:11–14

Finally, the last example from our survey of the first 7 chapters of the Gospel of John: this coming from the crowd of common people in Jerusalem, **"Yet many in the crowd believed in him and were saying, "When the Messiah comes, will He do more signs than this man has done?"** 7:31.

These are two more examples of a supernatural experience leading to belief in Jesus. The common people make the logical connection between the supernatural deeds they are seeing and the supernatural nature of **who** is doing the deeds.

Jesus expects people to make this logical connection. He makes this abundantly clear when He says, **"Very truly, I tell you, the Son can do nothing on his own, but only what He sees the Father doing; for whatever the Father does, the Son does likewise."** 5:19

The deeds that Jesus does are the deeds of God. These are the only kind of deeds that reveal the nature of God – anything less than supernatural deeds fails to reveal a supernatural God.

Later, Jesus goes on to say, **"But I have a testimony greater than John's. The works that the Father has given me to complete, the very works that I am doing, testify on my behalf that the Father has sent me."** 5:36

Jesus Himself is resting his credibility as the "one who comes from God" upon the supernatural signs that He is doing.

It may be tempting to say that Jesus is God and so we should expect supernatural conversions where He is involved, but we, being normal humans, cannot expect to operate as Jesus did. This of course would be a virtual denial of His humanity, but we can see how one could make this mistake.

The only way to rule out this errant conclusion is to examine the lives of His first fully human followers to see if this connection between a supernatural experience and faith in Jesus continues. So, on to the next chapter...

## Some questions to consider:

1. What have you learned from this chapter?

2. The supernatural things that Jesus did [knowing things only God could know, healings and miracles] are called "sign" gifts. What are they a sign of?

3. Jesus said, **"Unless you see signs and wonders you will not believe."** Do you think there are people today who need to see signs and wonders in order to believe in Jesus? Why? Why not?

4. If Jesus is fully human as well as fully divine where did His ability to do supernatural deeds come from?

5. If Jesus in His humility chose to rely on the power of the Holy Spirit to do supernatural "sign" gifts, do you believe you can rely on the Holy Spirit to do supernatural deeds through you?

6. Have you ever been used by God to do a supernatural deed? Explain.

# Chapter 11:  How Did the Early Church Do Evangelism?

The question we want to answer in this chapter is, "Does Jesus' method of 'supernatural' evangelism carry on through the lives of ordinary Christians after He has returned to heaven?" This is an important question, because if so, we cannot avoid a supernatural lifestyle simply by saying, "Well, it worked for Jesus, but who am I to put myself on His level?" Once again, we are running into the effect of focusing almost exclusively on Jesus' divinity at the expense of what we can learn from examining His humanity.

He is our example for what the Christian life is supposed to look like. After all, it is His life in us that defines us as Christians. The term first used to describe His followers, which we translate as "Christians", is legitimately translated as "little Christs." And we should note that this label was not self-proclaimed by Christians, but was given by non-Christians after observing the early church in action. To answer our question the Book of Acts is our starting point.

Most Christians have read the Book of Acts at least once. Many of the events found there are extremely well known. For that reason, we don't need to examine the book in detail, but there are a few incidents that are worthy of mention.

## The Church's Supernatural Birth

The church came into existence through a corporate supernatural experience. It was literally "born" into the supernatural. Can you imagine being one of the 120 waiting in the upper room for the Holy Spirit? We wonder if they had any idea of what they expected the coming of the Holy Spirit to be like. Do you think they expected to be speaking in foreign tongues, having no idea what they were saying, and then have foreigners coming to faith in Jesus after hearing a message in their own language; a message of which the speaker had no comprehension?

We doubt they expected to be overwhelmed by the Spirit of prophecy, to find themselves giving messages from God to people they

**The church came into existence through a corporate super-natural experience. It was literally "born" into the supernatural.**

hardly knew. It is not an exaggeration to say that this "Pentecost" experience was probably the defining moment for the remainder of their Christian lives. Their new confidence and boldness alone was worth the price of admission. These people have been radically changed in one encounter with the Holy Spirit!

Their experience was so overwhelming that those who watched them believed them to be drunk! We wonder if they expected that result! The experience is so radical and unexpected that Peter feels compelled to explain it. He explains it to the crowd of onlookers using the Old Testament promises of the outpouring of the Holy Spirit. He masterfully weaves in the story of Jesus and His unjust murder with the result that the spiritual eyes of the crowd are opened and they repent!

We need to pause here for a moment to consider that these people who are now repenting are those who, a short time before, demanded the death of Jesus. In this moment, there occurs a complete change of mind – a spiritual and mental about-face! We should also take note that Peter concluded his explanation with a promise that these listeners could receive the gift of the Holy Spirit as well. This promised gift was not some sort of theoretical theological understanding of the Holy Spirit. It was a promise to receive what these observers had just witnessed. The same experience they have just seen is for them as well! As a result of witnessing the outpouring of the Holy Spirit and hearing the explanation given by Peter, 3000 come to faith in Jesus! In one day! This is indeed an outpouring of supernatural power!

As we write about this Pentecost experience it brings to mind an experience Mark had in Northern Russia in the early 90's. In his words,

*"I took a team to Murmansk to do an outreach with the brand-new Youth with a Mission base there. We arrived in Moscow the day that Yeltsin was facing the attempted coup in Red Square. It was a very exciting time to say the least.*

*The town that we held our meetings in was a very rough place. Our Russian YWAM leader told us that this town was the place where criminals came to hide from the law. It was, in his words, the place where you go when you have nowhere else to go. My confidence began to lag...*

*We met in the "culture palace", a sort of community hall which was no palace and had no culture. The first night I spoke and failed miserably. My message was way too intellectual and frankly boring. I went to bed that night very ashamed. I told God, "I am so sorry, I was afraid to pray for the sick, so I just gave a salvation message. Please give me another chance and I will preach about Your power to heal and save!"*

*The next night I got up and preached about the power of God to heal and save. We prayed for the sick and I saw a blind girl healed! It rocked my world. After her mother shared about her healing, I gave an invitation for all those who wanted to accept Jesus as their Savior. The whole room put up their hands! I thought I must have promised them something wonderful like a new apartment or new car or something. I could not believe that they all wanted to know God just for His sake alone. I was conditioned to the Western sales pitch that involves promising prosperity, perfect health, perfect kids and a vacation home. The response actually caught me off balance.*

*I stopped the invitation and started from the beginning. I explained how being a Christian was a hard life - you lose friends, family may reject you, you may lose your job or apartment etc, etc. I made it as negative as I could. Then I gave the invitation again and again, all*

*the hands went up. I still could not understand what was happening.*

*I stopped and said to God, "What am I doing wrong? Why are all these people wanting to become Christians?" He dropped this thought in my mind, "Ask them how many of them have ever heard anything like this message before." I asked them and out of over 200 people in the room only a hand-full had ever heard anything to do with the Gospel before!*

*I asked them to come forward to receive Jesus and the whole room came forward. There was no room in front of the stage, so I invited them up onto the large stage. They all came up. As I was explaining to them how we were going to pray to receive Jesus, I noticed three teenage boys at the back of the group. They were punching and teasing each other while I was trying to explain how to become a Christian. It actually made me angry. I imagined saying to them, "I didn't beg you to come up here. I told you how hard it is to live as a Christian. I made it easy for you to say "no." If you have no interest in becoming a Christian, why did you come up here?"*

*God gently rebuked me and said, "Forget about them, focus on the ones who are sincere." So, I did. I finished the prayer of repentance and salvation and then I told them I would pray for them to receive the Holy Spirit so they will know they truly belong to God. I invited the Holy Spirit to come and touch them and give them evidence that God is real. People started to cry and laugh and then I noticed the three teenagers at the back.*

*The one in the middle was now shaking and twitching uncontrollably. His friends were trying to hold him up. He fell on the stage and continued to shake violently. This went on the whole time we prayed for the sick. Many healings occurred and then it was time to leave. The three teenagers were still caught up in the shakes. The problem was, the janitor insisted on closing the room and this kid could not stand up, let alone walk.*

*I watched as his friends carried him out of the building and down to the bus stop. They held him up until the bus came and when the front door opened they dropped him inside, the door closed and the bus left. I laughed.*

*The next night the shaker returned with more than 20 of his teenage friends. They all sat at the back and when the invitation came for salvation almost all of them came forward! I would love to know what he told his friends to get them to come to the meeting. I am sure he never mentioned my great sermon or clever illustrations, but I have no doubt he mentioned his experience with the supernatural power of God."*

Now back to the book of Acts.

## Taking the Gospel to the World

Thus far we have looked at the supernatural birth of the early church. Now we want to focus on how the truth about Jesus spread beyond the Jewish culture. How does the early church convince a non-Jewish culture of the truth of Jesus the Jewish Messiah? This is an important question because Judaism had no inherent credibility within the Roman Empire. It was perhaps the smallest of faiths competing against established Roman gods and religion. It had the disadvantage of being the faith of the occupied subservient nation. It was, in effect, a low class, low credibility, brand new, untried religion. It really had nothing going for it in natural human terms. It was certainly going to need a very good salesman.

Enter Paul. Paul is the perfect bridge to the Roman culture. He is a Jew, but he is also a Roman citizen. This means he has a common understanding of Roman culture. He "speaks their language" so to speak. He is also very highly educated. He is a successful, self-employed business man. He is also an intellectual. In our human reasoning, he is the perfect choice. Ditto, as far as God is concerned, with one important qualification. God will have to wean Paul of his dependence upon his human abilities before imparting him with superhuman abilities.

Paul's conversion is perhaps the most obviously supernatural of the New Testament. He is literally knocked to the ground and struck blind while he hears the voice of Jesus rebuking him. God provides two visions to bring about Paul's healing from blindness. One is to Ananias directing him where to find the persecutor of Christians [Paul] and one to Paul in which he "sees" a man named Ananias come and heal his eyes.

Ananias is skeptical about trusting Paul and God responds by saying, **"Go! This man is my chosen instrument to carry my name before the Gentiles and their kings and before the people of Israel. I will show him how much he must suffer for my name"** Acts 9:15–16.

Although Paul has every human ability necessary to make him a "best choice" for missionary to the Gentiles, we will see that these human abilities are often Paul's worst enemies. Much of what Paul "must suffer for my name" involves learning to rely not upon his human ability, but upon God's supernatural ability.

> **Much of what Paul "must suffer for my name" involves learning to rely not upon his human ability but upon God's supernatural ability.**

After Paul makes his debut with the leaders of the church in Jerusalem, he disappears for many years. We don't know where he went or what he did. All we know is that he experienced many years of obscurity. Sort of like Moses living in the desert for 40 years after running from Pharaoh's household in Egypt - a lesson in humility.

The next we hear of Paul he is a teacher in the church in Antioch. He is not famous, and for all we can tell, he has done no miracles. He is merely using his human abilities to serve the church he is a part of. There is a great little lesson here – while we wait for more of the power of God through us, we need only to be faithful to what we have the ability to do. Paul is an intellectual theologian, so he teaches.

Upon this foundation of faithfulness God builds a supernatural ministry. As recorded in the opening verses of chapter 13 of the

Book of Acts, one day while the church is worshiping, God speaks supernaturally through the gift of prophecy to commission Paul and Barnabas for the new work of evangelists to the Gentiles. It is important to notice that God used His church to commission Paul and Barnabas to their new ministry. They were not self-professed missionaries, but men who were commissioned by, and accountable to, their community. There is a truth to be found here: the greater the power - the greater the accountability. Budding revivalists take note.

## Paul's First Missionary Journey

Now the fun begins... Let's follow Paul and Company on his missionary journeys starting with his first. As we examine his adventure, see if you can discern a pattern developing.

Acts 13:4–13 First Paul and Barnabas go to Cyprus. Here they are summoned to explain the gospel to the Proconsul. The proconsul is reacting favorably to the message until his court sorcerer intervenes in an attempt to prevent him from believing the truth. Paul, under the power of the Holy Spirit, prophecies to the sorcerer the darkness of his heart and blinds him. The proconsul decides to believe in Jesus. From Cyprus, they go on to Pisidian Antioch.

Acts 13:13–52 In Pisidian Antioch Paul preaches, persecution results and they are expelled from the region. Next, they go to Iconium.

Acts 14:1–7 In Iconium Paul begins preaching in the Synagogue. They stay and "preach boldly" and the message is confirmed by miraculous signs and wonders with many converts. The reaction from the religious leaders is persecution, so they leave the region and go to Lystra and Derbe.

Acts 14:8–20 In Lystra Paul is preaching and heals a cripple in the middle of his message. The people start to worship Paul and Barnabas as gods. Paul corrects them and goes on preaching. Some Jewish leaders from Antioch show up and stir up a riot against Paul and Barnabas and Paul is stoned and left for dead.

The next day they leave for Derbe and then go back and revisit the previous cities, appointing elders in each local church as they make their way home to Antioch.

Here is the pattern we see: preaching, supernatural gifts, persecution, converts, and a church plant. Not necessarily in that order.

## Paul's Second Missionary Journey

Acts 16:12–40 Paul goes to Phillipi. Through the deliverance of a demon-possessed fortune telling slave girl, Paul causes a riot and they are thrown in prison. That night they are supernaturally set free and the jailor and his whole family is converted. A church is planted, which grows and prospers. Next Paul goes to Thessalonica.

Acts 17:1–9 In Thessalonica Paul preaches, riots break out, and he performs supernatural signs and wonders. He describes the experience in **1 Thess. 1:5, "... our gospel came to you not simply with words, but also with power, with the Holy Spirit ..."** From here he goes to Berea for a short visit and then on to Athens.

Acts 17:16–34 Paul arrives in Athens. This is a place of real significance for Paul because, being an intellectual, he is coming back to his intellectual home. It is his kind of place - a place where new ideas are discussed among the intellectuals. It is a proud and trendy city. There is a Starbucks on every corner. A contemporary analogue would be New York City. Athens is really where Paul feels at home - where he is surrounded by people much like himself. Here is the description of what took place; **"Paul reasoned in the synagogue with the Jews and in the marketplace"** Acts 17:17. We bet he had fun.

Here he preaches his famous sermon to the unknown god. Many theologians hold up Paul's sermon to the unknown God as the greatest sermon in the Bible. This was his presentation to the intellectuals intended to convince them of the truth of Jesus.

**Apart from preaching a great sermon, the stop in Athens was a failure, yielding only a few converts and no church plant.**

When you examine the sermon it truly is brilliant. He builds a bridge by complimenting them on their religious commitment.

Next Paul uses their altar "to an unknown god" to segway into an introduction to Jesus. He even quotes one of their poets [talk about bridge building]. His logic is flawless and his argument is compelling, but what was the result? No supernatural signs and wonders were done. Only a few converts were made and no church was planted there. And worthy of note, his message resulted in no persecution. Apart from preaching a great sermon, the stop in Athens was a failure, yielding only a few converts and no church plant. Now on to Corinth...

Acts 18:1+ Paul comes to Corinth having just come from his failure in Athens. Here he makes this telling statement: **"And so it was with me, brothers and sisters. When I came to you, I did not come with *eloquence or human wisdom* as I proclaimed to you the testimony about God. For I resolved to know nothing while I was with you except Jesus Christ and Him crucified. I came to you in *weakness* with great fear and trembling. My message and my preaching were *not with wise and persuasive words*, but with a *demonstration of the Spirit's power*, so that your faith might not rest on human wisdom, but on God's power"** 1 Cor. 2:1–5.

**Having just failed in Athens, Paul returns to his previous pattern – a demonstration of the Spirit's power.**

## Paul learns a valuable lesson

It is reassuring for us to see Paul make a mistake and learn from it. We often tend to make supermen out of Bible characters. We can't imagine Paul ever making a mistake or needing to change his approach, yet this is what he did. Even Paul must eventually come to the place where he rejoices in his weakness, because it is when he is weak that the power of God is most evident through him. Having just failed in Athens, Paul returns to his previous pattern - a demonstration of the Spirit's power followed by conversions and a church plant.

The church planted in Corinth was birthed as a supernatural church as are all the rest of the churches Paul plants. From Corinth Paul goes back to the pattern that works. This is Jesus' pattern, Paul's pattern and the pattern of the New Testament church. What does this mean for us?

The fact is, we live in a postmodern age. Of all the cities Paul visited our postmodern culture most resembles Athens. We in the West are culturally postmodern. Postmodernism is characterized principally as an age in which absolute truth is irrelevant – its existence is simply denied. People are no longer asking the question "Is your faith true?" The question they are asking is "Does your faith work for a better life?" They want to know if it has the power to solve their problems.

The lesson for us is simple; rather than mourn the good old days of truth, we should be able to answer their question the way Paul did – with a demonstration of the power of the Holy Spirit.

Allow us to return to what we said in a previous chapter. **Becoming a Christian is actually a supernatural event**. No one can be born again through human reason. If someone can talk you into it, someone else can talk you out of it. The new birth is a work of the Holy Spirit. Openness to God often comes through an experience of the supernatural, which is undeniable and which "opens the heart and mind to the reality and goodness of God." The Bible tells us that the minds of the lost are incapable of "seeing" the light of the Gospel. The problem is not one of being unwilling to hear, it is one of being incapable of hearing.

> **People are no longer asking the question "Is your faith true?" They are asking, "Does your faith work for a better life?"**

**"The god of this age has blinded the minds of unbelievers, so that they *cannot* see the light of the gospel of the glory of Christ, who is the image of God"** 2 Cor. 4:4.

At the risk of being redundant, even at its most rational, the decision to become a Christian is a supernatural event. **Until the Holy Spirit intervenes to free an individual from spiritual blindness, conversion is not possible.** The issue is not that people don't want to become followers of Jesus, it is that they can't! There is a power of supernatural blindness that is more powerful than their ability to reason accurately about the existence of a supernatural God.

When we truly understand this, we will approach evangelism the same way Jesus, Paul, and the early church did. We will pray with a supernatural faith for a supernatural work of the Holy Spirit. We will be open to every spiritual gift of power that might be the power necessary to open their minds for long enough to allow them to make a decision unhindered by the power of the enemy.

Notice we say, "long enough to allow them to make a decision". A demonstration of the supernatural does not force anyone to believe in Jesus as their Savior and Lord, at best it frees them from the lies of the enemy, which have dominated their minds [resulting in an inability to perceive the truth]. Once the mind and heart are free from the bondage of the enemy, a window of freedom is created in which a truly free decision can be made. Sadly, many still refuse to accept the life that Jesus freely offers, but because their minds have been freed of demonic deception, their decision is a true expression of their hearts. Because it is a true expression of their hearts, they are truly responsible for the dire consequences of their rejection of God's grace.

Before we go on to the next chapter, we want to answer what we anticipate may be a criticism you have at this point. By stressing the need for a demonstration of the Holy Spirit's power, we may be interpreted as devaluing reason within the process of evangelism. This is not the case. Our concern is that *reason alone* has been the "go to" means of evangelism for much of the Western church for at least the last 200 years. Our understanding of conversion as well as the Christian life has been unbalanced against the supernatural. **By stressing the supernatural nature of our faith, we are hoping to return to a place of balance between our natural gifts and our supernatural gifts.**

All of the spiritual gifts are necessary for a biblically normal Christian life, but a biblically normal Christian life is a supernatural as well as a natural life. Our goal is to see us living supernaturally natural and naturally supernatural lives.

If all the foregoing is true, we should be seeing supernatural evangelism taking place today. Now let's look at a few contemporary examples of clearly supernatural evangelism.

## Some questions to consider:

1. What have you learned from this chapter?

2. Do you think it is significant that the church was born through a supernatural experience of God's power on the Day of Pentecost? Why, why not?

3. Do you think there is a difference between the Christian life of someone whose birth into it was through a supernatural experience vs. someone whose birth was by intellectual assent alone?

4. Knowing that "The god of this age has blinded the minds of unbelievers, so that they <u>cannot</u> see the light of the gospel of the glory of Christ, who is the image of God." [2 Cor. 4:4] how does this change your approach to evangelism?

5. What is the role of prayer in opening the minds of unbelievers to receive the truth about Jesus?

# Chapter 12: Supernatural Evangelism: Alive and Well Today

An unbiased reading of the New Testament makes it easy to reach the conclusion that God's supernatural sign gifts are intended by Him to be a normal part of the life of everyday Christians going about their busy lives. So, are they?

**A trip to the doctor** – Mark's story

*A few years ago, my doctor sent me for a radiological CAT scan. I had the procedure and the attending nurse told me to drink water as soon as possible to flush the radioactive dye out of my system. As I was walking across the foyer to leave I saw a young man loading up a water vending machine. I went over and asked him if I could buy a bottle. I bought the bottle and headed for the door. About half way to the door this thought came very clearly to my mind. "Go back and tell him about Me."*

*I assumed this thought was from the Lord and to my shame I said, "No, I don't want to do that." I continued to walk to the door and when I went to open the door the thought came again, "Go back and tell him about Me." Again, I said I didn't want to. [I know; I am not much of a Christian]. I walked outside and when I got to the curb to cross the street the thought came again.*

*This time I paused and said to the Lord, "Every day I start the day with prayer and I tell you that my life belongs to You and so I will do whatever You ask me to do. Then as soon as You ask me to do something embarrassing or inconvenient, I say "no." OK, I will go back and tell him about You, but it is not an easy conversation to start, give me some help here. How am I going to start the conversation?" The answering thought that came to my mind was, "Go back and ask him if in the last 10 days he has been wondering how he can come to know God."*

That seemed easy enough so I went back and said, "Remember me, I just bought a water from you?" He said, "yes" [of course he said yes]. I said, "I know this sounds kind of crazy, but I am a Christian and sometimes God communicates something to me for someone else. I believe He just asked me to ask you a question. Are you OK with that?" He said, "yes." I said, "God told me to ask you if in the last 10 days or so you have been wondering how you can come to know God." He said, "Yes I have!" I said, "Do you want to know how you can know God today?" He said, "yes!" I explained the Gospel to him and led him to the Lord.

I don't know why I said this, but then I said to him, "You know; God wants to know you much more than you want to know Him." He reacted with a look of real surprise and said, "About 10 days ago this old man came up to me at the market and said, "Young man God wants to know you" and then he walked off. Then a few days later at the same market this old lady came up to me and said, "God says you are not to leave your wife" and then she walked away."

I asked him if he was planning on leaving his wife and he said yes, he was, but not NOW after this experience. I gave him good counsel as to how to find a Christ-centered church and how to buy a good Bible and the need to be part of a small group. I prayed for him and left.

Needless to say, I was full of joy as I drove home. There is no joy like knowing you are in cahoots with the Creator of the universe.

As I was driving home, I thought about the old man and old woman who encountered the young man at the market. I imagined them showing up at their church small groups after talking to the young man at the market. The group leader asks if anyone has a praise report and the old man says, "Yesterday at the market I felt like the lord wanted me to tell this young man that He wants to know him." The group leader says, "Well, what did he do after you explained the Gospel to him." The old man says, "I didn't explain it to him, I just told him what I thought God said to me." The group leader looks at the old man with disappointed eyes...

*The same thing happens to the old lady at her women's group. Same look of disappointment. Neither of them "closed the deal." And this is the way we often look at evangelism; it's all about the close. But look at what happened here. Two people risk speaking a message from God to a total stranger. They speak only what they believe they heard from God. They have no program in mind, merely speaking what they think God is saying.*

*When I come along, this young man has already had two subtle brushes with the supernatural. Neither one gives him enough information to come to belief in Jesus, but when I come along and speak to him about God's desire to know him, his prior experiences fall into place and he comes to belief. All three of our words were appropriate [prophetic] to this young man's spiritual state and taken together they make it crystal clear that God is seeking a relationship with him. I doubt he will ever forget how he came to know Jesus.*

### Shake up our youth group – Mark's story

*"Our youth group needs shaking up! I want you to come and teach our youth how to hear the voice of God and then I want you to take them out in public to prophecy over strangers!" so said my pastor friend from Houston. To be honest, I was a little intimidated. I had never done a field trip like this before. At the same time, I was excited, so I said yes. Friday night and Saturday morning, I taught the youth how to "hear" God's communication to us [which will be the subject of later chapters – you are going to love it!]. Saturday afternoon was the field test.*

*I always stay with the same family on these trips to this particular church. I had become part of the family, sort of the "Uncle Buck" of the household. The teenage daughter and I got along very well. She had no trouble sharing her doubts about her family's faith. She was also not excited about coming to my prophetic workshop. It seems she had said yes to a babysitting gig which provided the perfect excuse not to come, "Sorry, but I am making money and so obviously that must take precedence over learning to hear God's voice!"*

*I could not argue with her logic, so I decided to buy her attendance. I told her that I would match her babysitting income, if she would come to the workshop and field trip. She said yes and came. She was skeptical throughout the training, telling me that God would never use her because her doubts were just too high. I suggested to her that God loves a challenge and she presented the perfect challenge – a real doubting Thomas!*

*Our battle plan was simple. We go to the Food Court of the local mall and we walk around and look at people. When our gaze lands on someone and a thought pops into our heads we come back to Mark and decide what to do with it. My skeptical "niece" was the first to report back. She said she looked at a man sitting eating at a table and the word "divorce" popped into her mind. What do we do with this one word that might be from God?*

*I walked over to the man and said, "I am training some young people to hear messages from God for total strangers. That girl over there thinks she heard something from God for you. Would you be willing to help us determine if it really was God that she heard?" He said yes. She came over and said, "I think God told me that you just got divorced."*

*He started to cry. Immediately I "heard" God say to him, "You see yourself as a failure, damaged forever and no longer fit to be married. But God says to you that you are not doomed to be lonely. Can we pray for you?" He said yes and we prayed for God's comfort for him. He wept through the whole prayer time. He thanked us profusely. He was full of peace by the time we finished.*

*Another teen got a similar word for another person with similar results. In total, our two-person teams prayed over strangers for more than an hour. The accuracy of the words was amazing. My pastor friend reported weeks later that the youth group had completely changed, "The kids are different - they are on fire for God."*

**On the way to San Antonio** – Mark's story

*A few days after the field trip to the Mall, my pastor friend and I were driving to San Antonio for more meetings. On the way, we stopped at a sports bar for lunch. After we ordered, my friend asked me if I got anything from God for our waitress. I said no, did you? He said he had a thought come into his mind that maybe she has trouble trusting men. I suggested we find out. When she came back with the food I said, "I know this sounds kind of crazy, but my friend here thinks God told him something about you. Would you mind if we ran it by you to see if he really did hear God?" She said sure. Bill said, "I think God told me that you have a serious problem trusting men." She said, "Absolutely!"*

*At that moment, a thought came to me and I spoke it to her. I said, "Right now you are living with a guy, but you are not married. He is very kind to you and he really loves your daughter. You think he may be the one for you and your daughter, but because of the abuse you have received from men you can't trust him, but you want to." She said, "Exactly!" I continued, "There is one man who will never abuse or misuse you. He is the perfectly safe man for you. If you get to know him, you will get over your trust issues and be able to trust a man again. His name is Jesus."*

*On hearing this she said, "This is amazing! There is this girl who works here who is always giving me these little books about Jesus! She says I have to get to know him! This is amazing!" I went into counselor mode. I said, "You need to spend more time with this girl and you need to read those little books and you need to get a good Bible that is easy to read." She said she would.*

*Here is another example of natural and supernatural gifts working together to bring someone to Jesus. Her need has created an opening. Her co-worker has begun teaching her about Jesus. The prophetic words we brought to her brings experiential credibility to the words already spoken by her co-worker. Not only that, but now she has evidence that there is a God who cares enough about her life to send total strangers to tell her about her fears and her need to know Jesus. Wonderful!*

## Back home from Houston—just another day at the mall – Mark's story

*What happens when you come back to your home church and tell them about the field trip to the Mall? They want to do it too! So, ditto the whole experience. I teach for a weekend and then the next weekend we go to the Food Court at one of our local malls. It was about three weeks before Christmas and the malls were busy. We needed some kind of helpful introduction to shoppers. This is what came to me, "If you could have anything you wanted for Christmas from God other than the usual presents and gifts, what would it be?"*

*A few people blew us off, but most of them thought about the question and answered with surprising vulnerability. One woman told me that she had been estranged from her adult daughter for years and longed to spend a Christmas with her. An older man told me that his health was bad and he didn't have enough energy to be with his extended family. Others told of problems at work and with family relationships.*

*In each case we had an opportunity to pray for them. All those who answered the question were open to receiving prayer as well. We spent the better part of a day praying for people.*

*I wonder if any of you readers are thinking, "Nice introduction to praying for people, but what does this have to do with prophecy and the supernatural?" Good question. Let me answer that question by saying something about prayer. Much of the time prayer is little more than us asking God to give us what we want. This is fine as far as it goes, but the Bible tells us that Jesus is before the Father in heaven right now praying for us and for the lost. [Hebrews 7:24–25] I take this to mean that whenever I go to pray for someone, Jesus is already praying for them. If this is true, then I have a choice between praying my prayer for this person based upon my assessment of their needs or waiting and listening to the "voice" of God to tell me what Jesus is praying for him. Whose prayer has the best chance of being answered?*

*I approach every prayer this way; ask them what they need and then wait on the Holy Spirit with the expectation that He will tell me how to pray His prayer for them. In other words, prayer can be an opportunity to use a revelatory gift to direct our prayers. And these prayers tend to be more powerful prayers than those that come from our own minds. So, this is what we do. We listen to the need and then we quiet ourselves and wait for God to communicate His heart and mind for the person.*

*My prayer partner and I were taking a break from praying for strangers, so we sat down and had a coke. A past church member came by and sat beside us, asking us what we were doing at the mall. I began to explain how we were praying and prophesying over strangers. While I was explaining all this, two women were sitting to my left. I noticed that they were listening closely to everything I was saying. I turned to them and asked if they would like prayer. They said yes!*

**Prayer can be an opportunity to use a revelatory gift to direct our prayers.**

*It turned out one of them had just lost her job and would be out of her apartment in three days. Out on the street with nowhere to live two weeks before Christmas! I told them that we would pray for them, but that it was our custom to be still for a few minutes to listen to God to see how He wanted us to pray. I did this and this is what came out; "You have been terribly abused by men. All the men in your life have abused you. What is amazing is that you have never gotten bitter or hateful in all the pain and injustice. Jesus wants to be a spiritual husband to you for a period of time, while your pain heals. He does not want any more men in your life until He has healed your broken heart. When your heart is healed and you can trust again, He will bring the right man into your life."*

*Needless to say, she wept through the whole prayer. Her friend kept saying, "How could you know her so well? This is incredible!" Then we prayed for her friend and I told her how God saw her. I told her of her character strengths and what God wanted to make of her life. When we were done they were radiant with joy. With complete sincerity they asked, "Are you angels?" It was a hard question to answer because at that moment we were doing the usual work of angels – bringing messages of great joy and encouragement from God.*

*The next day I was scheduled to man our "free prayer" table in the Mall. We set up the table right in the middle of the main walkway in the mall. We wanted to make sure that everyone who passed saw our sign. I tried to look harmless and loving. My partner for the day was a guy from church whose wife thought it would be good for him to go out and experience a few supernatural spiritual gifts. He was a willing neophyte.*

*To be honest there were not many who took us up on the free prayer offer... until... a middle-aged couple were walking toward our table. I saw that they saw our sign and they saw that I saw that they saw me seeing them seeing our sign. [I love that sentence]. I could see them hesitate and look at each other. They were both waiting for a buy in from the other. I decided to do a little selling so I said, "Hey, what have you got to lose? It can't hurt." So, they came over and sat down. I said, "What would you like prayer for? They said, "We have found our dream house and we really want to buy it, but we haven't been able to sell our present house first and it has to sell or we lose our dream house."*

*What an easy thing to pray for! So, I gave them the spiel about not wanting to pray our prayer for them, but God's prayers for them – so we need to wait a minute or two. They were fine with that. Nothing came, so I just prayed for their house to sell. In the middle of this prayer a thought came to me; "His ex-wife has been cursing and slandering him." I had no idea if he had an ex-wife, but I decided to risk it and just give what I was getting.*

*I told him his ex-wife had been slandering him to his family and at his church and that as a result he was beginning to believe that he could not be a good husband to his new wife [the woman sitting beside him]. As I was speaking his head was nodding "yes" and his wife was crying and saying, "Yes! Yes!" Then I told him that as a result of this cursing and slander he has begun to believe that he*

107

*doesn't deserve his new wife and that maybe she is not God's will for him, and that these thoughts are undermining his new marriage.*

*At this point they both came apart – they just wept. I went on to tell them that God says, he is a good man and that with God's help, he is going to make a great husband and have a successful marriage - that they are God's gift to each other. We rebuked the lies that were trying to destroy his marriage and his intimacy with God.*

*My partner saw a mental picture of a train half way across a very high railroad bridge between two cliffs. The interpretation came to me - they are in a time of change and transition between the past [the bad marriage] and the future [the new marriage] and that a new stability is coming.*

*When we were done praying and prophesying over them they were thrilled! This is what they said, "We live way south of here [about 30 miles] and have never been to this mall before. When we decided to drive all this way to this mall, we didn't know why we wanted to come here. It made no sense to us, but we just wanted to come here. Now we know why we felt we needed to come here. Everything you said to us is absolutely true! You have no idea what your words mean to us!" Free prayer indeed!*

*One more and then I have to go to the gym. A few years ago, a man in our church had a friend who was a bi-vocational pastor – a construction worker and a pastor. He met a man on a construction site who said he was an atheist. The pastor had a prophetic word of knowledge about the man and told him, "Something bad happened to you and God didn't answer your prayer and so you stopped believing in God." The man said, "My daughter ran away three years ago and I have not heard from her in three years."*

*The pastor said, "If your daughter phones you in the next hour will you give your life to Jesus?" The man said, "Yes, and my whole family as well." The pastor started to pray that the man's daughter would call him within the next hour. While he was praying, the man's cell phone rang. He was too afraid to answer it, so he handed it to the pastor. It was his daughter reaching out to her father! He gave his life to Jesus right there on the job site!*

## Walking the streets of Tijuana at night – looking for the sick

Alone on the streets of Tijuana on a Friday or Saturday night is not a good idea... unless of course you like to take risks. Our friend Chris likes to take risks. He also likes to pray for the sick [or are we being redundant?]. He is the guy Mark told you about - the one who Mark prophesied over at church who asked to learn all he could about praying for the sick. The one who came on numerous ministry trips to empty the filing cabinets of Mark's mind, to learn all he could about supernatural ministry. Learn, he did!

The thing about learning to pray for the sick is that you need a constant supply of sick people to pray for. Waiting for sick people to come forward at church did not satisfy his "eager desire" for God's power in his life. His solution was to go out and find the sick. He started by taking his friends to shopping malls in search of sick people. Whenever they saw someone on crutches or with some obvious physical problem they asked if they could pray for them. Rejection is not one of Chris's issues, so he had no problem with hearing "No thank you." Perseverance brings its own reward.

One afternoon at a Target store Chris noticed a young man with a cast on his wrist. Chris asked him if he could pray for his wrist. The young man said "Sure." Chris asked him if he believed in God and he said "No." Chris asked him, "If God heals your wrist, will you believe in God?" The young man said "probably." Chris established a baseline from which to pray. He determined how much mobility the young man had in his fingers and how much pain there was. He began to pray and immediately the young man felt something happening in his wrist. When Chris suggested that he try to move his fingers, a long string of cuss words followed with the question, "How did you do that? My fingers move perfectly! There is no more pain! What the !!@# just happened?!?!" Chris led him to the Lord right then and there.

## Back to Tijuana

Chris walked the streets of Tijuana alone on the weekends looking for a sick person to heal who could speak English. Chris figured that if he could get an interpreter healed, then healing the next person would be easier. And that is exactly what happened.

Mark suggested that Chris keep a record to document his healing experiences. He did so with his smart phone. Over a period of 2.5 years Chris saw approximately 125 physical healings and led 55 people to Jesus. He calculates that his success rate for physical healings was approximately 60%. During that time, he saw Hepatitis C healed as well as Cancer and Cerebral Palsy.

The lady healed of Hepatitis C came to Mark's church to give her testimony and brought her medical reports from both before and after her healing. Mark read the reports that confirmed her diagnosis of Hepatitis C and the report coming after her healing confirming her free of the virus.

We are convinced that much of the success that Chris experienced came because he was willing to take risks to see the supernatural evidence of the Kingdom of God. Later, when we discuss the practical means of experiencing the supernatural power of God, we will see that risk is critical to developing these spiritual gifts. We applaud Chris, because he has taken risks that we have not taken and probably never will.

At one point, he told Mark he wanted to see a person raised from the dead. Mark told him that in our culture we have very little chance to pray for a resurrection from the dead because we have little exposure to dead bodies. Chris took this as a challenge. First, he put an ad in Craig's list letting San Diego know that he was willing to pray for a resurrection from the dead. When this brought no opportunities, he began contacting Morticians to ask if he could pray for a resurrection from the dead! Yes, I know, it's a bit crazy. Alright, maybe it's allot crazy, but when you get to heaven which do you want Jesus to say to you; "You took a few too many risks with My power" or "You took too few?"

After reading these testimonies of God's supernatural power we realize that we have seen far too many demonstrations of God's supernatural power to write them all down. This may have been the disciple John's experience that prompted him to write, **"Jesus did many other things as well. If every one of them were written down, I suppose that even the whole world would not have enough room for the books that would be written"** John 21:25.

We know this is hyperbole, but that is how it feels to look back on over 30 years of living a naturally supernatural lifestyle. And by the way, it feels great!

## Some questions to consider:

1. What have you learned from this chapter?

2. What is your emotional reaction to Mark's stories of God's supernatural power?

3. Risk is central to experiencing the supernatural power of God. What are you afraid to risk?

4. Can you use your imagination to see yourself prophesying over people and/or praying for their healing? If not, why not?

# PART THREE:

# HEARING GOD'S VOICE
# IS THE KEY

# Chapter 13: Defining and Explaining Revelatory Gifts

The current culture in America has a fascination with extrasensory perception, often called ESP. Movies, television and novels have explored this topic in depth to the point that it has become part of the common zeitgeist, or the spirit of our age. One of the moods of our times is an increasing interest in all things paranormal. Many people believe that they have either been born with some sort of extrasensory perception or that they can achieve it through meditation along with training from a spiritual guide. Sad to say, too many are turning to dangerous and false sources for these experiences. This is another reason why we believe that God wants to offer biblical alternatives to these displays together with clear instructions on how they are to be activated and operated.

There are many reasons for this modern interest with something so ancient and clearly tied to occult practices. Perhaps the greatest reason is that people inherently know that there is a realm beyond mere reason, where they can perceive things about themselves and others. C.S. Lewis, the brilliant English author of the Narnia books, penned the following words in his book, Mere Christianity. "If I find in myself a desire which no experience in this world can satisfy, the most probable explanation is that I was made for another world."[1]

> **People inherently know that there is a realm beyond mere reason where they can perceive things about themselves and others.**

It is this desire for another world that is growing in intensity today. Perhaps one of the additional reasons that this is happening is that the Church in America has left out this wonderful dimension in both belief and practice. In this chapter, we are seeking to respond to this lack with teachings on the scriptural approach to paranormal perception and its practice. We want to give biblical guidelines and teaching on what the Scriptures say about extrasensory gifts and abilities (the gifts of the Holy Spirit) and how they may be activated in a person's life.

## Four major categories of revelatory gifts

As we probe more deeply into this subject, we will examine four major categories of these revelatory supernatural gifts: the gift of prophecy, the word of knowledge, the word of wisdom, and the discerning of spirits. Each of these functions has clear scriptural instructions on their use and activation as well as their biblical precedent.  In Scripture, these gifts are known as the charismas or manifestations of the Holy Spirit. In the Apostle Paul's letter to the church at Corinth he explains the reason that these sorts of abilities are given to followers of Christ. **"Now to each one the manifestation of the Spirit is given for the common good"** 1 Cor. 12:7.

It is well to note from this passage the following: First, that the gift is for the "common good". In other words, it's not to show off spiritually or bring glory to the gifted one, but rather for the purpose of benefiting others. Second, the gift is a manifestation of the Holy Spirit, therefore it is not inherently a part of the nature of the individual who manifests the gift.  This establishes two principles. Number one; that it is available to every believer and number two; because it is a gift of the Holy Spirit, it does not require the person to have some unique, human ability to operate in this realm. The supernatural action happens because of the superhuman influence and empowerment of the Holy Spirit.

Before we get into the details, let us further add one more encouragement. It's important to realize that these gifts are not only available, but clearly promised in the Bible. The Apostle Peter, echoing the prophecy of the prophet Joel, spoke of the day when God would pour out his Spirit on all flesh. This would be during the last days and would be evidenced by both men and women, both old and young moving in the supernatural realm.

(Act 2:17–18) We call this "Every Member Involvement" or EMI. In some circles, it would be called the "priesthood of all believers."

The Apostle Paul in his letter to the church at Ephesus stated that his purpose as a spiritual leader, along with the other church leaders, was to train ordinary believers to serve His church. (Eph. 4:11–13) When God calls a person into the realm of service to others He always offers them the equipment necessary to do the work He's called them to. Followers of Christ are called to serve others not merely with human effort, but in the power of the Holy Spirit. Therefore, it is evident that our God, whose resources are unlimited, would not fail to adequately provide His servants with the abilities to operate in the realm of the supernatural. Take these promises to heart as you follow along with us in this study.

## The Gift of Prophecy

The first gift of the Holy Spirit that we want to explore is the gift of Prophecy. When it comes to this gift, let us begin with a few humorous stories from Bob, some of which may be true and others that may have become charismatic urban legends. One noted church leader tells the story of being in a service when a word of prophecy was given to the congregation. It went something like this: "Behold, as I said by my servant John Wesley or was it Charles?" Perhaps God was having a senior moment...

Another humorous one Bob heard is when a dear exhorter proclaimed to the congregation something close to the following: "The Lord says to rise up right this moment and go out into the streets and preach the word. Leave thy coat and hat behind for you must go quickly." The excited "prophet" went out the back door of the church only to return shortly with this addition to their declaration: "Correction, be sure to take your coat, it's cold outside."

**Followers of Christ are called to serve others not merely with human effort, but in the power of the Holy Spirit.**

In another, a misguided seer gave a "word" with a serious dramatic flair that

114

went something like this: "Thus saith the Lord, "There is fear in the east and there's fear in the west and there's fear in the south and fear in the north and sometimes I get kinda afraid myself.""

Let us round off these stories with this final zinger. A dear but misguided would-be prophet made this attempt at declaring on behalf of the Lord: "I am the mighty God who led my people out of Egypt by Joshua my servant. And I am the one who led you across the Red Sea by my servant Joshua and behold I am the one who brought you to mount Sinai by my servant Joshua." Then there's a momentary pause to be followed by this declaration. "Behold, the Lord hath made a mistake."

We've given the four earlier illustrations for two reasons. First, in the New Testament expression of the prophetic gift we're taught that all prophecy must be judged. (1 Cor. 14:29) We trust you've been able to discern the veracity of the ones we've just mentioned. Second, we mention these because too often we tend to take ourselves too seriously. Over the years we've seen too many self-appointed prophets who think that they have the "Word of the Lord," when they've missed it by a mile. **Humility is always our best defense**.

We have discussed how a cavalier attitude toward this important gift has often cheapened it and created cynicism towards its function in the church and the world. This is one of the reasons we've written this book. Our hope is that, as you seek to operate in this gift, you will not only take it seriously, but make the commitment to never abuse it in any way. Too many people have been led astray by so-called prophets. We hope this sort of thing is exposed and corrected amongst God's people.

It is clear from the Apostle Paul's instruction to the Corinthian church that the function of prophesying was encouraged and was to be actively sought after. It is the only gift that we are told to eagerly desire. (1 Cor. 14:39) This is because the gift has the power to encourage and guide the church and its members in significant and healthy ways when it functions properly. (1 Cor. 14:3, 5, 12, 26) It is also the medium through which other important gifts are expressed, such as the word of knowledge and word of wisdom. Often when someone is given divine knowledge it is expressed through the prophetic utterance.

**It's the word that carries the authority and not the spokesperson.**

**The definition of prophecy can be further expanded as "speaking God's immediate message for a person or group of people through the empowerment of the Holy Spirit."** Often it involves knowing facts which only God or the person[s] being addressed could know. This is what gives prophecy its supernatural character. It is not rational analysis, nor is it a particularly appropriate example of the teaching gift. It is not a matter of rational thought at all. It is something that the prophet "hears" and then speaks.

When we operate in this gift we must remember that we are speaking for God. The Apostle Peter exhorted the church that when we speak in this capacity it must be with a sense that God is personally speaking through us. (1 Peter 4:11) Why do we say this? Simply, because it is vital that we hear from God and confirm that fact through the Holy Spirit before we presume to be His mouthpiece. Prophecy is not expressing our personal opinion on a matter; it is speaking for God through His power.

Just as important is the fact that when a deep personal reverence for God's truth accompanies this operation it adds a gravitas to the message that is essential. It's important to note here that this doesn't mean that the vessel being used to deliver the message has some sort of exalted position. Remember, in the case of Balaam, God spoke through a donkey. It's the word that carries the authority and not the spokesperson. We will have more to say about this in a later chapter.

Sadly, sometimes people make a donkey out of themselves when they imagine themselves to be an exalted gift to the church simply as a result of delivering an effective message. Think of the absurdity of a UPS driver expecting to be thanked for a birthday gift he happened to deliver. When we take the credit for a gift God allows us to deliver, we open the door to allow pride to creep into our personality and lifestyle. Again, humility is our best defense.

## Purpose of Prophecy

When we move in this important gift it is crucial to remember that the Apostle Paul gave the church at Corinth three vital reasons for its operation. The NIV translation gives us three words to consider (strengthening, encouraging and comfort). First, it is for the building up of those who hear it. (1 Cor. 14:3) Many times when God initiates this function in a group or individually, it is to strengthen those who may be struggling and in need of refreshing. It is often given to move them forward through a trial or to guide them in the midst of spiritual warfare or to strengthen them during times of temptation or suffering. (Isa. 50:4; 1 Tim 1:18)

Second, the next purpose of prophecy is to move people towards God's perspective. The word "exhortation" in the original language carries with it the concept of making an appeal. Often when speaking prophetically we are appealing to the hearer to move closer to God and His purpose for them. Therefore, the message carries with it a certain energy that hopefully will motivate the hearer(s) to acts of obedience. (Heb. 10:24) Because genuine prophecy is a word from God, we should expect it to have not just the power to inform, but also the power to transform. And it does!

Third, in this passage we are told that the prophetic word can bring comfort. When balanced with the other words in this segment it is a vital part of the gift. People need to not only be strengthened and motivated, but often they need to be comforted. The church at Thessalonica was filled with anxiety concerning predictions that people were making concerning the Lord's return. In his letter to them, the Apostle Paul was able to comfort them with the prophecy he gave concerning the second coming of Christ. He instructed them to comfort one another with this accurate prediction. 1 Thess. 4:18

## Foretelling and Forth telling

The gift of prophecy in the New Testament functioned in a dual capacity. It was used both to forth tell and foretell. Forth telling can be seen in situations where prophets brought great strength and comfort to the church in the midst of controversy and uncertainty. It is God's word for a problem being experienced right now. By way of example; the early church had been in the midst of a controversy concerning the Gentiles' responsibility in relationship to the Law of Moses.

Paul and Barnabas had both gone to Jerusalem to settle this matter with the church leadership. Once it was decided that the gentiles were not required to keep the Law of Moses, the leaders in Jerusalem sent this message back to Antioch by the hand of Silas and Judas. Both of these men were prophets and the account tells us that they were able to encourage and strengthen the believers there. (Acts 15:32) No doubt the earlier disagreement concerning the Law of Moses had left many of them in a quandary. Now under the inspiration of the Holy Spirit, Silas and Judas were able to bring this matter to a close and settle any anxiety in the hearts of the believers there.

The foretelling function of prophecy speaks to the future. Usually this is either by way of a promise to be fulfilled in the future or a warning concerning a problem to be encountered in the future.

When the gift of prophecy was used in a foretelling function amongst the early believers in Christ, it often had a significant impact and had to be extremely accurate. (Acts 11:27–30) On one occasion recorded in the Book of Acts a prophet by the name of Agabus arrived in Antioch and predicted that a massive famine would occur, affecting the entire Roman Empire. Ancient historians have confirmed this report, but it is evident from the context that at the time no one knew that such dearth would occur.

In spite of no visible evidence of an impending famine, the church in Antioch received a considerable amount of money and sent it to Jerusalem with Paul and Barnabas. This is the wonderful thing about accurate foretelling. When the gift of the prophetic functions in this capacity, it can save lives and give much needed direction to God's people. It is important to consider that if this word had not been accurate, then not only would the integrity of the prophetic word and the prophet Agabus have been brought into reproach, but the money of the faithful in Antioch would have been misappropriated.

One of the most interesting displays of this in modern times came through the boy prophet of Armenia. The account of this prophecy is given in Demos Shakirian's book, The Happiest People on Earth. In his book, Demos tells how a young boy who could neither read nor write had a visionary encounter in which he saw the future persecution of the Armenian people and was given direction of how they could escape from what would become the first modern holocaust.

The boy not only received this warning in detail, but what he saw was written down. As well he drew a map giving direction for the people to settle on the west coast of the United States. This boy could not read maps and had no prior geographic knowledge of what he saw.

Those who followed the prophetic instructions escaped the horrible persecution that the Turkish government inflicted on nearly one million Armenians. This function of the prophetic gift was rare in New Testament times and is rare today as well. It's notable that Agabus is only mentioned two places in the book of Acts. In his second appearance, he warns the Apostle Paul concerning the future persecution he would face. (Acts 21:10–14) This warning was accurate, but not complete in all its details. This shows us the reason why all prophetic words must be judged. Agabus warned Paul that he would be bound by the Jews and handed over to the Gentiles.

The word proved to be true. Once in Jerusalem Paul was confronted by a mob of people in the temple who falsely claimed he had brought Gentiles into the sacred places. Ironically, it was

Gentile Roman soldiers and their captain that rescued Paul from what would no doubt have been his end.

**Intimacy with God brings not only His voice, but the confidence to risk speaking His words.**

Those who heard this word at the time Paul received it interpreted it as a warning giving Paul divine direction to avoid this evident arrest. Nevertheless, Paul chose to ignore this interpretation and continue his plans to go into a situation that might mean his arrest and possible death.

We can learn some important lessons from this account. First, we can see that God clearly speaks in a future tense to His followers. But when He does, it is important that we properly interpret these words. Over the last part of the twentieth century and during the current season of trouble in the new millennium, we've seen books written about possible futures for the church and the world. Most concern dire predictions.

When it comes to interpreting "End-Time" prophecies recorded in the Bible we find that many predictions have been extremely inaccurate. People have predicted the day of the return of Christ, the rise of the anti-Christ and the rapture of the church only to have egg on their faces when these things failed to occur. Like the instructions given to the church in Corinth, we need to judge these forecasts thoroughly.

When it comes to prophetic utterances given by those who claim to have divine insight into future events, it is just as important to weigh them closely under the inspiration of the Holy Spirit and against the clear lens of Scripture and with the best of our human reason. Modern prophets have predicted certain things and gained great notoriety today only to be proven completely inaccurate later.

The sad fact is that these failures not only discredit the self-proclaimed prophet, but the ministry of prophecy as well. To add to this sad scenario, often these seers have been exposed later in their ministries to have lived immoral lives and to have taught heretical doctrines. All of this will be discussed in a later chapter.

We write this not to diminish the importance of this gift, because we heartedly believe that it is a legitimate expression of God's economy in our day, but to caution believers each time such a prophetic message is given. Having stated these cautions, we must say that the ministry of prophecy must not be discounted simply because failures and counterfeits exist. To do so is nothing more than throwing the baby out with the bath water.

### Activation Guidelines

In Micah 3:8, the prophet declares that God's Spirit has filled him that he might proclaim God's word. Perhaps what is of greatest importance in the activation of this gift is that we seek to be continually full of the Holy Spirit. If we are empowered by the Spirit we will be more attuned to His voice. The prophet Amos clearly heard what God had said and explained that speaking for God was almost an automatic outcome of hearing what God had said. This is the crucial element in activating this gift in our lives – intimacy with God brings not only His voice, but the confidence to risk speaking His words.

As the leaders of the church in Antioch worshiped God in a season of fasting and prayer, God clearly spoke to them concerning the future ministry of the Apostles Paul and Barnabas. (Acts 13:1–3) So like them, as we spend time in God's word and in prayer and fasting we will clearly begin to hear from God and His message for others.

## Some questions to consider:

1. What have you learned from this chapter?

2. Do you have a desire for a supernatural dimension in your faith? In your relationship with God?

3. We have said in this chapter that God will not command you to do something that He will not equip or empower you to do. Does this bring a new confidence to you as you consider risking in order to experience the supernatural spiritual gifts?

4. We have stressed humility in the chapter. Why is humility so important when moving in the supernatural gifts of the Holy Spirit?

5. Why do you think the Apostle Paul stresses that the supernatural gifts are for the "common good?"

# Chapter 14:  More Terms to Define and Explain

### The Word of Knowledge

Every day most of us learn something new. We can learn about an event through the media or we can meet someone new through a casual acquaintance and get to know something about them or perhaps hear from a friend about a new event in their lives. On each of these occasions we are receiving a tiny part of the complete knowledge of all that God knows. We say God is omniscient because He knows all things. A word of knowledge in the biblical sense is God sharing with us some of the knowledge that He possesses through the supernatural means of the Holy Spirit.

**A word of knowledge in the biblical sense is God sharing with us some of the knowledge that He possesses through the supernatural means of the Holy Spirit.**

It is important to note that we did not gain this information by studying, talking with others or observing things personally, but rather by God imparting it to us through a supernatural means. This means it is a gift; something spoken or uttered to us by the Holy Spirit. Often this is knowledge of an event that is only known to God and the person experiencing the event. When we share what God has revealed to us, the person receiving this gift of a word of knowledge knows that God has a purpose in revealing this formerly hidden bit of information. It is an experience of God gently [or sometimes forcefully] intervening in their lives.

There are some great examples in Scripture of this gift in operation. This sort of gift occurred in the life of God's Old Testament prophets. God supernaturally revealed to Elisha that his servant Gehazi had gone behind his back to request a gift from a foreign general. This was something completely contrary to Elisha's wishes and as the servant approached the general, Elisha perceived the event even though he was in another place at the time. (2 Kings 5:20–27)

As Joshua commanded the invading armies of God in their campaign to conquer the promised land, God showed him why, in their second battle, they were defeated. God revealed to Joshua that their failure was because someone in their ranks had sinned. (Joshua 7:10–11)

We see this gift in operation in the life of Jesus as well. While taking a break from His journey He stopped to rest outside the city of Samaria where He spoke to a woman He had never met before. He revealed to her that He was aware that she had been married five times and was currently living with a man that wasn't her husband. (John 4:16–19)

On another occasion, He knew that Lazarus had died even though He was some distance away from Lazarus's home at the time. (John 11:11–17) He told His disciples about this event and later when they arrived at Lazarus' home, they then became aware of it.

It is tempting to say that Jesus knew these things because He is God and knows all things. Tempting as this conclusion may be, we need to consider the fact that Jesus had emptied himself of those innate powers and only came to supernatural knowledge like this through the gift of the Holy Spirit's insight. He did this to encourage us such that we can follow His example and receive supernatural knowledge as well. He promised His followers that once in heaven He would be imparting His gifts to us, gifts such as divine knowledge through the Holy Spirit. (John 16:13–14)

 We see this in the life of the early church. As the followers of Christ in Jerusalem were bringing their financial gifts to the apostles for the support of needy people, God showed Peter that a couple were attempting to deceive him concerning the amount they were donating. (Acts 5:1–10)

As the Apostle Paul was coming to the end of his third missionary journey, he told the elders of the church at Ephesus that he would be imprisoned. (Acts 20:23) Once he arrived at the home of Philip the evangelist, the prophet Agabus spoke to the gathering and told them that God had revealed to him that Paul would suffer persecution in the city of Jerusalem. (Acts 21:10–11)

This gift operates today as well. It has made a fresh appearance with the coming of the Pentecostal movement in the last two centuries. One of the great examples of this is the story told by Demos Shakerian concerning his grandfather coming into the fullness of the baptism of the Holy Spirit; while his family was still in the nation of Armenia. The elder Shakerian was somewhat skeptical of the Russian's belief that God still worked through His Holy Spirit as He did in the days of the apostles.

Demos' family was scheduled to host a group of Russian Pentecostals at their farm. To prepare for this event, instead of butchering a healthy cow, his mother chose one with a blemished eye. To cover up her indiscretion her husband put the head of the beast in a sack and hid it under a pile of grain in the nearby barn. When the caravan of Russians arrived, the meal was prepared and just before they were to eat the patriarch was asked to bless the food. Instead of giving a blessing he raised his hand to stop the event and then walked to the barn. He emerged a few moments later carrying the sack with the animal's head in it. When he dropped the bag in front of all that were there the head rolled out and the milky eye was exposed for all to see.

This sudden display of the word of knowledge opened the Shakerian elder to the reality of the Holy Spirit. Moments later he received the baptism of the Holy Spirit as the patriarch laid his hand on him.

This is a very dramatic example, but often a word of knowledge can be as simple as God giving you an impression about what someone may be declaring as fact. A dear friend of Bob's was speaking to a college group and had a group of youth gathered around him after his talk. One of the group began to challenge the speaker, suggesting that what he had shared was inaccurate and misleading. The antagonist claimed to know both the Hebrew and Greek languages and therefore was much more capable of giving a proper interpretation of the matter being discussed.

The person seemed to be very convincing and was difficult to deal with. Then our friend got a simple impression from the Holy Spirit; his adversary was lying. So, he turned to the man and said would you tell me the first letter of the Greek Alphabet. Suddenly the tables were turned. The man was nonplused and couldn't give an answer. Through this simple, but divinely inspired word of knowledge, my friend found his teaching defended by God Himself.

If we want to move in the word of knowledge, we must first be open to the fact that God wants to give us special knowledge for situations that require it. We've seen how God uses this gift in evangelism and ministry to other Christians. It's a truly helpful gift, if properly used. Here are a few guidelines for seeing the gift operating in the life of the believer.

## Activation guidelines

You need to be open to the right impressions. In other words, you must believe that God is interested in building his kingdom through you and that supernatural gifts are part of the kingdom building plan. Once you've settled that issue, you should expect that He will be giving you special knowledge when it is need. So, first of all, be aware of the fact that the Holy Spirit will be speaking to you about others' lives and the current situation that you're in. This is something that can occur even to young believers. Often it can even be more prevalent in them since they have not been programmed to believe that God doesn't give words of knowledge today.

An example of this is an event that occurred in Bob's life when he was a new believer.

## Bob's story

*"Just as Elisha was given secret knowledge dealing with the movements and location of Israel's enemies, I was given knowledge about an issue dealing with the location of a certain individual that I'd been praying for. Shortly after I became a believer I started to fervently pray for friends that had been involved in the same hippie life style that I had been in. Often, I would walk over to another believer's house that was also praying for my friends and we'd join together in prayer for our former hippie friends.*

*I followed a specific pattern to get to their home to join them in prayer. That path took me through the nearby college campus. Each time I would take the same route, but on one particular day I felt a strong impression to go through the children's park instead. This meant that I would be on an entirely different course to my prayer partner's home. It was irregular, but the impression was so strong that I went that way.*

*To my surprise, no sooner had I entered the children's park, then there was one of the friends we'd been praying for. As it turns out he had been wondering about me and where I was. I soon engaged him in the details of my transformation and the radical change God had made in my life. He was with a group of guys that soon invited him to go and smoke some marijuana with them. Interestingly enough, he was so intrigued by our conversation that he refused to leave with his friends and continued to listen to my testimony. Shortly after I finished sharing he excused himself and I later learned that he went to a nearby chapel and committed his life to Christ. He attended church that night at a revival service I was also attending. At that meeting he made a public declaration of his new faith. This rather simple but important impression resulted in a wonderful work of God."*

We believe that God is giving us impressions all the time and if we're open to what may appear to be simple changes prompted by the Holy Spirit in daily patterns, we will see wonderful things coming out of it. These impressions can be a word about someone's need for healing, or that someone is open to the message of the gospel, or a quiet whisper that someone is going through a difficult situation in their lives and needs God's encouragement.

By mentioning to others those impressions that we believe God is saying to them, His grace can confirm to them that they are loved and God is near. To add a word of caution, God was not asking Bob to do anything risky or odd, but rather, to make a simple change in his daily routine so that He might lead him to someone in need.

God can also give us words of knowledge through dreams and visions. A great example of this is another event that occurred in Bob's life both prior and after his conversion to Christ.

## Bob's story

*"When I was in my first year at college I found myself hitch hiking back and forth from the Bay Area and my hometown in northern California on the weekends to visit friends. On one occasion, I was picked up by a minister who shared the gospel with me. I was not that interested, but I was eager to let him know about my own explorations in the New Age drug culture. Despite my disinterest, God was at work in that situation.*

*Over the next three years God brought my face before that minister and he prayed for me over and over again. Shortly after I found Christ I began attending a small church in my home town. Within a week or two the pastor of that church got a call from a minister that was doing revival services in different churches in the area. The pastor began to explain how I'd been saved and some of my other hippies' friends had started to attend service at the church. The pastor was about to tell them my name when the evangelist interrupted the pastor and said, "Don't tell me his name let me tell you." Then to the amazement of the pastor he declared my name.*

*That conversation led to the evangelist coming to our church and holding a series of meetings that resulted in an outbreak of spirit blessing for that whole area. God had given this minister a vision of me over and over again and then confirmed it by arranging for our lives to come into contact again resulting in a time of spiritual renewal for many."*

**Knowledge without wisdom can be dangerous.**

It is important that you're open to dreams and visions concerning others and corresponding situations. These experiences may be the word of knowledge at work as it was for Paul when he received the call to bring the Gospel to Europe (Acts 16:6–10) or similar to Peter when he had a vision that prepared him to bring the good news to the Gentiles in Caesarea.

### Word of Wisdom

One of the most important gifts in God's array of blessings is the word of wisdom. Knowledge without wisdom can be dangerous. Just look at what mankind has done with some of the knowledge that has been acquired through science. When the secrets of the atom were unmasked, atomic power was unleashed that now produces electricity that enhances our lives, but it also opened the door to the development and use of weapons of mass destruction. The writer of Proverbs tells us that wisdom is supreme. (Prov. 4:7, NKJV) In other words, there are many gifts, but one of the best is wisdom. Therefore, we believe that one of the most excellent gifts is the word of wisdom.

Wisdom builds on the material that knowledge provides. That way, the word of knowledge and the word of wisdom often operate in tandem. **The kind of wisdom we're referring to is beyond the scope of human ability; it is divine.** It's not something that can be gained through study or experience and should by no means replace them. Nonetheless, when it's in operation, others recognize that it's from God and therefore it glorifies Him. A great example of this is found in the life of King Solomon. (1 Kings 3:16–28)

An example of the word of wisdom is seen in the life of Jesus when He was being questioned about the matter of taxes. He was asked if He should pay taxes to Caesar. We're sure those questioning

Him hoped He would make an inappropriate statement that would set Him at odds either with the government or with the religious people of the land. But God, through the Holy Spirit, gave Him a word of wisdom that confounded them all when He held up a Roman coin that carried the inscription of Caesar and said that which belonged to Caesar should be given to him and that which belonged to God given to God. (Matt. 22:15–22)

When it comes to biblical examples of this gift in operation in the lives of believers, we can see it in the life of the Apostle Paul before the Sanhedrin (Acts 23:23–35) or among the church leaders gathering in Jerusalem to seek an answer from God concerning a controversy in the early church. (Acts 15:1–21)

**Activation Guidelines**

When it comes to this gift, God provides us with some clear instructions from scripture. Solomon, who had great wisdom, was very aware of how this should be activated in one's life. His admonition was to have a listening ear (Prov. 2:1–2).

There's a great example of this in the story told about a man who worked in an ice plant. These facilities were common years ago before most people had refrigerators and when most ice was produced in a central location. These plants were highly insulated and their floors covered with saw dust. This type of protection kept the ice from melting until someone came to purchase it. One day, a worker who was employed at the plant, lost his watch there. Since the floor was covered in sawdust it would make finding the lost timepiece difficult.

The solution was simple. He waited for all the other workers to go home and then stood in the center of the building. The thick plant walls blocked the noise from outside as well as other distractions, like the voices of his fellow workers. He soon began to hear the soft ticking of his watch.

In the same way, if we allow our spirit to grow quiet and develop a listening ear, we can hear the still small voice of wisdom whispering in our spirit. Practicing being still and quiet is the route to acquiring a listening ear for the still, small voice of God.

Cultivating a teachable spirit is at the core of having a listening ear. God tells us that He will awaken us each morning with words of instruction, if we have the heart of a sincere learner. (Isa. 50:4) During a long sojourn in the desert, after he had fled from Jezebel, Elijah found God's word coming to him in a still small voice. (1 Kings 19:11–13) The instruction God had for him was not in a fire, earthquake or mighty wind, but in a whisper. The important thing to note about Elijah is that he was aware of the difference and knew enough to hear that quiet speech.

In the same way as we continue to wait quietly before God, His wisdom will become more evident to us. A wonderful example of this is a story that concerns a city dweller and a man raised in the wilderness. On a certain occasion, the city dweller was visited by a Native American who lived in an area where the loud noises of the city were not present. In that forested environment, he had become familiar with the sounds made by the tiny creatures that lived there. Therefore, when he was visiting his friend in the city, he was alert to the call of a tiny bug in a nearby bush. He asked his friend, "Do you hear that sound?" His friend responded, "What do you mean - the sound of buses, cars and pedestrians talking?"

After walking over to the nearby flowerpot and taking the tiny creature from it the Native American replied, "No, the sound of this insect?" The Native American had developed an "ear" for that sound and was familiar with it even in the midst of a busy city. In the same way, we can develop a listening ear for God's words of wisdom, if we actively seek to hear from Him.

## Discerning of Spirits

Before discussing this gift, we must first understand that there is an entire realm inhabited by beings that have the capacity to move in and out of the physical dimension that we usually think of as reality. In many places around our planet it is not uncommon for cultures to be very aware of this duel reality. In our postmodern world people, even godly believers, are naive as to the existence of trans-dimensional beings all around us. This is a consequence of what we discussed regarding our Western aversion to the supernatural.

The Bible divides these trans-dimensional beings into three categories; Divine (John 1:32–34) and the divine spirit in man (Job 32:8), Angelic; Holy (Heb. 1:7) and demonic. (Matt. 12:43–45) The gift of discerning of spirits allows us to discern among them so that we can properly deal with them.

We can ask God to give us sensitivity to this realm and He will allow us to properly perceive and understand it. This was the case in the life of one of Elisha's servants. While they were staying in the city of Dothan, they were surrounded by the cohorts of the Aramean army. When the servant became aware of the force that had come to capture Elisha, he was deeply concerned and questioned Elisha about what they should do. The prophet explained that there was a much larger contingency of forces with them than against them. Then he prayed that his servant's eyes would be opened and immediately he was able to see that the city was surrounded by the forces of God. (2 Kings 6:8–17)

It is this spiritual perception that functions when the gift of discerning of spirits is operating. We may not see it with our physical eyes, but we will be able to perceive beings and things in the unseen realm.

Some excellent examples of this are found in Scripture. Peter, when confronted with a former sorcerer who thought that he could buy the gift of God, was able to see that the man's human spirit had been polluted with bitterness and bound up with rebellion. (Acts 8:18-23) During a season of ministry in the city of Philippi, the Apostle Paul was confronted by a young woman who was continually prophesying over him. What the woman was saying was correct, but Paul perceived that the spirit animating the girl was demonic. He finally became so frustrated with the situation that he cast the spirit out of her. (Acts 16:16–18)

Another example is found when Paul and Barnabas arrived in the city of Paphos, located on the island of Cyprus. There Paul confronted a false prophet who was resisting Paul's instructions to the governor of the island. Paul clearly exposed the demonic influences that were at work in the man and rebuked him by causing the man to be blinded for a season. (Acts 13:6–12)

Scripture identifies various types of demonic spirits and we see that Jesus and His followers were able to also identify them and deal with them effectively. Some of the categories of evil spirits mentioned in the Bible include: dumb, unclean, blind, deaf, infirmity and lunacy. (Mark 9:17, Luke 13:11, Matt. 17:15–18, Matt. 12:43, Matt. 12:22–32) In each of these cases the source of the problem was identified as a wicked spirit and then dealt with accordingly by the power of God. This gift doesn't operate solely for the purpose of making us aware of the presence of evil, but also so that we can aggressively deal with it. God, through His word and the power of the Holy Spirit, gives us the authority to overcome these spirits once we have identified them. (Luke 10:19)

**The Spirit of God vigorously resists all the forces of evil in the world and will alert us, and give us insight into how to deal with the demonic.**

### Activation Guidelines

First of all, it's important to recognize what this gift is not. It is not the gift of suspicion, criticism or some form of spiritism. Sometimes you will meet people who say that they are discerning an evil spirit at work in another person and it's really their own jealousy, bitterness and suspicion that is operating. Even some of Jesus disciples felt that they should rebuke others who were casting out demons because they were not part of the group traveling with Jesus. (Mark 9:38–39) Jesus corrected His disciples' lack of discernment. So, we need to be careful that our human judgment does not take precedence over God's gift of discernment.

At the same time, there are groups of so-called spiritists that claim to have spiritual discernment and are actually living under demonic influence. Such people are those involved in new age religions and occult practices. The gift of discerning of spirits is not a human gift, but rather a divine ability granted by God. One of the best ways to have this gift active in our lives as believers is to be full of the Holy Spirit. The Spirit of God vigorously resists all the forces of evil in the world and will alert us and give us insight into how to deal with the demonic.

In dealing with the demonic it is important to ask God for discernment. Paul instructed the church in the city of Corinth that a spiritual person has the ability to spiritually discern. (1 Cor. 2:14–15) The Apostle John also teaches us to test the spirits. (1 John 4:1–2)

We hope that through this examination of scripture you are convinced that all of these revelatory gifts are both biblical and available to us today. Even though you may believe they are for the Church today you may still wonder, "Are they really for me?" The next chapter will help to answer that question.

For more on the practical aspects of activating the revelatory gifts in your life, see Chapters 17, 18 and 19.


## Some questions to consider:

1. What have you learned from this chapter?

2. In Bob's story of taking a different route to his prayer meeting he had nothing more than an idea that he should take a different route. It turned out he was being led by the Holy Spirit. Why do you think the Holy Spirit did not make His message more obvious?

3. How sure would you have to be to risk obeying what you thought might be a message from the Holy Spirit? 40%, 50%, 60%, 70%...?

4. How do you think the spiritual gift of wisdom differs from the human wisdom we accumulate through life experience?

5. Many Christians shy away from the spiritual gift of the discerning of spirits because it has been badly misused in the past. How could it be wrongly used? How could it be correctly used?

# Chapter 15: Is Prophecy Really for Everyone?

We wrote this book because we believe that of all the supernatural gifts of the Holy Spirit, prophecy is the most useful and accessible. Jesus told us that His sheep hear His voice. (John 10:27) This is a nice, easily dismissed, pastoral image that conveys a profound promise: His sheep can actually hear His voice! Even more so, He expects His sheep to hear His voice! Handy little truth, isn't it? Prophecy is nothing more than "hearing His voice" and repeating what He said. So why is that so important? After all, we have the Bible which gives us true principles to live by. Do we really need to hear His immediate voice? And what difference does it make to our lives to hear His voice right here and right now?

> **Prophecy is nothing more than "hearing His voice" and repeating what He said.**

The Apostle Paul tells us that prophecy is important. He tells us to desire it above all the other spiritual gifts. He tells us not to reject it or devalue it. Further, he tells us that the church is built on the foundation of the Apostles and Prophets. This raises the question; what is so special about hearing the immediate voice of God? Fortunately, Paul answers that question for us when he says: **"... faith comes from what is heard, and what is heard comes through the word of Christ"** Rom. 10:17.

The word "faith" used here means, "to believe to the extent of complete trust and reliance." It is the kind of certainty that moves mountains [to use a Biblical phrase]. It is the kind of faith that is referred to in James 5:15 where it tells us that the prayer of faith will heal the sick. It is the kind of faith that Jesus referred to when He said it would result in answered prayers.

Obviously, faith is instrumental in most answered prayers, but the real question is how do we get this kind of complete trust and reliance? The answer is through the "word" of Christ. This means the word "word" *is* the word! The Greek word used here is "rhema." It means the actual spoken word. It is very immediate. Literally, it means to hear His spoken voice.

## How do we hear his "voice"?

Jesus tells us that we will "hear" His voice and Paul tells us it is the route to powerful faith which brings the supernatural power of God into our present circumstances. This raises an important question: how do we "hear" His voice? There are two main ways. The first, which is self-evident, is through the Bible. We have all had the experience of reading the Bible and having a passage "jump off the page" and touch us with life-changing truth. This is a work of the Holy Spirit which goes beyond our mere intellectual understanding of what we are reading. This work of the Holy Spirit, in illuminating and applying scripture to our minds and lives, is a gift of supernatural "revelation."

> **Prophecy has the power to engender faith in the hearer, which faith brings the power to fulfill the prophetic word.**

The second way we hear God's voice is through His immediate word to us, which is also revelation because it is a work of the Holy Spirit. It has the same effect of revealing His truth to our minds and our lives, but it comes directly rather than through Scripture. It is always consistent with what Scripture teaches us, but it is not dependent upon Scripture for its delivery. **When the message comes through another person, we call this the gift of prophecy**. How we recognize His voice to us, for ourselves and for others is the subject of a later chapter. For now, we need to understand the power of prophecy and its importance to our lives.

When a true prophetic word is spoken, it is a word of Christ that is coming through an authorized representative. It has the authority and power of God delivered with it! It has the power to engender faith in the hearer, which faith brings the power to fulfill the prophetic word. One prophetic word can produce the kind of faith that perseveres no matter what the enemy throws at you. Here is an interesting example:

A number of years ago the denomination Mark was a part of did a survey of all their church plants – both those that succeeded and those that failed. They tested for a variety of factors believed to be important to a successful church plant. These included adequate startup funding, level of theological education of the pastor, training for the startup leadership team, demographic studies of the proposed region, etc. One of the questions asked was; "Did you hear God tell you to do this church plant?"

As it turns out, approximately 90% of those who succeeded "heard" God tell them to do the plant. Conversely, approximately 90% of those who failed said they did not "hear" God tell them to do the plant. All of the other factors were inconclusive. Hearing God imparts faith and prophecy speaks for God. Here is another example of 8 words from God changing the course of a person's life. The life changed was Mark's. Here is the story in his words:

*"A few years ago, Shell and I were on vacation in Moscow, Russia. It was a beautiful spring day. We were walking down the sidewalk when I saw someone walking towards us who I recognized. It was my interpreter from the ministry trip I had taken in the early 90's – the one I have already told you about. This in itself was an amazing co-incidence. As we drew closer, I noticed something unusual about him. He was wearing all the same clothes I had been wearing when I was there over 20 years ago – the same shirt, belt, pants and shoes. This struck me as very odd, but out of concern not to embarrass him I said nothing.*

*The three of us sat down at a sidewalk café to have a coke. As we were talking I heard music coming from a second story window two doors down. Someone was playing an acoustic guitar in a finger picking style that sounded familiar. In fact, the song sounded strangely familiar. He started to sing the song in English and in a moment of utter shock I realized it was a song I had written when I was 20 years old! It had never been recorded and I had only played it for a few friends. It was a surreal experience! And then I woke up. I had been dreaming.*

*Like all dreams, it seemed completely real. While I lay in bed thinking about it, it still seemed real – real and very significant. I was sure it had to have been from God. I was also sure it meant something important for me, so I asked God what it meant. I said, "Father this has to mean something. The guy was wearing my clothes from 20 years ago and then another total stranger is playing my song from almost 40 years ago! What are You trying to say to me?"*

*Before I tell you what He said to me, it would help if you knew my life situation at the time of the dream. To my regret, I had reached a point in my ministry where I no longer felt I was accomplishing anything. I am in the people-changing business, and as far as I could tell, business was not good. I was discouraged and retirement was looking better by the day. I was actually counting the months as the big 65 approached. It was not that I didn't like my ministry; it was that I no longer believed I was making much of a difference in people's lives. I believed I no longer had influence for God.*

*After pondering the strangeness of the dream and realizing it must have come from God, I asked Him what He was trying to tell me. This thought came immediately, "You are far more influential than you think." I realized that was the point of the guy wearing my clothes and the second guy singing my song. I took some comfort from this word from the Lord, but in my heart, I still believed whatever influence I had must not be much, even if it was more than I thought.*

*Ten days later I was having lunch with a friend from our church. We ate at our usual place, a very good Chinese restaurant. At the end of the meal the fortune cookies came. I took one and opened it. What do you suppose it said? Yup, "You are far more influential than you think." Word for word.*

*I have been eating at Chinese restaurants since I was a child. I always open the fortune cookie, read the fortune and eat the cookie. To the best of my recollection I have never received that fortune before [not that I pay much attention to fortune cookies].*

*The fortune cookie experience iced the prophecy cake for me! I guess I needed to hear the same word twice. My attitude completely changed. It did not matter what I saw or didn't see. I had a new lease on ministry. My mind was renewed. My energy increased. I wrote my first book. Invitations to speak increased dramatically [I have no idea why]. I decided not to retire and that magic age has come and gone. I am more excited about my ministry now than I have been in decades.*

*God used a dream and that fortune cookie to renew my life by giving me a gift of faith that does not need continual positive feedback in order to carry on. Interestingly, I have noticed that my teaching has more impact and power and the prophetic words I give seem to have more effect as well. Objectively, I have to say that I can see my influence increasing. The amazing thing is that I am not doing any more than I was doing before. In fact, the work is getting easier even though I am getting older. The real change is that now I am believing for much more!"*

In the interests of maintaining peace with our anticipated critics let us say this about fortune cookies: We do not believe fortune cookies are a valid means of discerning God's will for our lives. The fact that God used a fortune cookie to confirm His previous message must not be taken as some sort of divine endorsement of seeking direction from such means. Mark could have just as easily noticed a $1,000.00 bill on the ground and picked it up only to find "you are far more influential than you think" written in divine script on the bill. We also refuse to walk up to every donkey we confront and expect it to prophesy to us. [LOL]

We want to take a moment to analyze how the dream and fortune cookie worked together to bring about life-changing faith. There was nothing obviously supernatural about the dream itself. It could have been nothing more than Mark's subconscious wishing that he had more influence. This would be a fair interpretation given his disillusionment with his ministry.

Even though he took the dream as from God and believed that God had spoken to him regarding its meaning, he was little more than encouraged. This is a sad admission because he readily admits that hearing God's thoughts of encouragement in his mind should have been enough to get him back in the saddle, but it was not. It was just a measure of encouragement.

Had the dream not occurred and he not "heard" God's thoughts in his mind, the fortune cookie experience would have been insignificant. He would have thought, "That is a nice thought, I wish it were true." What made the fortune cookie experience so powerful for him was the juxtaposition of it following the dream and the fact that the two messages were word for word. Neither the dream nor the fortune cookie encounter was a supernatural event in itself, but taken together they were conclusively supernatural to him and in their effect.

What we believe happened was that two events, sharing a common message, could not be dismissed as mere co-incidence. The timing of the dream and the fortune cookie defies coincidence. Something beyond natural chance was occurring – something "super" natural was happening. This brush with the supernatural presence of God in Mark's life produced a supernatural gift of faith that he still draws from two years later.

In retrospect Mark was humbled by the experience, because he recognized himself in the class of people Jesus described when He said, "Unless you people see signs and wonders you will never believe". [John4:48] Sad as it is, we believe that from time to time we are all in that class with doubting Thomas and that is why the gift of prophecy is so wonderful. It is God's help to us in our moments of disbelief. Because faith comes by hearing God's words [and because prophecy is a supernatural gift], prophecy gives us what we need, beyond our natural abilities, to believe in God's goodness to us. If we are correct in our belief that from time to time all of us need supernatural help to believe in God's promises to us, then prophecy is truly for everyone.

**Is Prophecy for Everyone?**

Given the importance of prophecy, we can see that the question; "Is prophecy for everyone?" becomes critical. Is this kind of miracle-working faith only for those who hear God regularly? Does God really intend all of His sheep to hear His voice? If so, why are some called by God to be prophets and others are called to be teachers, etc? This is a legitimate question given what Paul tells us in 1 Corinthians 12:29.

After re-enforcing our unity in our different gifts and callings, Paul underscores our unity in diversity by asking the rhetorical question, **"Are all apostles? Are all prophets? Are all teachers? Do all work miracles? Do all have gifts of healing? Do all speak in tongues? Do all interpret?"** 1 Cor. 12:29–31. The answer to this rhetorical question is obviously "no." This would be the definitive negative answer to our question, but for the fact that Paul seems to contradict himself in the first verse of Chapter 14 where he says, **"Follow the way of love and eagerly desire spiritual gifts, especially the gift of prophecy"** 1 Cor. 14:1.

On the one hand, Paul tells us we are not all "prophets" and on the other hand he tells us to eagerly desire the spiritual gift of prophecy. How do we reconcile these two seemingly contradictory passages?

The best answer we know of comes from Dr. C. Peter Wagner.[4] In the hopes of accurately representing his analysis, we will present our humble efforts as follows:

To understand the distinction Paul is making we need to understand four categories or terms relevant to the exercise of a spiritual gift. These are: 1. the role attached to a spiritual gift, 2. the occasional expression of a spiritual gift, 3. the ministry of a spiritual gift, and 4. the office of a spiritual gift. These are not biblical terms used to describe spiritual gifts, but rather a categorization of how spiritual gifts can be organized and better understood given what the Bible teaches. We are not trying to develop doctrine here, just a helpful way of reconciling two potentially contradictory passages. Here are the terms:

## 1. The Role

When we refer to the role attached to a spiritual gift we are referring to the activity that God empowers and expects from every Christian. The spiritual gift of evangelism provides a very good illustration. The Bible makes it clear that all of us are to be prepared to give a reason for the hope of our salvation in Jesus. We call this being a "witness." Witnessing is the role expected by God for all of us. It requires no supernatural ability, we just tell our story.

Speaking personally, both of us take every good opportunity to witness to non-Christians about our faith, but we have to say that most of the time they do not end up accepting Jesus as their Savior. However, there have been more than a few times in which

**At any time or in any situation we should expect the occasional expression of any spiritual gift as the situation and need requires.**

something supernatural happened - just like the young man who accepted Jesus during Mark's trip to the doctor's office or Bob being guided to witness to his friend in the park. These were as easy as holding a basket under an apple tree and having the fruit fall into it - effortless. The Holy Spirit was obviously doing something supernatural. This is an example of what we call the occasional expression of the spiritual gift of evangelism.

Let's take another example regarding the gift of giving. God expects all of us to support our local church. The role God expects from all of us with respect to the gift of giving is the "tithe." Tithing does not require a supernatural empowerment in order for us to tithe. Tithing is just a matter of obeying God's word – it is our role.

We hope many of you have experienced something like this: you are tithing faithfully without ever thinking of giving beyond your tithe when some special need is announced at church. All of a sudden you find yourself convicted to give to that need. It is such a strong conviction that giving in this case is an easy and joyous choice. This is a work of the Holy Spirit directing and empowering the spiritual gift of giving. This is an example of the occasional expression of the spiritual gift of giving. It's time we defined the term.

**Our responsibility is to discover our spiritual gift ministry and steward our ministry by making time for it.**

### 2. The Occasional Expression of a Spiritual Gift

At any time or in any situation we should expect the occasional expression of any spiritual gift as the situation and need requires. In our example of evangelism there are situations in which you find your words have real power. You watch as the hearer becomes emotional. It is as if every one of your words has spiritual power. You know they are receiving truth from God. You know something beyond your persuasive ability is taking place. This is the occasional expression of the spiritual gift of evangelism. We should all expect this kind of occasional expression of any of the spiritual gifts as the situation and need requires.

### 3. The Ministry of a Spiritual Gift

The occasional expression of a spiritual gift becomes a ministry when it is no longer occasional. **When a spiritual gift occurs in your life with regularity you should consider it one of your principal ministries.** Because the gifts of the Holy Spirit are His gifts and because He lives in each of us, all of the spiritual gifts are resident in all of us. We should all be prepared to pray for the sick, cast out demons, prophesy, teach, evangelize, and even do a miracle, as well as all the rest of the gifts.

Although this should be our mindset, it is readily apparent that none of us have enough time in our lives to do all of the gifts all of the time. We would literally not survive our giftedness. Add to this the fact that, because these gifts are the gifts of the Holy Spirit, we do not decide which of the gifts we will operate in most of the time. He chooses our "ministry" of the spiritual gifts for us. Our choice is whether or not to obey the delegation He has given and to further develop our ministry[ies]. What this means is that we should expect to specialize in a few spiritual gifts with the remaining being occasional.

This may sound rather complex, but in practice it is easy. All you have to do is to be open and experiment with all of the spiritual gifts and watch which experiments are helpful to people and which are not. **The gifts that bless people the most will be your ministries**. Amazing how practical the Bible is! It tells us that the gifts are for the common good in order to build people up, so **all we have to do is watch and see which gifts do people the most good**. It's almost too easy...

Our responsibility is to discover our spiritual gift ministry and steward our ministry by making time for it. We are responsible before God for what we do with the spiritual gifts. If we use our time wisely for the Kingdom of God then God will expand our ministry until it reaches the full potential that He has ordained for us. Let's use the gift of evangelism to illustrate how this might work.

Imagine having the spiritual gift of evangelism. In the beginning, you notice that many times when you witness to someone, they come to Jesus. You compare results with your friends and find that you have a much higher success rate than they do. As a result, you decide to be very intentional about finding opportunities to witness. You overcome your fear and start going out to malls to do "cold calls." People actually get saved!!

You drag your newly caught fish back to church where they will be cleaned. Soon the church notices these new converts and your leadership asks if you are willing to lead others on these evangelistic field trips. You are hesitant because you never considered yourself to be a leader, but because leaders speak for God, you decide to take the risk. On your next adventure, you find that a few of your teammates are leading people to the Lord as well!!

Next the church asks you to teach a weekend course on sharing your faith with strangers! Serious fear arises, but you realize that you have noticed that a few techniques work better than others, so you reluctantly say yes. The first class is a big success. People are being released to witness who were paralyzed with fear prior to taking your class. Now you are truly excited!

A few months later your pastor is bragging you up at a regional pastors meeting and soon other churches are asking you to come and teach your evangelism class and take their wanna-be evangelists out with you on your next field trip. At this point you realize that something is definitely up! You debate the time commitment and wisely decide that God is calling you to a ministry that goes far beyond anything you ever imagined. You say yes and the adventure grows. So, does your joy and sense of fulfillment. Welcome to the Ministry of Evangelism!

What happens if your ministry grows to where you are asked to teach and lead evangelism training all over the country or even the world? Welcome to the "office" of Evangelist!

### 4. The Office of a Spiritual Gift

A ministry of a spiritual gift becomes the "office" of a spiritual gift when the ministry becomes recognized by many churches over an extended area. Billy Graham occupied the office of Evangelist throughout the whole world. He was an evangelist to the nations.

Within the local church, offices also exist. Paul makes this clear in the Book of Ephesians: **"So Christ himself gave the apostles, the prophets, the evangelists, the pastors and teachers, to equip his people for works of service, so that the body of Christ may be built up until we all reach unity in the faith and in the**

**knowledge of the Son of God and become mature, attaining to the whole measure of the fullness of Christ"** Eph. 4:11–13.

It is tempting to see these offices as some sort of honorific position, especially in legalistic circles. Nothing could be further from God's intent. Calling someone a prophet to the church in Los Angeles is not a label used to bestow honor, but rather a descriptive term used to describe his/her function in the body of Christ. **It does not mean he/she is special. It means he/she is specialized**.

It is much like the coaching positions on an NFL football team. There is a head coach, an assistant head coach, an offensive and defensive coach and then several coaches on both the offense and defensive teams. The title of "coach" makes it clear what their function is; to make the players they coach the best they can be. The word which comes before the word "coach" describes which players he works with. Just as these are functional titles, so also are the offices within the church locally and regionally, nationally and internationally.

All of the spiritual gifts operate at the levels of role, occasional expression, and ministry. Only the 5 mentioned above in the Ephesians' passage can carry the further functional description of "office."

## Summary

Our hope is that after reading this chapter you are convinced that God intends all of His children to receive revelation from Him in a direct manner and further, that our responsibility is to discover our spiritual gifts and steward them to the level of ministry He has ordained for us. We can leave the level of "office" in His hands.

## Some questions to consider:

1. What have you learned from this chapter?

2. In this chapter we have said, "When a true prophetic word is spoken it is a word of Christ that is coming through an authorized representative. It has the authority and power of God contained within it! It has the power to engender faith in the hearer which faith brings the power to fulfill the prophetic word." Try explaining this in your own words.

3. In Mark's story of the dream and the fortune cookie, it is clear that the supernatural nature of the message comes from the coincidence of the message from the dream and the message from the fortune cookie. Have you had experiences that mere "coincidence" cannot adequately explain? Could such experiences be God communicating with you? How would you find out?

4. In your own words explain the difference between: 1. The role associated with a spiritual gift, 2. The occasional expression of a spiritual gift, 3. The ministry of a spiritual gift, and 4. The office of a spiritual gift.

5. What is your personal responsibility with respect to your undiscovered spiritual gifts?

# Chapter 16: Old Testament vs. New Testament Prophecy

Is there a difference between Old Testament and New Testament prophetic ministry? If so, who cares? The answer is; yes, and you should. Allow Mark another personal story to illustrate why the difference matters.

*"When I first discovered the prophetic gift, I was amazed. Other than obvious physical healings, like a blind person being healed, there is no better display of the supernatural nature of God than a truly accurate prophetic word. If a picture is worth a thousand words, then an accurate prophetic word is worth a thousand pictures. An accurate prophetic word is truly a wondrous moment. As a result of my enthusiasm, I opened the door wide to prophetic ministry within our church.*

*The church attendance was about 600 at the time. We were running two services and so keeping to a rough timeline was very important to our Children's Church workers. We wanted to open our services to prophetic ministry, so we allowed an "open mike" time for prophetic words to be given. I know... but we were young and idealistic. You know what happened... people who should not have spoken did and those who should have didn't. We had some moments of pure embarrassment, which I will not go into. I still cringe to this day!*

*We also missed some words that would have underlined the teaching and led to powerful ministry. How do I know? Because those who didn't get up to speak came forward after the service to tell me what they would have [should have] said. At these moments, I often had visions of ringing their necks! [that's a joke by the way]*

*Sadly, the Sunday service prophetic problems were the least of the problems we faced. As we encouraged the gift, I began to get pages and pages of notes coming from the self-professed prophets within our church. It seems all of them were having dreams, writing them down, giving them to me and expecting me to interpret them and then have them presented to the church on Sunday morning. When I said no to most of them, the Old Testament prophetic ministry started in earnest.*

*When you think of an Old Testament prophet, what do you see in your mind's eye? Many [falsely] see a grumpy old man, who lives by himself, who is always angry with someone, usually the King or the Priest. You see a guy who makes a living correcting his leadership. He is strange, other-worldly and socially awkward. A party animal he is not. The word "winsome" never comes to mind. At the heart of their prototypical Old Testament prophet is the belief that bringing criticism to his leadership is within his God given job description.*

*I began to receive "helpful" letters from our "prophets." These followed a predictable form: 1. You are a great pastor. 2. You are destined for greatness, 3. The Holy Spirit was going to do a powerful work last Sunday UNTIL you missed His leading and failed to listen to His voice, 4. You know I love you and respect you, 5. The Holy Spirit has given me to you as a gift to help you guide the service BUT, 6. You are not listening to me [us], 7. If you don't start listening to us, your ministry will fail and you will end up driving a cab and eating fast food for the rest of your wasted life!! [I exaggerate somewhat, but you get the drift]*

*My reaction to these kinds of messages was entirely predictable – I shut down the prophetic ministry and licked my wounds, but a problem remained. I could not understand how a small group of nice people could become such a problem. My question became, "How could nice people be so critical of another nice person like me? What makes them think that treating their leader like this is OK with God?" This question got under my skin. I began asking God what went wrong. What follows is the answer I believe He led me to and it has to do with the difference between Old Testament and New Testament prophetic ministry."*

Before we embark on our investigation into Old Testament prophecy, there is one more important point to make. All of the spiritual gifts have temptations uniquely tailored to them by the enemy. Take for instance the gift of teaching. Teachers are tempted to believe that if they just explain the Bible accurately, people's lives will change. When they don't change or don't change quickly enough, the temptation is to consider the people hard-hearted or hard-headed, or as in Mark's experience a few years ago, to believe that your ministry is accomplishing too little to justify continuing.

For those who have a ministry of compassion, the temptation is to believe that a good hug is all most people need to get them off their disabling sin and back into the saddle. Those who have a deliverance ministry are tempted to believe that behind every problem there lurks a demon, which when cast out, will result in a person who becomes a model Christian.

**All of the spiritual gifts have temptations uniquely tailored to them by the enemy.**

**In the case of immature prophets, the temptation is to harshly judge those who do not receive their word as from God or who do not do with it what they wanted done.** In many cases the judgment is against their leaders. The singer/song writer Joni Mitchell once said that her songs are like her children and she wants everyone to love her children as much as she does.

For budding prophets, the same applies to their words, but with greater force. They are sure their words are from God and therefore must be proclaimed in the church. This means that whoever says no to this must be out of God's will, and who better to point this out than the prophet who gave the word. The perfect storm is created when this temptation meets the Old Testament model of prophetic ministry.

## The Old Testament Model of Prophetic Ministry

Let's start the discussion with a question; who is the first Old Testament prophet? So, who is it? When Mark asks this question when he teaches this material most people say Isaiah or Jeremiah or Samuel. Once in a while someone says Moses, and they are correct. He is the first person to function in the office of prophet for the nation of Israel. He said of himself, **"The Lord your God will raise up for you a prophet like me from among your own people; you shall heed such a prophet"** Deut. 18:15.

What is interesting about this fact is that we do not usually think of Moses as principally a prophet. This is because he was much more than that. He was also Israel's priest. A prophet speaks to the people on behalf of God and a priest speaks to God on behalf of the people. Moses did both equally, but he did even more than that. He also acted as leader, judge and governor over the people. He functioned in three ways: prophet, priest and king [only in the sense of acting as the government over the people].

**God's leadership mechanism in the Old Testament was a man who was prophet, priest and governor in one leader.**

Moses exemplified God's plan for His leadership over His people. God's leadership mechanism in the Old Testament was a man who was prophet, priest and governor in one leader. In other words, these three roles operating in unity comprised God's design for leadership. Sadly, this unity came to an end. Gradually three distinct functions or traditions began to form; prophets, priests and kings.

The divide accelerated when Israel demanded a King. The story is really quite simple. Israel was a theocracy surrounded by nations ruled by a King. Israel was the odd man out. Israel's reaction was predictable, "Everyone else has a king, so we should have a king too." One of Satan's greatest lies is this; "Everyone else is doing it, so you should too." The people took the bait and began demanding a King.

They presented their demands to their prophet Samuel who took the matter to God. Samuel was not pleased. **"But the thing displeased Samuel when they said, 'Give us a king to govern us.' Samuel prayed to the Lord, and the Lord said to Samuel,**

**'Listen to the voice of the people in all that they say to you; for they have not rejected you, but they have rejected me from being king over them'"** 1 Sam. 8:6.

It is important to note that it is not the choice of who will be king that God objects to - it is the institution of kingship that God does not want. (1 Sam. 10:19) It is after Israel's rejection of God's form of leadership, that we see the separation of the three functions of leadership. From this point onward, we see an almost constant struggle between the three institutions of prophet, priest and king. It is within this separation that the Old Testament role of prophet becomes one of opposition, not just to bad kings, but to the institution of kingship itself. (Hosea 8:4; Amos 5:26)

We know how it goes from here on; prophets angry with kings, kings angry with prophets, prophets angry with priests, priests angry with kings, etc. etc. This is inevitable once God's design for leadership is violated. The resulting description of an Old Testament prophet now becomes; one who lives apart from the people, is not a part of the normal life of the community, who shows up occasionally to criticize the king or the priests and who is always right. (Elijah in 1 Kings 18 or Jonah in chapter 4)

He is easy to picture as this grumpy old man who rides his donkey up to the city wall, lights the fuse on his bomb and lobs it over the wall. Then he rides back to his cave to eat bugs and wild honey and sleep on his camel hair blanket.

Is this what God had in mind for the leadership of His people? We think not. God had in mind something much more like Moses, where the leadership governs, but it does so by combining the three functions in unity, in one body as it were; speaking for God to the people, speaking to God for the people and leading the people in obedience to God.

### New Testament Prophetic Ministry

Moses expressed a prophetic longing that someday a leader would arise who would be a prophet like him. I wonder if he was longing for more than just a prophet like himself? Perhaps he was longing for a leader who would be for the people what he had been – prophet, priest and leader/governor. Whether or not this is what Moses had in mind, God certainly had a plan to combine the functions of prophet, priest and king into one perfect leader. He of course is Jesus.

When we think of Jesus, we rarely think of Him as only our prophet or priest or king. We recognize in Him the perfect unity of all three of these functions. He speaks to us from and for His Father God as our prophet. He speaks to His Father for us as our priest. He brings the Kingdom of God to the earth as our king because He *is* the King. What a magnificent thing to see God's perfect plan for His government finally restored in His Perfect Son! Moses must have cheered from heaven when Jesus was born!

As wonderful as the restoration of God's design for leadership is, there are consequences of it that will significantly change our understanding of the gift of prophecy in the age in which we live – the Church Age.

The Church is referred to repeatedly in the New Testament as the "body of Christ." This is not just some sort of nice compliment to us without real meaning. We are to embody the very nature of Christ. As we said earlier, we are new creations in Him. We partake together in His divine nature. We are His hands and feet with which to continue His ministry. The Holy Spirit is His Spirit living in us to re-present Jesus to the world. **We are literally His body here and now. He lives His life through our bodies**.

What this means in practice is that our local churches are to be led in the same way that He would lead if He were physically present with us. **Because the rift between prophet, priest and king has been healed through Him, and because we are His body, there must be no rift between these functions in His church**. The same unity of these functions that exists in Jesus must exist within His church. There is as much room for the prophetic ministry to criticize the ministry of leadership as there is room for Jesus' hand to attack His foot.

What this means for us today is that the Old Testament model of prophetic ministry is no longer applicable, because the church is the body of Christ. **Love is to rule over all**. There is no place for the "gift" of criticism. Unity through love has been restored to all of the gifts and ministries within the church. This is certainly the conclusion Paul reaches in 1 Corinthians chapters 12–14. These chapters are so important to any discussion of the gift of prophecy that it behooves us to examine them in detail. Here is a summary of those chapters:

1. Ignorance of spiritual gifts is bad. 12:1

2. Gifts differ, but they all come from the same Spirit. 12:4 [unity]

3. We are to use our spiritual gift[s] for the good of others 12:7 [unity]

4. Paul lists a number of spiritual gifts and reminds us that we do not choose our gift[s]; the Holy Spirit decides what gifts we will specialize in. 12:8–11

5. Although our gifts may vary by function, we are one body – **unity** is paramount. 12:12–13

6. There is no room for self-criticism because my gift may be hidden or humble and there is no room for pride, because my gift may be obvious or spectacular. We need each other. 12:14–24 [unity]

7. There must be no division within the body and each should care for the others equally. When one of us suffers, we all suffer. When one of us receives honor, we all receive honor. 12:25–26 [unity]

8. Paul lists the offices of spiritual gifts as well as other spiritual gifts and closes with the rhetorical question; "Are all apostles, prophets, teachers, workers of miracles..." Paul sets forth the "office" gifts. 12:29–30

9. After teaching on the importance of spiritual gifts, Paul shifts emphasis to the necessity and centrality of love in the body, calling it "the most excellent way." 12:31 [unity]

10. Spiritual gifts used without love are pointless and those who use them without love are "nothing." 13:1–3 [unity]

11. Paul describes the nature of love as it applies to relationships [the wedding passage]. 13:4–7 [unity]

12. When Jesus returns we will no longer need prophecy or the gift of tongues, because we will see Jesus clearly and know as we are fully known. 13:8–12

13. Chapter 14 returns to teaching about the usefulness of spiritual gifts telling us to eagerly desire them, especially the gift of prophecy. 14:1

14. Paul describes the value of prophecy over the gift of tongues, because prophecy speaks to people for their "strengthening, encouragement and comfort." Prophecy is superior because it is focused on building others up – it is other-focused. 14:2–5 [unity]

The remainder of Chapter 14 deals with the proper use of tongues in church meetings [which is not relevant to the present discussion], but Paul does include these comments about prophecy as it is used in church meetings: **"But if an unbeliever or an inquirer comes in while everyone is prophesying, they are convicted of sin and are brought under judgment by all, as the secrets of their hearts are laid bare. So, they will fall down and worship God, exclaiming, 'God is really among you!'"** 1 Cor. 14:24–25.

This kind of supernatural experience for a non-believer attending a church meeting is a **"demonstration of the Spirit's power, so that your faith might not rest on men's wisdom, but on God's power"** which Paul has already referred to in 1 Corinthians (1 Cor. 2:1–5). It is an opportunity for an experience of the supernatural nature of God which enables faith, as we have previously discussed.

These three chapters have a very significant progression. First, Paul teaches us about spiritual gifts. Second, he teaches us all about love for one another. Third, he returns to teaching us about how spiritual gifts are to be used in our church meetings. Paul makes a theological sandwich; two pieces of nourishing whole wheat bread [spiritual gifts] with the meat [love] in the middle. Paul is underlining the message that spiritual gifts are not as important as how they are used in love. Love is the truly valuable commodity here. The gifts are just the Holy Spirit's expression of love and when love rules, unity results.

This should be self-evident, but in our experience power trumps love for many of us. Moving in spiritual power is very intoxicating and wonderful … for our pride. Loving people without being noticed is not intoxicating or exciting, and it certainly does not appeal to our pride. Putting others first means putting ourselves second and pride hates second place.

We may be laboring the point somewhat, but when it comes to the use of power, we need a constant reminder that love and not power is the goal. Our New Testament model of prophecy will have much more to do with love than with supernatural power. When we forget this, we will be tempted to return to prophecy as

**Power trumps love for many of us. Moving in spiritual power is very intoxicating and wonderful … for our pride.**

criticism and correction. Fortunately, those days are over.

To summarize our discussion thus far, Jesus restores the unity between prophet, priest and king in Himself such that church government will be the result of these three functions working in unity together through love. This fact alone will be responsible for several very significant differences between prophecy in the Old Testament and prophecy in the New Testament or "Church Age."

## The Holy Spirit's role in the Old Testament

We will discuss these practical differences shortly, but there is more regarding the difference between life with the Holy Spirit in the Old Testament and life in the Holy Spirit in the New Testament. These differences have to do with the changing role of the Holy Spirit from the Old to the New Testament. Let's look at them.

When we examine the language used to describe the work of the Holy Spirit in the Old Testament, we see a common phrase used repeatedly. The phrase describes the Holy Spirit's activity as one of "coming upon." The picture is one of the Spirit coming upon someone, empowering them to do something powerful, and then leaving. He blows in, blows up, and blows out. There are only a few instances which suggests the indwelling of the Holy Spirit and in these cases the reason for His indwelling was to empower someone for some godly task.

### The Holy Spirit's role in the New Testament

When we examine the language used to describe the work of the Holy Spirit in the New Testament, we see a new concept being emphasized - His "indwelling" within the believer. The language changes because a fundamental reality has changed. We divide the Old and New Testaments because of the coming of Jesus, but we must not forget that the coming of Jesus brought something we call the New Covenant. We can rightly divide the Old and New Testament as between the Old and New Covenant. Everything changes under the New Covenant. Let's examine the change.

Under the Old Covenant, man lived under law. That is to say that **for most people in Israel their relationship with God was really a relationship with God's law**. This was not God's plan for man. It came as a result of man rejecting a "face to face" relationship with God. This rejection occurred very specifically at a certain time and place. At Mount Sinai God told Moses to have the people ready themselves for an intimate encounter with their God. God told Moses He was going to *reveal* himself in front of all the people. He was offering all of the people a "face to face" relationship with Himself.

We refer you to Mark's first book, "Is God Religious?" [7] where this encounter and its consequences are dealt with fully. Suffice it to say that the people clearly rejected an intimate father-child relationship with God and as a consequence, lived under law until the coming of Jesus. The way the prophet describes it is to say that God's law was written on stone tablets rather than on the hearts of God's people. In other words, **because the people have rejected an intimate/personal relationship with God, their relationship with Him becomes legalistic rather than relational.** Jesus came to change that, but for the purposes of our present discussion what concerns us is the means by which this change was brought about.

The means of moving from a life under law to a life of intimacy with God is made possible by the fact that after Jesus dealt with the legal ramification of human sin on the cross, a new reality is made available. The new reality is the indwelling of the Holy Spirit in every believer. Just think about it. The kind of relationship Moses had with God is now available to every Christian! Actually, our relationship with our Father God is far better even than Moses'. Moses came and went from the face to face presence of God and over time the glory faded from his face.

We cannot leave God's presence, because He lives *within* us! Our experience of His presence is only a pause away. **All you have to do to enter into the experience of the presence of God is to stop your busyness and remind yourself that He is here with you now!** Even more than that, He is here **in** you right now!

The reality of the miracle of God living *within* us changes forever the role of prophecy under the New Covenant.

> **The kind of relationship Moses had with God is now available to every Christian.**

At Mount Sinai, the people substituted a relationship with the law and a prophet for one of intimacy with God as their Father. This is how Moses describes their rejection of God and the consequences; **"The Lord your God will raise up for you**

**a prophet like me from among your own people; you shall heed such a prophet. This is what *you* requested of the Lord your God at Horeb on the day of the assembly when you said: 'If I hear the voice of the Lord my God any more, or ever again see this great fire, I will die'"** Deut. 18:15.

What the people are doing here is rejecting a direct relationship with God and substituting representatives of Him in His place. The representatives are three; prophets who speak to them for God, priests who speak to God for them and kings who lead them [often not for God], but for themselves. [Sort of like our politicians today]. All of this takes place under an overriding legal relationship with God's law.

Regarding the gift of the direct revelation of God's voice [prophecy], it means that instead of each member of the community hearing God for himself [because he indwells them], they must rely on the office of prophet. Sadly, there were not enough prophets to go around. They were few and far between. Prior to Jesus' coming, Israel had gone for over 400 years without hearing a prophet speak to the nation! Talk about feeling like God is distant! This is sad, but the consequences go far beyond merely feeling the lack of God's voice.

Through some of Israel's history, the common people did not even have the written law through which to relate to God. The only voice of God they could hear came through prophets. This meant that prophecy must be 100% accurate or the nation is in serious trouble. In fact, this is the test of whether or not Old Testament prophecy is genuine. To be genuine it has to be 100% accurate. The standard was so high that the consequence of inaccurate prophecy was death! We are always tempted at this point to ask our "wannabe Old Testament prophets" if they really understand what kind of burden they are striving for.

At the risk of redundancy, it is important to reiterate that this state of affairs was not God's intention for His people or for the gift of prophecy. It was the logical outcome of His people rejecting intimacy with Him. In fact, the Old Testament prophets looked forward to a time when all of God's people would hear the voice of God;

**"No longer shall they teach one another, or say to each other, "know the Lord," for they shall all know me, from the least of them to the greatest."** Jer. 31:34

**"And it shall come to pass afterwards, that I will pour out my spirit on all flesh; your sons and your daughters shall prophecy, your old men shall dream dreams, and your young men shall see visions, even upon the menservants and maidservants in those days, I will pour out my spirit.** Joel 2:28

Sadly, because there was no personal voice of God for each person, there had to be a prophet to say, "know the Lord", but the day is coming when no one will have to rely on a prophet to hear God speak to them. God will speak to all of them directly [from the inside, not the outside]. This changes the nature of prophetic ministry in the New Testament church in a very interesting way.

**Prophecy in the New Testament church does not have to be the final [100% accurate] authority on what God says**. We now have a direct relationship with our Father – we can ask Him. As well, we now have the Bible with which to judge a prophetic word and it tells us *almost* all of what we need to know to live a successful Christian life. Why do we say "almost"? Because the Bible will not tell you which job to take, which house to buy, what city to live in, or whether to marry the doctor, the lawyer, the nurse, or the teacher.

What we find in the New Testament church is what we should expect: prophecy is not the final authority for what God is saying to us. It is not always accurate. It must be judged. God indwells all of us and speaks to all of us, but none of us hear perfectly.

**"For we know in part, and we prophesy in part, but when perfection comes the imperfect disappears ... Now I know in part; then I shall know fully, even as I am fully known."** 1 Cor. 13:9–12

Paul holds prophecy in very high regard, but he does not expect it to be perfect. He tells us that it is partial. Because it is partial he also tells us that it must be judged. (1 Cor. 14:29) This raises a very interesting question. Why would God allow those who presume to speak His words to be partial or wrong in part? Why would God actually set it up so that none of us, not even gifted prophets, hear perfectly?

We believe the answer has to do with God's extremely high value on unity, humility, and love. He has designed His body [the church] to be a living example of His nature – the Trinity – love in love with love. The Trinity displays perfect humility – each of the three constantly diverting attention and glory to one of the other two.

By God's design, the church is to reflect the unity we find in the Godhead. This means that no one in the church is complete alone. No one hears or understands God fully. **No one's gift is perfect. The result is that we truly need one another in order to understand God**. God is a family [three in one] and He cannot be understood apart from being a part of His family – His church.

We are designed to need each other and each other's spiritual gifts. Our understanding of the very nature of God demands this interdependency. When we come to understand that the church is to exemplify the love and unity found in the Trinity, we will see that there is no place in the church for a perfectly accurate Old Testament prophet. Allow us to illustrate.

Suppose God gave each local church at least one perfectly accurate Old Testament prophet. Each member of the church can phone the prophet anytime to hear God's unique immediate message to them. After a few months what would the life of the prophet be like? As we ask this question, perhaps you are beginning to see why Old Testament prophets lived alone in the desert! We wonder how long our Old Testament prophet would last before burning out. Imagine the phone calls all day and all night! He is to be pitied.

As bad as it would be for the prophet, imagine what its effects would be on the rest of the people in the church. Why bother having a prayer life if you can phone the prophet? Why bother reading the Bible for yourself? Who needs the gift of wisdom or counseling? What good is the teaching gift, if all we have to do is phone the prophet? Why should I develop my own spiritual ears when I can use the prophet's?

Unity and interdependency require that all of the gifts operate together to bless the community. There is no place for one gift displacing any of the others. The presence of a partial prophetic gift in the church means we need sound Bible teaching, wisdom, wise counsel and compassion in order to judge the word. It means that all of the gifts become important in understanding how a prophetic word is to be interpreted and applied. We will look at this issue of interpretation and application in greater detail in a later chapter when we look at the relationship between the gift of prophecy and the gift of leadership. For now, it is enough to say that all of the gifts of the spirit are partial because **being a Christian is a team sport.**

It should be clear at this point that the criteria for testing whether or not a prophetic word is genuine changes between the Old and New Testament age. In the Old Testament age, the criteria were very simple: was the word 100% accurate? In the New Testament or Church Age the criteria involve more relational factors. Is it edifying? Does it build up people? Is it encouraging? Is it loving? Not just, is it perfectly accurate?

Let's summarize what we have learned about the difference between Old Testament and New Testament prophetic ministry with a quick chart answering 7 questions about the Holy Spirit and the gift of prophecy in the Old and New Testament.

| QUESTIONS: | NEW TESTAMENT | OLD TESTAMENT |
|---|---|---|
| 1. Who has the Holy Spirit? | - every believer | - only a few occasionally |

| | | |
|---|---|---|
| 2. Who has the gift of prophecy? | - every believer | - only a few occasionally |
| 3. What is the means of the gift? | - indwelling | - "coming upon" |
| 4. What is the accuracy of the gift? | - in part [to be judged] | - 100% [or die] |
| 5. What is the test of the gift? | - is it edifying, comforting, etc. | - 100% accuracy |
| 6. Place in the community? | - a part of the body | - outside of the community |
| 7. Purpose of prophecy? | - encouragement | - largely correction |

Our prayer for this chapter is that we will be set free from the negative results of seeing the prophetic gift through the lens of the Old Testament model of prophetic ministry. **We are now free to risk prophetic words, because we do not have to be perfect**. We can rest in the fact that we are simply one part of a family of gifts that operate together to communicate from God to one another.

We can also be encouraged to learn to listen for God's direct and immediate voice to each of us and we can take comfort in the fact that we are surrounded by other spiritual gifts that will help us to judge correctly what we think we are hearing.

Under grace we can truly relax and enjoy developing our spiritual gifts, free from the tyranny of perfect performance.

## Some questions to consider:

1. What have you learned from this chapter?

2. At the beginning of this chapter Mark shared his negative experience with prophetic ministry in his church. Do you think this is an isolated problem or do you think other churches have experienced the same sort of problem?

3. Prior to reading this chapter, what was your image of an Old Testament prophet? Has that image changed? If so, how?

4. Can you explain in your own words how and why the rift between prophets, priests and kings developed in the Old Testament? If you can't you might consider rereading this chapter – it's important.

5. Can you explain in your own words how and why the rift between these three has been healed in the New Testament Church through Jesus? Ditto... it's important.

6. Is it clear why God has not designed our Church Age prophecy to be 100% accurate? Explain.

7. What is the effect of this chapter on your attitude toward the gift of prophecy?

# PART FOUR:

# HOW TO HEAR AND SPEAK GOD'S WORDS

# Chapter 17: Okay, Show Me How to Do It

We don't know about you, but we have a recurring frustration about life in the church. It seems there is no shortage of messages that tell us what we need to do to grow as a Christian. We each have a looooong list of what we must do. The problem is that most of us have a very short list telling us *how* to do it. Have you experienced this problem? For years Mark was told he needed to have a "quiet time" with God, but no one told him *how* to do it. Prophecy is much like that. It is clear that all of us can prophesy, but how do we learn to "hear God's voice?" The questions become: how does God communicate with us and what do we mean by His "voice?"

To get very practical we are going to review the 5 "Ws" of prophetic ministry; who, what, where, when and why? Then we will look at the "how" which will comprise the bulk of this chapter and the next.

## WHO?

We have answered this question, but by way of review; all Christians have the gift of prophecy within them because the Holy Spirit lives within each of us and the gifts are His gifts [they are of Him not of us]. This means that all of us should desire and expect to prophesy, but not all of us should expect to function in the ministry of prophecy or the office of prophet. **As we risk exercising our spiritual gifts, it will become clear to us and to those we serve which gift[s] we will specialize in.**

## WHAT?

Prophecy may be defined as "a supernatural work of the Holy Spirit which allows one to hear and communicate a message from God to a person or group or persons which communicates God's knowledge and perspective regarding the present or future circumstances of the hearer[s]." It includes both "forth telling" and "foretelling." It often includes the revelation of facts, which only God and the hearer could know. This is what gives it its supernatural credibility.

Here is an example in Mark's words:

*"I was with a group of evangelical pastors many years ago and during our prayer time for one another I asked the leader of the group if I could give him a prophetic word. He was skeptical, but open. I told him what he was asking God about and then told him what God had to say in answer to his questions. He was shocked! He said, "you just told me what I wrote in my prayer journal yesterday! This is incredible!""*

An accurate prophetic word brings the immediacy of God into our life in a way that nothing else does.

Prophetic words can pertain to any subject. In the Bible, prophetic words were used to:

1. Reveal sin
   o Elisha to Gehazi (2 Kings 5:20–27)
   o Jesus to the Samaritan woman at the well (John 4:7)
   o Peter to Ananias (Acts 5:1–6)
2. To locate a lost possession
   o Samuel to Saul (1 Sam. 9:15–20; 10:22)
3. To reveal thoughts
   o Jesus to the Scribes (Matt. 9:1–7)

In Mark's experience, the Holy Spirit will often reveal what a person has been thinking and often the lies that he has been believing, which have sabotaged his life. Routinely, after revealing what he has been thinking, God will respond with His thoughts for the person's situation and His truth which brings freedom from the lies that has dominated the person's thinking.

4. To aid in physical or emotional healing
   o Jesus and the paralytic (Matt. 9:2)
   o Jesus and the man sick for 38 years (John 5:1–9)

Mark's example:

*"Very early in my new experience of the gift of prophecy I was asked to pray for an older woman who was suffering from arthritis. I thought the point of our prayer was physical healing, but as I waited on the Lord for direction as to how to pray, the name "Frank" came strongly to my mind. It meant nothing to me, but it came with such clarity that I had to ask her, "Who is Frank?" She became very agitated and told me that Frank was her brother who had died in a very violent accident. The next word that came very clearly to me was "death." I asked her about deaths in her family. She told me a list of those she loved who had died prematurely.*

*She was very angry as she told me of those that had been "taken" from her. I told her that she was angry with God and she said she was. I told her that if she wanted to be healed, she would have to let go of her anger toward God. She flatly refused and her anger again flared up. She walked away with her anger and arthritis intact."*

5. To provide warning
   o Agabus to the Antioch church (Acts 11:28)
   o Agabus to Paul of persecution by the Jews if he went to Jerusalem (Acts 21:11)
6. To prepare one spiritually and psychologically for a coming trial
   o Agabus to Paul (Acts 21:11)

It is interesting to note that the Holy Spirit spoke to Paul through Agabus about what he would face if he went to Jerusalem. The logical inference to make is that God was warning Paul not to go. Interestingly, what we find as the story progresses is that the Holy Spirit confirms to Paul that he is to go to Jerusalem. The warning was actually given to Paul to prepare him for what was to come, which actually culminated in his execution. By knowing what to expect, Paul was prepared to face his own death with a sense of peace and the comfort of knowing God would be with him in his trial.

7. To identify and call into effect the spiritual gifts which God has ordained for a person and to speak to their God-ordained ministry and destiny:

**"Timothy, my son, I am giving you this command in keeping with the prophecies once made about you, so that by recalling them you may fight the battle well, holding on to faith and a good conscience, which some have rejected and so have suffered shipwreck with regard to the faith"** 1 Tim. 1:18–19.

There are many more biblical examples of the many uses of prophecy, but to summarize we can say that prophecy can deal with any question or circumstance that comes in life. God is interested in all those things that matter to us, no matter how trivial. In the context of prophecy, being childlike means asking Him about whatever concerns us, and being mature means accepting whatever He has to say.

## WHERE?

> God longs to speak to those who do not know Him, and we are His voice.

Can you imagine any situation in which knowing God's perspective would not be helpful? We can't. Sadly, many of us live our Christian lives within a small box called "church." We often default to viewing prophecy as something that only happens in church and through senior leaders. This small box is of our own creation and does not exemplify the heart of God. God longs to speak to those who do not know Him and we are His voice.

Mark's example:

*"A few years ago, I was taking a road trip into Baja, Mexico. I had to buy Mexican car insurance before entering Mexico. I was in a hurry and people were waiting for me in the car. I presented my registration to the 20-something girl behind the counter. As she was filling out the forms, this thought came to my mind, "She is in a relationship with a guy who she thinks might be the one to marry,*

*but she is not sure if she can trust him. She doesn't know what to do."*

*I gave her my usual opening line; "I know this sounds kind of strange, but I am a Christian and sometimes God tells me things about strangers. I think He just told me something about you, would you like to know what He said?" Almost all the people I have said this to say "yes." I think it is because we humans are essentially self-centered and a possible message from God about us is just too interesting to pass up. She said yes.*

*I told her exactly what I thought I heard from God. She was shocked! She said, "How did you know that?!?!" I told her that God had more to say to her and that if we could just be still for a few moments, I believed He would tell her more. She said fine. I closed my eyes and waited. Almost immediately this thought came, "He is not trustworthy. He is not My choice for you. If you wait and trust Me I will bring someone who will be a good husband for you." She was thrilled and thanked me profusely."*

Another story from Mark:

*"A few years ago, our elders' meetings took place in the same restaurant, on the same day, and at the same time. We were usually served by the same young waitress. One day my senior pastor and I were waiting for our third elder to show up when our usual waitress came by to refresh our coffee. She said, "I see you guys in here at this time every week. Who are you guys and what do you do?" My senior pastor said, "I am the senior pastor of the Gathering Place church and this is our prophet." She looked at me and said, "What is a prophet?" I looked up at her intending to try to explain what prophecy is, but as I looked at her I began to speak. I said, "When you were a young girl about 8 years old you were in a church service where an older, returned missionary was speaking about her life on the mission field. You received a call from God to be a missionary. Right now, you are dating a guy who has no interest in God and so you have never followed up on the call that is on your life. God wants you to start planning to take some short-term mission trips so you can reassess your future."*

*She was overwhelmed! She said, "How did you know what happened to me when I was a kid in church?" I said, "This is called the spiritual gift of prophecy." She said, "This is the most amazing thing that has ever happened to me!" It made me laugh to realize that while I was getting ready to deliver an explanation of prophecy, God was getting ready to give a demonstration. I wonder which would have had the greater impact?"*

For non-Christians prophecy operates to provide an experience of the reality of a God who loves them and who takes a personal interest in their lives. He does this when He reveals the secrets of their hearts through the prophetic words of a stranger. (1 Cor. 14:22–25)

For Christians, prophecy is designed to be a normal part of our life together. Wherever we have Christians who need encouragement, comfort, strengthening and/or building up of faith, we need the gift of prophecy. Paul considers it such a part of church life that he sets out guiding principles to govern how it is to be used in church meetings, which we will deal with next.

## WHEN?

The answer to the "when" question, as it pertains to non-Christians, is *anytime*. We assume that if God gives us a word of knowledge or prophetic word for a stranger, it is because He wants us to deliver it. There are exceptions to this assumption, but in the interest of developing our tolerance for risk, we should start with the assumption that it is better to fail by commission than omission. There are several exceptions to the general rule of "speak what you get."

The first exception concerns the timeliness of a prophetic word. Most of us think that in prophetic ministry we are only responsible for delivering the word. The fact is: we are also responsible for the timing of the delivery. There are many reasons for delaying the delivery of even a perfectly accurate prophetic word.

This fact was impressed upon Mark by an experience his father had. His Father [David] and his regular prayer partner [Pat] were asked to pray for a young girl who was fighting severe depression. As they were listening to the story of her life, David had this thought enter his mind, "She had an abortion in her teens." He began to gently probe as to anything traumatic that might have happened to her during her teens. She assured him that nothing bad happened. He went on to ask if she had ever done anything that she was particularly ashamed of. Again, she said no.

He was getting ready to suggest to her that she had an abortion when the thought came very clearly, "Don't bring up the abortion!" The prayer counseling ended and he was bothered by the word he thought he had received about her abortion. He asked his prophetic prayer partner [Pat] if she received anything unusual during the session. She said, "Oh yes, the Lord told me she had an abortion in her teens." David said, "Why didn't you ask her about it?" Pat said, "The Lord told me not to." They came to the conclusion that the abortion was not something this girl was ready to deal with.

Their conclusion raises the obvious question, "If this was not something for them to question her about at the time, why did God show it to them?" This brings us to the second exception as to timing. Often God will give us a prophetic word, which He wants us to intercede for long before we speak it. Immature prophetic ministers tend to make the mistake of confusing a prophetic word intended by God to be used to direct intercession, with one that He wants given immediately. This is particularly true of words that reveal sin.

**Confrontation always goes better after we soften the ground of their heart with intercession.**

**Our practice when God gives a word about the sin of another person is to spend much time in prayer for them before confronting them with their sin**. The fact is; confronting people about their sin is sometimes counter-productive. Their reaction is often one of extreme defensiveness and even counteraccusation.

Many times, as pastors we have heard this retort, "Who are you to be telling me what I am doing wrong?" [said with a tone of righteous indignation] Our response is usually, "I am your pastor and it is a part of my job I really hate, but not as much as I hate failing God and you." Confrontation always goes better after we soften the ground of their heart with intercession for God to grant them the spirit of repentance and openness to truth. The time spent in prayer also softens our hearts toward the person who is failing. This fact alone will result in a better response to a corrective word.

It is not only prophetic words about sin that should be committed to prayer before speaking aloud. **Many prophetic words are given solely as direction for intercession by the person who receives them.** This is why so many intercessors also have the ministry of prophecy. Prophecy is like military intelligence. It gives us insight into the plans of the enemy and allows us to mount a counteroffensive of prayer.

Immature prophetic ministers often rush to speak a word when a better course of action is to go to more experienced prophetic ministers to help determine the application of the word. **How the word is applied is just as important and often more important than the word itself.** We will deal with this issue in a later chapter dealing with the relationship between the gift of prophecy and the gift of leadership.

There is another reason to delay giving a prophetic word and it involves "preferring your brother." Mark has been in meetings in which he received a word he was certain was to be spoken to the group, but he decided to wait for the appropriate moment to share it. Many times, a few minutes later, a less experienced prophetic minister gave the same word. He then had the pleasure of confirming their word.

Other than these exceptions, we should deliver the word even when we are not sure if it is accurate. **Fear of being wrong is what prevents most of us from developing our prophetic gift**. The risk of being wrong is actually a greater gain than the false security of avoiding being wrong.

Most of us reject opportunities to speak a prophetic word, because we fear the embarrassment of being wrong. This is really just pride at work. There are the more noble among us who fear being wrong because to claim to speak for God and then to be wrong may bring discredit to our God. This is a legitimate fear, but one which is easy to avoid. Humility in the delivery is the key. If we claim to be speaking God's word and are wrong, we bring discredit to our faith. But if we claim to speak only what we THINK we may be receiving from God, then if we are wrong, we are the ones who look foolish. God's reputation remains intact.

In Mark's words: *"As well as being humble, simply saying what we think we are receiving is more truthful. Much of the time, when I am giving a prophet word, I am not sure the word is from God. I am sure enough to risk giving it, but not sure enough to announce it as a perfect word from God. In my experience, this is good for four reasons;*

*1. It is more honest to how I am experiencing the word [as a thought coming into my mind].*

*2. It leaves the task of judging the word in the hands of the person who should actually be judging the word – the person who it pertains to and who will have to determine how to apply the word.*

*3. It does not risk bringing God and prophetic ministry into disrepute, if I am wrong, and*

*4. It lessens the pressure the hearer feels to please the speaker by falsely affirming that it was an accurate word from God."*

There is another reason for not introducing our potential prophetic word by saying, "Thus saith the Lord." We are emissaries of a supernatural God in a culture that continues to view the supernatural as suspect. The more natural we can be when we move in the supernatural, the more accessible it becomes for those who have not experienced it. Our jargon and language do matter. When we are teaching about prophecy [hearing from God] to evangelicals we try to avoid language which acts as a theological barrier.

By referring to a potential word from God as a thought that just came to my mind, it is much less controversial or confrontational than announcing the FACT that I am now going to give a PROPHETIC WORD FROM THE LORD. The rule that should govern how we model and teach supernatural gifts should be determined, not by our traditions, but by what will be easiest for the listeners to hear and apply. We think this last sentence just made God smile.

**The more natural we can be when we move in the supernatural, the more accessible it becomes for those who have not experienced it.**

### Prophecy in Church Meetings

The biggest issue for most leaders who are considering developing a prophetic ministry within the church is how to integrate it into the Sunday morning service [if at all]. This is a subject that pastors inherently understand; while church members usually do not. The average congregation is composed of a large group of watchers and a smaller group of passionate performers. We are not using the term "performers" in a derogatory sense. We are talking about those who are very passionate about their calling or area of ministry. They naturally want to see it featured on Sunday morning which, despite our efforts to the contrary, remains the major church meeting of the week.

The missions people want to see missions featured every week. The small group leaders want to see home groups discussed every week. The worship team wants 10 more minutes of worship. The altar prayer teams want a longer ministry time. The Children's Church teachers want church to end on time. The youth pastor wants a regular call for more volunteers [as does the Children's Church co-coordinator]. Finally, the pastor just wants peace. The Sunday morning meeting is, at best, a compromise of equally important values. So, what do we do with prophetic ministry?

**Prophecy, like a good joke, requires the right timing.**

Without realizing it, many immature prophetic ministers apply tremendous pressure upon their leaders to feature prophetic words in the Sunday morning service. They feel a genuine justification for demanding that their words be heard regularly because they truly believe they are hearing from God. They reason that because God gave them a word just before or during the service, it must mean that it should be given before the service ends. This results in a demand [a forcefully polite request] that the church have a regular time set aside for prophetic words. Thus, we have the origin of the "open microphone time."

**Having experimented with an "open mike", we can tell you that it is not a good idea**. As we have already said, often those who should not speak do and those who should don't. For most churches, Sunday morning is in large part as much about reaching the lost as it is about taking the saints deeper. We, who believe that Sunday morning service should include a demonstration of the power of the Holy Spirit, walk somewhat of a tightrope. On the one hand, we want to take risks with the supernatural gifts so as to accurately portray the nature of God to the non-Christian who visits our church. On the other hand, we do not want him or her to be exposed to something that is obviously inaccurate or nonsensical.

The Apostle Paul raises this issue with respect to the gift of tongues. He reaches the conclusion that unless the gift of interpretation is present to make sense of the utterance, it is better not to give it. (1 Cor. 14:13, 19) His criteria for excluding a word in tongues in the absence of an interpretation is whether or not the word is intelligible, that is to say understandable, as well as edifying. This criterion may be equally applied to prophetic words in church. The words we need to hear are those that are understandable as well as edifying.

In our experience, many prophetic words are not understandable to the non-Christians who visit our churches. A word that describes an allegorical vision made up largely of obscure biblical symbols, which require a bible dictionary and a degree in end-times eschatology should not be given on Sunday morning. Not only is it not intelligible for non-Christians, it is often nonsense for average Christians as well.

Mark has an interesting example:

*"A musician friend of mine was asked to play in a worship band being assembled to play at a large prophetic conference coming to our city. He played for all of the worship sessions and attended all of the teaching/prophecy sessions.*

*A few weeks after the event [which I did not attend] he asked if he could ask me some questions about prophecy. We got together and he explained that he could not understand what these prophetic people were talking about. He was concerned that there might be something wrong with him as a Christian. When I asked him to explain what they had said, it was just as we have already described; largely obscure Old Testament references, largely symbolic in nature, which sounded very religious, but were so vague as to leave most of the hearers mystified."*

Sadly, we have been in many of these kinds of meetings and have left more confused than when we arrived. We wonder if perhaps we are dealing with some kind of prophetic Gnosticism. Just as an interpretation is essential to make sense of a word in tongues, so also an interpretation is essential to make sense of highly symbolic and allegorical prophetic words, assuming that the words are actually coming from God.

At the risk of giving in to the temptation of cynicism, we wonder at times if we are not dealing with a situation akin to "the emperor has no clothes." The small child in us wants to stand up and say, "What on earth are you people talking about and why do you pretend that you understand what was just said?" Now that we have vented, we can return to the discussion of prophecy in the Sunday morning service.

Our conclusion is that, **unless we are content to make the Sunday morning service only for seasoned Christians, we need some sort of filter for our prophetic words.** It would be helpful if the prophetic word could be judged before it is given. This is in fact what Mark's church has done. The protocol they developed is as follows; anyone who wishes to give a prophetic word must first seek out one of our senior leaders and speak the word to him or her. If a senior leader believes the word is applicable to what God wants to do in the service, he or she will interrupt the service when appropriate and ask the person to give the word.

This may sound cumbersome, but it works very well because, as we have already said, the timing of speaking the word can be more significant than the message itself. In Mark's experience. several times he has had a person approach him with a potential word which they believe was for the church. When this occurs, he asks them to run it by him. Often, he believes that it is a word for the church. When this is the case, he asks the person to sit with him in the front row until he "knows" when the word should be given.

Many times, the preacher will make a point that is exactly what the prophetic word said. Mark will interrupt the preacher to ask if a prophetic word affirming the message can be given. When the congregation hears the word, and understands that it was given BEFORE the preacher spoke the same message, the message is supernaturally underlined. Prophecy, like a good joke, requires the right timing.

There are exceptions to this protocol. When we have come to know our budding prophets, and know we can trust their good judgment we allow them to interrupt the service whenever they want to give a word. The same applies to our senior leadership and senior prophetic people. What we have found is that mature people do not abuse the privileges they are given. Our services are orderly, but not lacking in good comprehensible prophecy.

The key to the operation of prophecy in the Sunday morning service is the vital point made by Paul in 1 Cor. 14:32 "The spirits of prophets are subject to the control of prophets." What this is telling us is that **the Holy Spirit does not force anyone to give a word at an inappropriate time.** The bottle does not have to explode! **The fruit of the Spirit of self-control is just as powerful as the gift of the Spirit of prophecy**. We can trust the Holy Spirit to give us prophetic words to speak, but we can also trust Him to guide us to the right moment in which to speak.

Another of our protocols which is helpful in integrating the gift of prophecy into the Sunday morning service involves our pre-service prayer. Our best intercessors and prophetic ministers meet before the service to wait to hear from the Holy Spirit as to what He wants them to pray for the service. The waiting is for prophetic guidance as to what to pray. Often prophetic words will be given which outline the message the pastor is going to give without the prophetic intercessors having any idea of what the message will be.

Interestingly, the worship leader will often choose a song or two that highlight the message perfectly. We think this is an example of what we like to call a "spirit led" service. It is a regular experience of the immediate involvement of the Holy Spirit in leading His church and it results in a greater faith in the congregation to expect more of His presence.

## WHY?

We have already dealt with the why of prophecy. Simply, there is no situation which does not benefit from an immediate word from God. No matter how great our faith, we all grow in our devotion to our Father when we experience His voice. Prophecy is encouraging. Now let's get even more practical.

## Some questions to consider:

1. What have you learned from this chapter?

2. Can you see yourself risking by giving a possible prophetic word to a total stranger? What is the risk? What is the risk, if you don't?

3. Can you see yourself risking by giving a possible prophetic word to another Christian? What is the risk? What is the risk, if you don't?

4. Why do we suggest being careful about the use of prophetic words in the Sunday morning service?

5. Would you be comfortable with your potential prophetic word being filtered by leadership before being presented to the church? Why? Why not?

# Chapter 18: "No more "W's", Now for the "How's"

How do we hear the voice of God? Or perhaps better put, how does God communicate with us in an immediate and personal way? God is capable of communicating to us through all of our senses, but most of the time He communicates to us through our minds and our emotions. He places thoughts and images in our minds, which do not originate with us, likewise, with our emotions.

Ironically, we have heard people say that God cannot plant a thought in someone's mind. We say ironically because these are the same people that tell us that Satan tempts them regularly. What is temptation, but a thought that arises in our mind, which comes from the enemy? God has promised us the "mind of Christ" through the indwelling Holy Spirit. Surely God is capable of dropping His thoughts into our minds. So how do they come?

## 1. Mental Images

In Mark's words:

*"When I first experienced the gift of prophecy it was mostly through mental images. By mental images I am referring to images seen through your mind's eye when your eyes are closed. We all know what it is to have someone tell us to "picture" something. This is what I am talking about except that the mental image is placed within our mind by the Holy Spirit. It is important to note that when we are waiting to hear from God with our eyes closed we do not try to "conjure up" an image. We do not need to prime the pump. In fact, trying hard to see something will usually impede the process. If God is going to place an image in our mind, He does not need our help to do so. Quiet trust is the best posture whenever we listen to God. Here are a few of my favorite examples.*

*Although our Sunday mornings were orderly and relatively normal, our Sunday nights were experimental and risky. I taught regularly* to a smaller group of enthusiasts hungry for more of God – what a privilege! I was teaching on hearing the "voice" of God. The subject for the evening was "mental images." After teaching on how they come, we went into a time of waiting on God to give mental images to us. Everyone was reminded that risk is essential to growth and so everyone should share whatever they "saw" even if it made no sense to them. The goal was to receive guidance from the Holy Spirit as to how to pray for one another. Then we waited...

After a few minutes, someone shared an unusual image. It was of a very nice large desk with a huge leather bag tied with a chord around the top and having the $ sign on the side of the bag. The way he described it was like the money bags you see in cartoon shows. The bag was just sitting on the desk. I asked the group if this image meant anything to anyone in the room. A man at the back of the room, who was a world class effluence engineer with a very large engineering firm, spoke out. He said that on Tuesday his firm was going to a meeting with their bank to ask to borrow a very large sum of money. He said that if they did not get it, many of their engineers would be out of work. I asked the person who got the money bag image to link up in prayer with the engineer and off they went to pray.

The next person to share was a woman named Lucy. With some measure of embarrassment, she said she saw a cat sitting. I asked if this image meant anything to anyone in the room and no surprise, no one claimed it. A minute later a woman named Joy, who was sitting two rows behind Lucy said, with great reluctance, that she saw a large bear standing upright on its hind legs. She said she wasn't going to share it, but since Lucy mentioned the cat, she would risk mentioning the bear. Again, no one claimed it.

The evening went on with more images being claimed by more people until only a few remained seated in their chairs [the rest had gone off to other parts of the room to pray]. Remaining seated were; the cat lady, the bear lady and between them a new lady I had never seen before. I asked her if she had come to our meeting wanting prayer and she said yes.

*I asked the cat and the bear ladies if they would pray with our visitor. They said yes and off they went. About 40 minutes later Joy came back full of joy [no pun intended]. She said, "You will never guess what happened, it was amazing!" She said, "The lady we prayed for is Russian and her last name in Russian is "bear" and the nickname her parents gave her is "Cat!""*

*Imagine being this lady who hears about a church that prays powerful prayers for people. You come to the meeting not knowing whether or not God knows your name. You come hoping to encounter God. You are surrounded by strangers. God gives your name to two total strangers who end up praying powerful prayers for you! Do you suppose she was encouraged? Do you think she will ever forget that night?"*

This story illustrates a very important point having to do with mental images and prophetic words in general. **Often the message that comes to us may seem nonsensical or even irrational**; after all, seeing a bear or a cat is not much of a message from God. The temptation with such a cryptic word is either not to give it or to try to add some sort of meaning or interpretation to it, e.g. "God says you are like a little kitten resting in His lap" or "With God's help you are as strong as a bear!" We have great admiration for both Joy and Lucy because they risked looking foolish by simply giving exactly what they saw without attempting to interpret it.

Another story from Mark:

*"Early in my prophet experience I had the privilege of being a part of the ministry team for a John Wimber conference in New Zealand. After the conference, we did a satellite conference in Christchurch [that's a city not a church]. I was minding my own business when a middle-aged man came up to me and asked for prayer. As I was waiting on the Lord for what to pray for him, I saw in my imagination his chest open to reveal his heart. His heart was wrapped in several layers of cellophane. It was wrapped quite tightly, but it was beating normally. As I was "seeing" this I asked God, "What does this mean?" Without thinking I looked up at the*

*man and said, "You spend much of your time counseling people, but you have been hurt by people in the church and you have been protecting your heart from those you minister to. You have wrapped your heart in cellophane. God wants to free your heart so you can be vulnerable with people again."*

*He told me that the word was 100% accurate. He said he was in leadership in the church and counseling was his ministry. He said he had been protecting himself from those he counseled. He was very excited and said, "Stay right here, I'll be back."*

*A short time later he returned with a woman. He put her in front of me and said, "Do what you did to me with her!" I got annoyed and thought, "You can't just presume that because God gave you a word you can just order up another one for someone else." I started to say this to him, but I glanced at the woman in front of me and immediately began to speak, "You have a mother's heart. Your gift is in mothering younger women in the skills of being a mother. You have raised your own children and have thought that your mothering is over, but the Lord says you are going to teach other young women how to be a good mother."*

*She was shocked and so was her husband. He said, "You need to know something. We have been on staff at this church, but we are going to Singapore to run a home for unwed mothers. She is going to be training them in how to mother their new babies, we leave in two weeks!"*

*What I remember most clearly about this experience was the fear I had while I was speaking. Both sides of my brain were very active in what was going on. One side was receiving a message from God and speaking it and the other side was watching and saying, "You need to stop right now, you are being presumptuous, you don't know if any of what you are saying is true, you are making a fool of yourself, who do you think you are? You are not a prophet, you need to stop."*

*After I finished the second word, the woman ran off and brought her friend back. She said, "Do it to her!" Again, I thought, "These people have no right to presume that just because they heard from God they can just order up words for their friends." Again, I was about to say this to them when I gazed at the woman in front of me. Again, a message came immediately and again it was accurate. When I got back to my bed that night I recalled 11 prophetic words in a row - all for total strangers. I remember telling God, "That was the most fun I have ever had - please make sure this lasts for the rest of my life!"*

Back to mental images...

Mental images may come as still images or as "movies" [a scene being enacted in our mind's eye]. The scene may be purely imaginary, or it may be something that we have actually seen [a memory]. Here is one example of the "movie" variety. In Mark's words:

*"I was scheduled to do a conference in a city a few hours north of ours. I was brushing my teeth in the morning and talking to God about the conference to start that night. I said, "I don't want to just teach like I usually do, I want to do something different and more "Holy Spirit.""" Immediately this thought came to me "Take a paper and pen and find a place to sit during the worship where you can look at the people. Scan the group and I will give you words for certain people. When you get up to speak, start by giving the words I have given you."*

*I have to admit I was excited and intimidated at the same time. That night I sat at the front, to the side, where I could watch the people. Sure, enough my gaze would pause at certain people and a thought about them would come with a message. That night I gave several which were accurate.*

*The next morning, I did the same thing. As I was scanning the people my gaze stopped on a young girl of about 9 or 10 years old. As I was looking at her I saw a film clip in my mind of a black and white movie taken at a Katherine Kuhlman conference. It was a short clip of her in one of her diaphanous gowns seemingly floating across the stage calling out healings in the audience. I knew it was a real film clip that I had seen sometime in the past. I said, "God, why are You showing me this?" The thought came very clearly, "I am giving this girl the same gift that I gave to Katherine Kuhlman. She will hear my voice clearly even from her youth and she will have the gift of physical healing."*

*I told the Lord, "There is no way I am telling her parents that she is the next Katherine Kuhlman! That is irresponsible and dangerous!" I decided to de-emphasize the word as much as integrity would allow.*

*When I got up to speak I pointed to the young girl and said, "I have a word for you." She ran up to the stage, jumped up, ran over to me, put her arms around me, and clung to me. I was completely taken by surprise by her enthusiastic response. I told her, while addressing her parents, that she is gifted in hearing God's voice very easily. Also, that she has the gift of physical healing which will show itself more and more as she grows older. I told them not to treat her as special or different, but just to trust God that in His time He will bring her gifts to their full potential. To be honest, I didn't want to give the word at all. It seemed very irresponsible, but I decided to obey God and take the risk.*

*After the morning session ended a man came up to me and said, "That girl who came up to you is my daughter and there is something that you should know. When we were driving here this morning she was in the back seat with her brother and she told him, "That guy who spoke last night is going to give me a message from God this morning"". He continued saying, "I don't understand any of this. We don't go to church. We only came here because our neighbor invited us. What am I supposed to do?" I told him to start attending this church and ask as many questions as he needs to in order to come to know God for himself and for his family. Later that afternoon, I saw him receiving prayer from our team as he was being overcome by the Holy Spirit. Oh well, just another changed life.*

This story illustrates the truth of the importance of the timing of a prophetic word. The word that Mark was going to give to this young girl and her [then] non-Christian family was beyond their understanding. The only thing that gave the word credibility was the fact that on the way to the meeting she heard God tell her Mark was going to give her a message from Him that morning. The timing of what she heard and what Mark then said was just too co-incidental to easily dismiss.

The application of prophetic mental images may have nothing to do with the presenting problem we think we are supposed to pray for. Here is another example of this from Mark:

*"I remember one woman coming forward for prayer for a physical health problem. The obvious solution was to pray for physical healing, but following what I had been taught, I decided to wait for a few minutes and ask God how I should pray.*

*While I was waiting I saw a "movie" in my mind's eye. It was of her sitting at a kitchen table with her mother standing behind her brushing her long blond hair with a wooden hair brush. It was a very domestic and pleasant image so I began to describe it. As I was describing it the movie changed abruptly when her mother struck her in the head with the brush. I described what I just saw. The woman began to cry, telling me that her mother used to hit her in the head with a hair brush. As it turned out, forgiving her mother was an unresolved issue in her life which we were able to resolve that night."*

Mental images are often instrumental in prayer for physical healing. Mark again:

*"I was a part of the ministry team for a John Wimber conference in Canada when a woman came forward for healing from almost complete blindness in one eye. The first thing I did was establish the degree of blindness by testing her bad eye; while her good eye was closed. She could only see about 12 inches with her bad eye. I then began to pray a healing prayer for her bad eye. After about 5 minutes of prayer, we tested her eye again. This time she could see about 2 feet. We were both excited by the improvement so, we continued to pray.*

*The next time we checked the eye there was a slight improvement. We prayed again with no improvement resulting. I was very frustrated because I truly believed God was going to heal her. I asked her if she would mind if I just took a few minutes to be still and wait on guidance from God as to how to continue praying. She said fine [what else was she going to say?].*

*I began to still my mind and heart and wait. Very quickly I saw an image of a blackboard with a chalk drawing of a cross section of the human eye, like something a biology teacher might draw. The lens was on the left and the nerves leaving the eye going to the brain were on the right of the diagram. Some distance along the nerves was a large X chalked across the nerves and next to it there appeared a cylindrical chalk drawing with the nerve running through the center of the cylinder. Like a wire running through a tube.*

*At first, I was baffled, but then I remembered my biology. Nerves are covered by a sheath of material which is essential to the conduction of a nerve impulse. I said to the Lord, "Are you trying to tell me that she has something wrong with the sheath covering the optic nerves from her eye?" He said, 'Yes."*

*I know it sounds kind of crazy, but I began telling the sheath over her optic nerves to be healed in the name of Jesus. I did this for about 5 minutes with genuine faith, because I truly believed I had heard from God. At the end of 5 minutes, we tested her bad eye and it was completely healed. Her vision in that eye was equal to that of her good eye! Amazing!"*

Normally it is a mistake to try to interpret a mental image, but in this case, it helped Mark to understand how best to pray. Most of the time, the key to using mental images well is to try to avoid adding to what you have seen by interpreting the image. If the image is from God it will mean something to the person receiving it

**The key to using mental images well is to try to avoid adding to what you have seen by interpreting the image.**

either immediately or later. We should be secure enough to have the attitude of a UPS driver. He just delivers the packages, he doesn't feel the need to open them up and explain the contents.

## 2. Unbidden Thoughts

God is capable of planting His thoughts in our minds. When the thought is for ourselves, we call it guidance or conviction or comfort, etc. When it is for someone else, we call it "prophecy." Although mental images are often the most common form of God's communication in the early stage of prophetic ministry, they are often superseded by thoughts. These thoughts are unbidden in the sense that you are not trying to come up with something to say. Trying to come up with something to say is usually a recipe for something other than a word from God.

The key to hearing from God is to relax, wait and trust Him to speak. By saying this we are not talking about emptying our minds as is taught in Eastern meditation, but rather a focusing on the presence of the Holy Spirit and the peace that He brings. Dead air may be anathema on the radio, but it is life when trying to hear from God. He really does speak in a still small voice most of the time. Our job is to create a place of interior stillness in which He can speak without yelling. I do not know why He does not yell more often. We think maybe it is because He does not want to compete with our cherished distractions – why should He have to?

> **The key to hearing from God is to relax, wait and trust Him to speak.**

By spending daily time in stillness, we have become very sensitive to any thought that might be from Him. We say, "might be" because His thoughts in our minds sound very much like our own. They are just thoughts popping up in your mind. They don't come with special effects most of the time. They don't yell or demand attention. In other words, they are easy to miss. For this reason, we need to assign a part of our mind to the task of listening to our thoughts.

It may sound strange, but it can be done. In our experience, we believe the Spirit of God living in us quietly reviews our thoughts and points out the ones that should be rejected and those that should be valued. Either He is doing it or the best part of us is doing it, but we know that most of the time it is happening – thank God! Honestly, we take no credit for it other than the choice to spend time in stillness listening to Him daily. We don't always hear His thoughts, but we always receive His peace. Back to thoughts...

Although in the beginning it may be hard to recognize His thoughts in your mind, there is one time when the likelihood of hearing His thoughts is seriously improved. That, of course, is when you are praying for someone. When someone needs to hear from God the likelihood that He will do it through you increases and so, in these moments, you need to pay close attention. Let Mark give you an example.

*"One Friday night years ago my father was sitting in his recliner reading [an image burned into my memory]. There was a woman in his church who had been suffering with suicidal thoughts, but at the time she appeared to be doing well. The thought came to him, "You should phone Lucy and tell her how much she has grown as a Christian in the last year." He dismissed the thought and kept reading. The thought came again and again, he dismissed it. Finally, after the third time, he called her and gave her this small message of encouragement. She seemed to receive the message with genuine thanks. On Monday, he had lunch with her psychiatrist and happened to ask him how Lucy was doing. Her psychiatrist told him that on Tues night the week before her home group leader had told her that she had not grown as a Christian at all in the last year. The next day she attempted suicide and was hospitalized. Her psychiatrist went on to say that he was very worried about her, but when he saw her on Saturday she was so normal that "It was as if those damaging words were never spoken." He admitted to being at a total loss as to how things could have changed for her so quickly. My father told him of his conversation with her on Friday night.*

[Lesson: we need to pay attention to every encouraging thought that crosses our mind and be fearless in speaking them – they might just be prophetic.]

*Many years ago, I was doing a conference in Northern Canada. During the ministry time, a young man came up for prayer. I asked him what he wanted prayer for and he said that he was soon going to the mission field and he just wanted a general prayer of blessing - easy enough. I started to pray a general prayer for safety and opportunities for evangelism, etc. As I was praying, this thought came very clearly "He was sexually abused by a member of a religious cult." I immediately dismissed this thought as some sort of perverse distracting thought from the enemy. The thought came again and again I dismissed it thinking, "This is rural Canada. There are no cults around here. This is a well-adjusted Christian young man. Nothing like that could have happened to him." After a few more moments of general prayer the thought came again and again, I dismissed it.*

*After I finished praying for him, as he was about to leave, I asked him if there was anything else he might like to receive prayer for. He hesitated and then said, "When I was young my family belonged to this religious commune in the area. The leader was a woman and she molested me." We dealt with his forgiveness issues and he went on his way. That experience was a turning point for me. I decided that I will risk saying what I am hearing unless God specifically tells me not to.*

**One of the difficulties we face in sharing a prophetic thought is that often they come as just one word** e.g. fear, anger, unforgiveness, abandonment, sorrow, rejection, etc. The temptation is to believe that the word is too cryptic to share or too simple to have meaning. In Mark's experience, most of his prophetic words start as just one word. He has found that if he takes the risk to speak that first word, the rest of the message will follow. Mark has a story that illustrates this point:

*"I was doing a conference [not a prophetic conference] in Canada in Nelson British Columbia [one of the most beautiful places I have*

*ever been]. Shell and I had stayed up very late Saturday night talking with the pastor who hosted us. I got very little sleep that night. In the morning I was so tired, I didn't think I could teach. I got through the teaching and asked the Lord what He wanted me to do to apply the message during a ministry time. While I was waiting for His answer, I noticed this woman at the back of the church. As I looked at her, the word "business" came into my mind. I thought it might be from God so I asked her to stand and told her that I heard the word "business" for her. She stood up expecting more. I was expecting more as well, but I was too tired to even try to think of something to say so I just waited. This thought came to my mind, "You are very gifted in business, but you are desiring a change. You want to start a new business, but you are not sure if the opportunity before you is the right one. God says it is."*

*After the service, she came up to me and said, "I have never been to this church before and I don't know what this all means, but this morning my husband and I had a fight because I want to start a new business with a friend of mine and my husband doesn't think it will work. We had an argument and I needed to leave the house so I went for a walk. As I was walking by this church I felt a strong urge to come inside, so I did. I don't know why I stayed, but what you told me has answered my questions about the new business. I am going to do it and I feel completely at peace with that decision! Thank you!"*

We can learn an important lesson from that experience – if we will be faithful to share the first word, God will be faithful to add to that small act of obedience. It is now normal for Mark to give just one word and then wait for the rest of the message. In fact, it

**If we will be faithful to share the first word, God will be faithful to add to that small act of obedience.**

is not unusual for Mark to identify a person he believes he is supposed to prophecy over have them stand up and then tell them. "I have no message right now, but if you don't mind a few moments of stillness I believe the message will come." Mark cannot remember a time it did not come. **There is always an element**

**of risk involved in moving in the supernatural gifts of the Holy Spirit, but fortunately, most of the time it is nothing more than the risk of appearing foolish.**

Prophesying in Tandem

When we are praying with others for someone, it is not unusual for one person to receive just one word and then for another person to receive the next part of the message. The prophetic word can even involve three or more people. Prophetic teams are very useful and should be encouraged wherever more than one prophetic minister is present. Prophesying with a team takes the pressure off of each prophetic minister to receive the whole message. It reduces the risk factor and so encourages more people to exercise their prophetic gifting.

Here is one more story Mark really likes:

*"I was on the ministry team for a very large conference. It was an amazing event; 7000 people attending the conference and a ministry team of 500. There were so many people to be prayed over that the organizers taped lines on the carpet at the back of the room and hundreds of people stood almost shoulder to shoulder waiting for the ministry team to get to them. I had a whole row to myself!*

*At the beginning of the ministry time I was full of the Holy Spirit and physical energy. After prophesying over dozens of people for almost two hours, I was exhausted. I came to this young lady in her mid-20's and she stood with her hands open and a smile on her face waiting for a word from God – she was in the "I am ready to receive" posture – happy and enthusiastic. I waited and waited and she went from being ready and enthusiastic to "what's the problem, how come he isn't saying anything to me?" Still nothing came. Finally, this thought came, "Tell her I like her." I said, "God, she has probably driven for hours to get to this meeting and she is expecting a powerful word from You. Is "I like you" really what you want to say to her?!?" He repeated, "Tell her I like her."*

*I have to admit this was one of the hardest words I have ever given. It just seemed so "vanilla." He didn't even say, "I love you!" What is*

194

this "like" business?? In obedience and full of doubt, I delivered the word. Her reaction was very strange. At first, she had this puzzled look on her face and then she began to cry. It was not gentle crying, it was full of pain. She cried so hard she fell on the ground and continued to cry for about 20 minutes. I could not figure out how I had hurt her so badly. I felt terrible. I got down on the ground beside her while she was crying and then the rest of the message came to me.

I put my head on the ground next to her ear and this is what God said to her, "You think I only love you when you are serving me and when you are in church doing religious things. But I love you when you do the things you like to do. I love you when you sew and when you take your walk in the woods behind your house. I actually like being with you when you are not trying to be religious. I really like who you are!"

As I was speaking this message the crying stopped and she began to smile, then she began to laugh and then she laughed uncontrollably for another 20 minutes. When the laughter stopped she stood up and said, "My husband has been telling me for several years that he doesn't like me and that there is nothing about me anyone could like. I believed him. When you said God says He likes me I could not believe it and I just felt worse than ever. But when God started telling me what He likes about me I knew it was true. I feel so happy. I can't believe it! I don't have to hate myself anymore!" It brings tears to my eyes just remembering what He did for her."

Next, more "how to's" but first...

## Some questions to consider:

1. What have you learned from this chapter?

2. How would being used by God to deliver these kinds of prophetic messages change your Christian life? Can you imagine yourself doing something like this?

3. Do mental images ever come to you while you are praying for people?

4. Do unusual thoughts ever come to you when you look at strangers; something about what is going on in their lives?

5. Will you begin to pay attention to the unbidden mental images and thoughts that come into your mind, especially when you are praying for someone?

# Chapter 19:  More "How To's"

So far, we have discussed two "How to's" on the road to a successful prophetic ministry; mental images and unbidden thoughts. Now we will finish the "how to's" starting with unbidden emotions. Sounds like a title to a romance novel doesn't it...

### 3. Unbidden Emotions

God can communicate to us through our feelings and emotions. Often God's prophets were touched with powerful emotions as He touched their hearts with His concerns for the people of Israel. **God can plant an emotion in our hearts just as He can plant a thought in our minds.** Have you ever had this experience? You come into a place full of people and you are feeling content, happy or at peace when all of a sudden you have some strong negative emotion. Maybe you suddenly feel lonely or sad or fearful. You dismiss it or wait for it to leave believing that maybe you ate something that disagreed with you. Most of the time you probably did, but sometimes God is communicating what someone else in the room is feeling.

How do you know if it is indigestion, your own emotion rising to the surface, or a prophetic gift of empathy for someone God wants you to pray for? Short answer: you don't. The only way to find out is to speak it out and ask.

Mark's example:

*"We were in one of our Sunday night Holy Spirit ministry training sessions in which I had explained the various ways God communicates when it was time to apply the teaching. I invited the Holy Spirit to speak to us in whatever way He wanted to. Very quickly I had a very strong emotion of loss come up within me. I felt as if I had lost a best friend or family member. The only word I could associate with the emotion was "loss." I described the emotion and*

gave the word "loss." No one claimed it. About a minute later a woman said she received the name "Jane." Moments later a woman in the front row said, "This is amazing, my sister Jane lost her baby two days ago!" Now we know what to pray for.

Here is another example of unbidden emotions:

*A few months ago, Shell and I were ministering at a large church in Guadalajara. Before the service the senior pastors asked us to prophesy over their senior leadership team. It was a large team and I did not know many of them; not even their names. I asked the Lord what He wanted me to tell them and this thought came, "Go around the circle and tell each of them what I like about them." As I lay hands on each of them the Lord showed me what He liked about each of them. I came to a man I did not know at all. I put my hand on his shoulder and waited for a word.*

*Almost immediately I felt what I can only describe as an overwhelming compassion coming from him into me. I have never experienced anything like this before. It was so powerful I could not speak. I just started to cry. I tried to speak, but all that came out was "Oh God, Oh God, Oh God." I was emotionally undone. It took quite a while before I could speak. When I did, this is what came out, "You have this incredible gift of compassion for the poor. You have a ministry to the poor. I see you giving food and clothing away. I see you working with the poor. You are going to plant a church, but it is not going to be here with this church. It will be some distance away. You are going to build your ministry on service to the poor."*

*All the while I was saying this, I was thinking I should not be saying this, I am tampering with their leadership team, I am basically telling him he is going to leave this church. I should not be doing this. When I finished the word, the whole team was very excited. They were laughing with one another and I had no idea why.*

*The service started and I went out to join the congregation with my interpreter. At the end of worship, the senior pastor called the man to the stage who I had told was going to plant a church elsewhere amongst the poor. This was the Sunday he and his family were being sent out to plant a work among the poor in a city 5 hours away! At lunch after the service one of the elders took out his smart phone and showed me photos of the man and his team handing out food and clothes to the poor. What a confirmation to him of the new work God was commissioning him to!*

## The emotion of sorrow

*Some years ago, my wife Shell was on a ministry trip to England. People were invited to come forward for prayer. Shell joined a group praying for a woman, but Shell did not know what the prayer was for. As she put her hand on the woman's shoulder, she was overcome by sorrow. The emotion was so strong that all she could do was weep inconsolably. Shell found out later that the woman had come forward for prayer because she was to attend a court hearing the next day to determine whether or not she could keep her young children. She had been unable to express any emotion with respect to her potential loss of her children. Shell was weeping "in her place."*

Have you ever wondered why Jesus was weeping at Lazarus's funeral when He knew that He was about to resurrect Lazarus from the dead and restore him to his sisters? **We are called to "weep with those who weep" and to share their grief with them. We can do this prophetically when God allows us to feel their pain.**

**A prophetic emotion can initiate a prophetic word or it can be the substance of the prophetic word.**

Sometimes the emotion we experience is God's emotion toward the person being prophesied over. The point is that whenever we find ourselves in a ministry or prayer situation we should take note of our unbidden emotions just like we take note of our unbidden thoughts. These emotions should be shared just as we share a mental picture, e.g. "I am experiencing this strong emotion; does it mean anything to you?"

## 4. Unbidden Scripture

What do we mean by "unbidden" scripture? How is scripture used prophetically? We are all familiar with the use of scripture in the teaching and counseling gifts, as well as in the gift of wisdom, but how is scripture used prophetically? It is prophetic when it comes to us through the prompting of the Holy Spirit and is the appropriate message God wants to speak in the moment.

Have you ever had the experience of thinking of a person and having a scripture reference come to mind? Often that reference is coming from the Holy Spirit. It is either a passage He wants you to use to pray for the person or it is a passage He wants you to share with them. We have made lists of all the scriptures that we have received over our Christian lifetimes. Many of them came from God through someone else. There are a few that we often return to for encouragement and they remain as powerful for us today as the day we first received them. Prophetic scripture should be shared in the same way as mental images or unbidden emotions; "I am getting this scripture passage that I think God may be speaking to you. Here it is."

## 5. Strong Impressions

This one is hard to put into words and for that reason we debated leaving it out as a category. If what we try to express here means little to you, just ignore it. We will let Mark try to explain it:

*"Sometimes, before a thought becomes articulated in my mind, I have a vague impression of something trying to find words in which to be expressed. It is almost like a pre-thought. This often happens when I see someone and know I am supposed to prophesy over them, but as yet have no message. At first when these impressions occurred I would just ignore them. But then it occurred to me that maybe if I waited, the message would become clear. This proved to be true.*

*The kind of impression I am talking about is much like intuition. I will get the intuition that something is not right in the person's life. I may have no idea what is wrong, but I "know" something isn't right. Or maybe I sense a change is coming for them. Whatever the issue, the impression is not strong enough to be put into words, but it is present enough to be attended to. These are the moments when it is very important to be free to say, "I am getting some sort of strong impression about you that I want to pray about, but I am not sure yet what it is. Would you mind if we just waited for a few minutes to see what might come to me?" Most of the time a prophetic word materializes, but sometimes I just have to say, "I am sorry, but nothing came. Thank you for allowing me to try." Attempting to help someone is never something to apologize for – the effort alone is an expression of love.*

*As I am rereading what I have just written I realize the key to so much of prophecy is being willing to be still and wait on the Lord for His words. We must become comfortable with stillness and silence in one another's presence. It occurs to me that one of the reasons God delays in speaking is simply so that we will learn to be still and to wait and trust Him. In a world, full of busyness and noise this is no easy discipline to establish, but it is essential not just to prophetic ministry but also to deepening our relationship with the lover of our souls. It is sad to write these words because there is a subtle suggestion that time spent in quietness with God is just another means to some sort of ministry end. The truth is, **time in stillness with God will increase our prophetic gift, but the time we spend in stillness with our Father is its own reward.** Nothing should ever be more eagerly sought than time spent resting in the love of our Father. For so many of us, getting to Heaven is our goal. **We need to remember that Heaven is a relationship much more than a place."***

> **The key to so much of prophecy is being willing to be still and wait on the Lord for His words.**

## 6. Dreams

One of the most consistent themes within the Bible is the place of dreams in God's arsenal of communication. We find them in Genesis through to Revelation. Dreams are still a way God speaks to us today. The fact is, we dream every night, but we remember few of them. We have found that the dreams that we wake up remembering are often from God. The ones that are very vivid and unforgettable are the ones we need to examine. There are many books written about dream interpretation, but this book is not one of them. Our purpose for including dreams as a category of God's prophetic communication is to honor His ways. Prophetic dreams are legitimate.

Our advice regarding a dream which you think might be from God is to write it down in full as soon as you awake. If it occurs in the middle of the night and is so vivid that it wakes you up – get up and write it down while it is clear and fresh. At that point ask the Lord what He was trying to say to you. Then write down any thought that comes to you in answer to that question. When you get up find a quiet place and read the dream and ask Him again what He may be trying to tell you. Again, write down whatever comes to you. In our experience, He will often tell you very clearly what the dream means.

One of the reasons God uses dreams is because of their nature. Dreams are "real" to us while they are occurring. It is as real to us in the dream as it would be if it were happening in time and space. This is why one dream can be heavenly and another a nightmare. **When the dream has a message from God we do not merely hear the message in the dream, we *experience* it!** Allow Mark one very disturbing, but life-changing example.

*"Approximately 35 years ago I was a young Christian and an obnoxious jerk. I was arrogant, impatient and judgmental toward my Christian brothers and sisters, but I truly loved Jesus. One night I had a terrible dream. In my dream Jesus was standing naked in front of me and I was holding a three-pronged garden fork [used for digging weeds] in my hand. In my dream, I was taking the garden fork and stabbing Jesus with it and tearing it down His body, opening huge gashes in His chest and stomach. As I was doing this I was horrified! I tried to stop, but I could not. I cried out over and over again, "Jesus, why am I doing this to You?!?"*

*The dream ended and I was overwhelmed with shame and confusion. I could not understand why I was treating Him this way. I lay in bed and I said to Him, "Jesus, why did You show me this?" He said very clearly in my mind, "This is what you do to Me when you criticize your brothers and sisters."*

I was well aware that criticizing my brothers and sisters was wrong. The Bible made that very plain to me, but the dream made it **real.** I have never forgotten that dream. The image returns to me whenever I need to be reminded.

## Prophetic dreams give guidance, protection, wisdom and preparation for ministry.

Here is one from Mark that illustrates a prophetic preparation for ministry:

*"The dream was vivid, but strange. She saw herself praying for a woman with odd shoes. All she saw in her dream was the woman's shoes. They were old and substantial - the kind of shoes old ladies wear when they have turned their backs to fashion in favor of comfort. Thus, was the dream that one of our prayer team had a few days before we left for a John Wimber conference in Frankfurt Germany. At the conference for 2 days, Susan joined the prayer team at the front of the auditorium praying for whoever asked, all the while watching for those unusual shoes. On the third afternoon, she saw them! They belonged to an older returned missionary who was suffering from severe arthritis of her hands.*

*The arthritis was so bad that she could not close her fists. Her fingers were bent and gnarled, almost immobile. The effect of the shoe dream was immediate. Susan was filled with faith for physical healing. After all, God had already shown her who she was to pray for. Several minutes of prayer time followed during which full mobility was restored to the lady's hands. Much rejoicing ensued!"*

## 7. Open-Eyed Visions

What do we mean when we refer to a vision as being "open-eyed?" Although rare, visions which superimpose themselves upon our natural sight are possible. Mark has only experienced such a vision once or twice in his life. It is a strange thing to see something beyond what you know as physical reality, yet there it is. We have friends who see these kinds of things regularly. If we did not know them well and know that they are not flakey or given to spiritual strangeness, we would assume they were simply strange otherworldly type Christians. Interestingly, their gift of "seeing" particularly into the demonic realm has proven to be useful and accurate.

One friend often sees demons "attached" to people – clinging to some part of their bodies. Her husband has a very powerful healing gift and when she sees what she believes is a demonic afflicting spirit he will approach the person and ask them if they are having pain in the part of their body that she has identified as afflicted. He is a lawyer and a stickler for integrity.

He never tells them what his wife has seen prior to asking his question about any pain they may be experiencing. Repeatedly, they will describe pain in the very spot where she has seen the afflicting spirit. Usually the pain ends when my friend takes authority over the spirit of affliction and commands it to leave. Amazing and wonderful! The thing we enjoy most about their ministry is the fact that she doesn't see herself as especially gifted or highly spiritual – she just describes what she sees in a very natural and matter of fact way. This has great credibility with us.

At other times, she has described angels present in her church service, not in some sort of public statement, but privately to one of her leaders. Because of her credibility and otherwise normal personality and good character, they take her visions seriously and if an application presents itself during the service, they will go with it. More on this subject in a later chapter where we discuss the interplay between the prophetic gifts and the gift of leadership.

An open eyed-vision should be treated like a mental image. It should be discerned as to whether it is direction for intercession or whether it should be shared with the person it concerns. If it is something to do with demons or angels in the church meeting, it should be shared with the senior leadership whose job it is to determine the application of the vision. The mere fact of an open-eyed vision does not, of itself, mean it must be spoken.

## 8. Sanctified Imagination

We are using the term "sanctified imagination" to describe something that has only happened to Mark twice. Of all the ways God has communicated to us, this is the most unusual. It is probably better for Mark just to describe what happened.

*"One Wednesday morning I was having my quiet time with God and my mind began to wander. I imagined myself at our home group meeting that night. It was my turn to lead in the communion portion of our meeting. I imagined myself serving the bread and wine [grape juice if it makes you feel better] to people as they came forward.*

*I was imagining myself giving powerful prophetic words to people as they came up. I imagined myself giving a word to a relatively new girl to our group named Jane. In my imagination, I told her the negative words her mother used to say over her when she was a young child. I then told her the lies that she was believing about herself based on the words her mother had cursed her with. Then I told her the truth God had to say about her in answer to the lies she had been believing.*

*As far as I was concerned the whole purpose of my imagined scenario was seeing myself as this amazing powerful prophet. I actually caught myself at the end of it and repented of cluttering up my time with Jesus with my self-focus, my "mighty man of God" movie. I left my quiet time humbled and forgot all about my fantasy.*

*That night in our meeting the communion time came and I began praying for those who came forward for the elements. Jane came forward and I began to tell her the negative words her mother used to say over her when she was a young child. I stopped her and said, "I am having this strange déjà vu experience right now, have I ever said these things to you before?" She said, "Absolutely not, but that is exactly what my mother used to say to me, how did you know that?"*

*I had forgotten about my mighty man of God prayer time fantasy so I said, "I don't know, but this is what God wants to say to you about the curses your mother spoke over you..." Jane was thrilled and I was happy, but the feeling of déjà vu continued to linger. When I went to bed that night I suddenly remembered my quiet time fantasy. It was word for word what I spoke to her that night!*

*The second time it happened to me I was on vacation at the coast in my parents' home. I had been working very hard and all I wanted to do was to go fishing with my father. I had no desire to do any kind of ministry. After a few days of fishing, my father asked me if I would go with him and mom and a friend to pray for a lady friend of their friend. They did not know her and neither did I. In fact, we did not even know her name, just her address.*

*As we were driving to her house, I began my mighty man of God fantasy. I pictured myself at the front door of her house. We ring the doorbell and my father's friend answers the door with her friend. She says, "Hello, let me introduce my friend..." At that point in my fantasy I interrupt her and say, "Don't tell me her name!" I turn to her and I say, "Your name is Jean and this is what the Lord says to you..." At this point, right before giving my imaginary prophetic word, I caught myself in this moment of self-focus and I stopped and repented. I said, "God, I am so sorry to be making this about me!"*

*I turned from my self-focused imagination and thought about something else entirely. When we got to the door, my father's friend answered the door and said, "Let me introduce my friend **Jean** to you." I was shocked! I realized that my silly imaginary ministry fantasy was from God and that I had stopped it just before giving the word God would have given me for this woman. I began begging God to give me another chance to speak His message to Jean.*

*After introductions, we discovered that she had terminal cancer and was not expected to live. We discovered we had been asked to come and pray for physical healing. We prayed for healing, but I knew that was not why I was there. God had a message for Jean and I had missed it! When the prayer was over and the small talk finished we were heading for the door when the message came. The thought [God] said, "You have two teenage boys and your fear is that when you are gone there will be no one to guide them toward God. You fear that they will not come to Me."*

*I gave her the word. She started to cry and said, "I am not afraid to die, but I can't get rid of the fear that they will not continue with God." I said, "I believe God has a word for you, so let's just wait to hear what He wants to say." The message followed which gave her the peace she needed to face her death without fear.*

*It is a measure of God's creativity that He will use even my self-aggrandizement to accomplish His purposes. Perhaps it is time to pay attention to even your imagination? I do."*

As unusual as this experience sounds, it is not outside the power of God to influence our imaginations even when we are not aware of Him doing so. As the scripture says, in Ephesians 3:20 regarding God's power, He "is able to do immeasurably more than all we ask or imagine...." What this means in our present context is that not all of our imaginations are vain. In fact, we may not be sufficiently amazed at what He can do.

## Some questions to consider:

1. What have you learned from this chapter?

2. Have you ever had an unbidden emotion come to you while praying for someone? What was the emotion you experienced? Looking back at the memory, was your emotion one that the person receiving the prayer was actually experiencing?

3. Have you ever gazed at a stranger and had an emotion that you believed they were experiencing as you looked at them?

4. Can you imagine going up to them and saying, "Excuse me, but are you feeling ___ right now? What would you do or say if they said "Yes"?

5. Have you ever had an unbidden scripture come to you while you were praying for someone or as you gazed at them? What did you do with it? What would you do with it after reading this chapter?

6. Have you ever had a dream you believed was from God? What did you do with it?

7. Has this chapter inspired you to risk delivering potential prophetic words? If yes, why? If no, why not?

# Chapter 20:  Being Natural with the Supernatural

We will let Mark open this chapter:

*"For years I refused to attempt being a Christian, because I was sure God couldn't love me. I actually wanted to be a Christian, but I was very aware of all my sins and character flaws and I knew I could never be good enough to be a Christian. I could not believe that God could love me and accept me the way I was.  It took years of hearing the message of God's unconditional love before the day the love of God actually touched me. When it happened, it was only for a moment, but it was the start of my experience of the grace of God. I came to believe that God actually loved me and it changed my life.*

*The trouble was that although I was experiencing the love of God, I continued to have a problem.  I didn't like myself. I was always comparing myself to other Christians and coming up short.  When I was with one successful Christian, I would compare myself to him and see all the ways I was not like him.  I would be around quiet, gentle and meek Christians and I would feel like a bull in a china shop.  I could never keep my mouth shut. I would spout off at home group and go home and beat myself up for speaking too much.*

*Then, when I was around outgoing and powerful leaders, I would see that I was not outgoing enough - never liking the person I was. I was sure that who I was could never have been God's idea. I was sure that my life needed to be a process of changing myself into whatever was the current model Christian most unlike me.  I could not believe that God intended to create extroverts. I was sure that the real Christians were all introverts. Let me give you an example of what an extrovert I was.*

*A long time ago in a land far away we did not have computers in church. This meant that all of our songs, sermon illustrations, etc. had to be produced on plastic film which was then laid on an overhead projector – can you believe it? We were a very free, fun-loving church at the time. Our worship leader decided to do his best to humiliate me in front of our congregation. He found a catalogue of priestly vestments and monks robes and he cut out the photo of a monk modeling a brown robe and pasted my head on the monk's body. During my sermon, my head on the monk's robed body came up on the overhead.*

*The church thought it was wonderful! Part of their joy was the thought of me finally being humiliated in public. Sadly, I actually liked the attention and wanted them to leave the photo up during the message! An extrovert is happy as long as he is the center of attention even when the attention is not particularly flattering. As much as I enjoyed being an extrovert, I secretly judged myself for being one until one day I discovered something.*

*What I discovered is good news and it is this profound truth;* **God does not just love you, He likes you**. *This is much harder to hear. We all know that God loves us, at least intellectually, but how and why could He like us?"*

We have this idea that before we knew Jesus as Savior, we were worthless lumps of corruption. After we became Christians, we received the Holy Spirit and He began expressing His gifts through us. But for many of us, we continue to see ourselves as little more than fallen nature getting in the way of His Spirit – sort of like He expresses Himself despite ourselves. This is not what the Bible teaches us. The Bible tells us in Psalm 139:14 that we are **"fearfully and wonderfully made."** It also tells us in Genesis 9:6 that we are **"made in His image."** These are things that happened to us when we were conceived, before birth. They do not depend on being a Christian or receiving the Holy Spirit.

## Each of Us is Unique

Everyone is made in His image, even that guy at work you can't tolerate. What does this mean? It means many things, but the one we want to look at now is the matter of our uniqueness. We share His most significant attribute. He is unique and so is each of us.

We think original thoughts and we are capable of creating things that have never existed before we made them. We are both unique and capable of creating that which is unique.

How does this natural attribute of being unique fit in with our expression of the spiritual gifts that come only after receiving His spirit? Are our natural talents now just a remainder of our pre-Christian, fallen human nature? Should they be ignored, or even worse, opposed? Are they "the flesh" that we are at war with?

To answer these questions, we want to look at two more texts: **"For freedom Christ has set us free,"** and **"for you were called to freedom brothers and sisters"** (Gal. 5:1, 13). We know that these verses are referring to freedom from sin and life under the law, but freedom *from* something also means freedom *to* something. What is it that we are free "to?" The short answer is "Christlikeness." His character is formed in us. The long answer is that His character is formed in *US* - as we are as humans; as He created us and designed us originally.

Our freedom is toward becoming all that He designed us to be and this includes all those talents and creativity built into us at conception, but it also means the temperament, humor, and personality that He uniquely designed each of us to have. We are free to become "more ourselves." This is very liberating news, but why is it important in the context of prophecy and the supernatural gifts? The answer has to do with honesty, authenticity and authority.

It starts with honesty: **"This is the message we have heard from him and proclaim to you, that God is light and in him there is no darkness at all"** 1 John 1:5. What this verse means is that God is entirely truthful. In fact, He **is** truth. By His very nature He is incapable of having anything to do with dishonesty. He is only integrity. He will not honor that which is not true. He will not work through untruth or dishonesty. This is not merely because He doesn't like dishonesty, it is because He is only truth and cannot be anything but truthful. This has profound implications for how He lives and works with and within us humans.

## Authenticity and Authority

The significance of this point will become clear when we understand the operating system of the Kingdom of God. Without going into too much detail, the Bible makes it clear that God, as our Creator and King, has chosen to delegate His authority to us to speak and act on His behalf to further His Kingdom. We see this in the earliest days of creation when God delegated His authority to Adam and Eve to rule over the garden. He gave Adam His authority to name all of the animals [in the ancient near east naming is an act of exercising authority over that which is named]. Throughout the Old Testament God continued to delegate His authority to humans to carry out His commands. Jesus did the same thing when He sent his disciples out to carry on His ministry.

**The more you grow in being just who He made you to be [authenticity] the more you will grow in spiritual authority.**

When we combine our understanding of the absolute nature of God's truthfulness with His choice to advance His Kingdom by delegating His authority to us, we can see the relationship between authenticity and authority. God's authority flows most fully through those who are true and who are true to who God made them to be. This does not mean He will not use you, if you are uncertainty of who you are or are going through a phase of imitating someone you admire. What it does mean is that the more you grow in being just who He made you to be [authenticity] the more you will grow in spiritual authority. We have a powerful illustration of this truth in the story of David and Goliath and King Saul's armor.

**"Saul clothed David with his armor; he put a bronze helmet on his head and clothed him with a coat of mail. David strapped Saul's sword over the armor, and he tried in vain to walk, for he was not used to them. Then David said to Saul, 'I cannot walk with these; for I am not used to them.' So, David removed them."** 1 Sam. 17:38

It was an honor to be allowed to wear the King's armor. It would have been an insult to refuse to wear it, but David knew it did not fit him. It was not what he was used to. It was not the way he had learned to fight. In short, it just wasn't him. Rejecting what is not him, he goes out armed only with what "is him" and he is victorious. Here is the question that reveals the heart of the matter: Do you think he would have defeated Goliath if he had stuck with [literally] King Saul's armor? We think not.

There are two very important lessons here:

1. **God doesn't just love you, He likes you! He designed many of the character traits that you have been trying to rid yourself of.** We are not talking about sin, but those quirks that make you unique.
2. When it comes to exercising God's authority to move in all of the spiritual gifts, being naturally yourself will be far more effective and powerful than trying to be someone you are not. This means that prophesying should sound just as natural as talking to a friend. There is no need for religious jargon or "preacher voice." The fact is, anything that is not truly you will just get in the way. The more authentic you are the more authority you have.

This is not just true spiritually it is true psychologically as well. We live in a world of falsehood. We are lied to every few minutes throughout the day. Our politicians lie to us, our advertising agencies lie to us, sales people lie to us and everyone has something to sell. Most of us have become very cynical – we expect to be lied to and most of us are very good at sniffing out that which is not authentic. It is a self-defense mechanism we need just to survive as consumers.

The problem is that when we come to witness about our faith we are coming to people who are on the lookout for that which is not authentic. They seem to be much better than many of us are at recognizing a religious spirit when it presents itself. The prophetic ministry is weird enough to most people without presenting it with any hint of unnatural affectation or religious trappings. The truth is that people who are comfortable with who they are, and speak and act with authenticity, are disarming to be around. One of the greatest compliments we can give a person is to say that they are "real." As prophetic ministers, we need only to be ourselves. In practice, this means:

1. Speaking as we would naturally speak – no special "godly" voice.
2. Using as little religious language as possible. It may take a few more words to express a religious concept, but using plain speech removes the possibility of being misunderstood.
3. Avoiding starting the message with "The Lord says" or "Thus saith the Lord."
4. Not introducing yourself as a "prophet". Just tell them the truth; "I am a Christian and I think God is giving me a message for you. Would you mind if I tried it out to see if it was Him?"
5. Not embellishing or exaggerating the word – as detective Joe Friday used to say, "Just the facts, ma'am."
6. Don't "sell" the word. You don't need to add human enthusiasm to the message. If it rings true, it will not need any salesmanship to sell it.

## Some questions to consider:

1. Do you ever compare yourself to other Christians and come out the loser? If so, why do you think you do this?

2. Why do you think it is harder for us to accept that God likes us as much as that He loves us?

3. Has God ever told you that He likes you? How about you ask Him what He likes about you?

4. Can you explain in your own words the relationship between authenticity [being true to who God made you – being yourself] and spiritual authority? Try it.

5. Have you ever experienced someone presenting a prophetic word using any of the 6 "don'ts" listed above? If so, what was your reaction?

# Chapter 21: How to Respond to a Prophetic Word

## Interpreting and Applying Prophetic Words

Thus far this book has concerned itself with how to recognize and deliver a prophetic word from God. This chapter will deal with the other side of prophecy – how to correctly receive and apply a prophetic word. It may not seem like an important issue, but it is. **A word improperly applied is a word wasted.** It is much like any resource, take money for instance. Someone hears of an urgent need in your family's life – you need a new car. They believe God is prompting them to give you the money you need for the car so they give you $20,000.00 for a new car!

Your family rejoices and gives God all the glory for the gift, but dad comes up with a great idea; "We have never had a family vacation, let's use the money for a trip to Disney World in Europe! It will be educational and fun at the same time!" Of course, you know where we are going with this; the trip lasts two weeks and upon coming home the family realizes that they have no car. The money was wasted.

A prophetic word can amount to nothing, if it is not interpreted and applied correctly. **Prophecy is composed of three aspects: the actual data, the interpretation of the data, and the application of the interpretation of the data.** Often the receipt of the actual data [the thought, image, scripture, etc.] is the easy part. Because the data comes by way of revelation, it requires no thought or intellectual effort to receive. It is truly serendipitous. But, like most of the Christian life, in any work God undertakes through us there is both His part and our part in achieving the result He has intended.

In the case of prophecy, God's part is largely accomplished by the delivery of the data. He will definitely be involved in the interpretation and application of the data, but it will usually be through spiritual gifts other than the "supernatural" ones. In regard to interpretation, God may give the person prophesying the interpretation of the word, but more often the matter of interpreting the word falls to the person receiving the word and those close to them who know them well and have the gifts of wisdom and counsel.

If you are familiar with a little brain science the distinction in function between the left and right sides of the brain is helpful in understanding what is involved in receiving prophecy. The right side of the brain is the place our emotions, artistic expression, music, and other non-logical functions are processed. This is the place where the prophetic data is received. There is no mental effort involved. It just comes spontaneously.

With the opposite side of the brain [the left side] we do our planning, logical analysis, mathematics and reasoning. The interpretation and application of a prophetic word is processed here. Unless the interpretation comes serendipitously [through revelation] there is mental work involved at this stage. We have to actually think about the word and about the circumstances of our lives. This is where the gifts of counsel and wisdom come into play. This is also the place where having someone objective to "bounce the word around with" is very helpful.

We say "objective" because, in our experience, people often have a vested interest in the interpretation of the word. They will often approach the word with a particular interpretation in mind. More often they will "force" an interpretation onto the word, which it will not logically support. The same happens with respect to interpretations that good biblical counsel and wisdom will not support, hence the need for objectivity. There truly is wisdom in the counsel of many.

It is helpful to understand that what we are really talking about regarding the interpretation of prophetic words is guidance. **Prophecy is often a means of divine guidance. As a means of guidance, it is subject to the same rules of determining God's**

**guidance that we face in any decision.** Let's look at the principles we use when we are trying to determine God's guidance as they relate to prophecy.

## Principles of Divine Guidance

Previously we discussed the balance between revelation and reason in discerning the application of a prophetic word. The same issue of balance applies to any issue of divine guidance. The question is, "How can I know that my subjective experience of 'hearing God's voice' is really God?" We said that subjective "hearing" must be balanced by the use of reason [the logical application of Biblical principles to the decision we must make]. This is true, but incomplete. The fact is, our reasoning from Biblical principles can be just as faulty as our subjective "hearing."

Everyone has heard friends justify extremely selfish choices by coming up with a Bible verse. "God puts a high value on hospitality, so I need a 7000-sq. ft. house." They get the house and never use it for the good of the church/kingdom of God. This is called "rationalization." What is happening in rationalization is we are contriving a Biblical "reason" to justify our own selfish choice. Sadly, this is a regular occurrence. So, given faulty subjective hearing and faulty reasoning, how can we truly discern the guidance of God? Here are some steps that will help:

**There is no point in asking for God's divine guidance until we actually desire God's rule and reign in our lives.**

## 1. Make a Choice to Obey

The question we usually ask is; "What is God's will for my life?" This is the wrong question. The right question is "What is God's will?" Our focus is usually on "my life." His focus is on His Kingdom and His will. We will never know His will for our lives until we first know His will. That is to say, His purposes and His agenda and His goals and His means to accomplish those goals for humanity. There is no point in asking for God's divine guidance until we actually desire God's rule and reign in our lives. The level of our commitment/motivation has to be at least greater than 50% for the Kingdom of God.

God doesn't waste guidance on people who have no intention of obeying what He gives. Those who have begun to obey what little they already know to do will receive more. The wheels of a car are very hard to turn when the car is sitting still, but when it is moving forward, even very slowly, it is easy to turn. And so, it is with guidance – applying the little guidance we already have will ensure more.

Psalm 37:4–5 is often quoted with respect to guidance; **"Take delight in the LORD, and He will give you the desires of your heart. Commit your way to the LORD; trust in him, and He will act."** What we need to notice before we apply this verse is that it is conditional. We get the "desires of our hearts" when we "delight in the Lord." Delighting in the Lord is the key. Unfortunately, in the circles we run in, this verse is often taken to mean something like this; "As long as I have warm feelings toward God and throw myself whole heartedly into worship on Sundays I can count of God's guidance." To avoid this sad application of the verse, the word "delight" is the word we need to focus on.

This Hebrew word comes from the root "to be soft or pliable." It translates as "easily yield to pressure", be "sensitive and gentle", be "delicate", and finally, "luxuriate in." **To delight in the Lord is to "be pliable and easy to lead."** To luxuriate in Him is to make Him the center of our pleasure. In vs.5 God promises to act, but He does so *after* we have "committed our way to Him." This means our focus and our actions are centered on knowing and obeying Him.

The New Testament teaches us the same principle: **"If any of you lacks wisdom, he should ask God ... But ask in faith, never doubting, for the one who doubts is like a wave of the sea, driven and tossed by the wind; for the doubter, being double-minded and unstable in every way, must not expect to receive anything from the Lord."** James 1:5–6.

At first glance, this verse appears to be saying that the key to receiving wisdom from the Lord is just asking "in faith" and "never doubting." When we see what James means when he calls someone a "doubter" and "unstable" the whole meaning changes. A doubter is one who is "double-minded" and "unstable in every way." "Double-minded" literally means "one who has divided loyalties." "Unstable" means one who is "unable to be controlled by something or someone."

**Obedience starts with our attitudes and our attitudes lead to our actions.**

The verse could be translated, "Don't expect to receive guidance or anything from the Lord when you come to Him with divided loyalties [between his will and yours] and don't expect to receive from Him when you choose to be out of His control." This is very similar to the sense of being soft and pliable and sensitive to God in Psalm 37.

James makes his meaning even clearer when we read James 4:2 **"... You do not have, because you do not ask. You ask and do not receive, because you ask wrongly, in order to spend what you get on your pleasures."** To ask wrongly means to ask with a bad motive, that being to get what you take pleasure in rather than what God wills for you. To ask wrongly is to ask without regard for His will. It is to be uncommitted to God's way for you. Jesus puts it another way, **"But strive first for the kingdom of God and his righteousness, and all these things will be given to you as well."** Matt. 6:33.

It is very tempting at this point to think that the only way you are going to hear God's guidance is if you are obeying perfectly, sort of like His guidance is a reward for perfect scores on the pop quizzes of daily life. The fact is, He is more concerned with the motivation of your heart than with your perfect actions. What He is looking for is a genuine desire in us to seek His will above all our other desires and concerns. If we can fix our hearts on Him and His will, our actions will generally take care of themselves. Obedience starts with our attitudes and our attitudes lead to our actions. So where do we start?

When we seek to hear God's guidance, the first thing to attend to is letting go of our desires – these are the things that run our lives – our unmet "needs" and our hopes and dreams. **What we are striving for is "holy indifference." It is the state of not preferring one alternative over another. Only when we are neutral can we really hear God tell us what is best for us**. We know what you are thinking, "my desires, dreams and hopes are my most valuable possessions. How can I let them go?" The answer is, by trusting them to God's care.

This letting go is never completely accomplished in this life, but the attempt to let go of our personal dreams and "needs" brings us closer to true holiness. True holiness is being completely set aside to be used where, when and how God desires – just like Jesus. "Not my will, but yours be done" should be our prayer as well.

## 2. Know the Bible

**"Your word is a lamp to my feet and a light to my path"** Ps. 119: 105–106. **"All scripture is inspired by God and is useful for teaching, for reproof, for correction, and for training in righteousness, so that everyone who belongs to God may be proficient, equipped for every good work."** 2 Tim. 3:16.

There are only two ways that God reveals His guidance and will to us: naturally and supernaturally. The natural means are those ways by which we can apply the natural gifts that God has given us to discover His will and guidance. He has given us minds that reason and He expects us to use them. In physiological terms, we are talking about the left side of the human brain, the part of the brain that uses logic and reason to navigate the terrain of this physical world we live in. By the use of our left brain we can study God's written word and find out all we need to know about His general will, agenda, plans, priorities, goals and means for human life.

Long before Paul began to move in supernatural power and guidance he was serving in the local church as a teacher of the

Scriptures. Stephen is the first person [after the disciples] in the New Testament Church to have a supernatural ministry of miracles and signs and wonders. This did not occur until well after he had been serving by waiting on tables in the local food outreach. He began by obeying the general will of God and once the "car was moving", God added the supernatural. This is the Biblical pattern of how God directs our lives. Know the Bible and you are 80% there!

The reason this is so important is because our subjective perceptions of what we think God is saying are subject to error. Not only do we have to contend with our own bias toward our own selfish desires, but we also must contend with a supernaturally powerful enemy who lives to plant lies in our minds. He is very good at deception. It is his title and job description. As an angel of light, he attempts to mimic genuine prophecy and Godly guidance. We need a plumb line by which to judge our subjective revelation. The Bible is that plumb line. The believers in the church at Berea are our example of people who search the word to confirm the alleged message from God.

**Every potential word we think might be from God must be judged against what we know of God's character, values, priorities, principles, plans, modus operandi, etc. as revealed in His Word**. It is helpful to remember that He will not contradict in His direct communication what He has said in His written communication e.g. He will not tell you to violate what He has clearly commanded in the Bible.

This does not mean that we must find a biblical example of the exact circumstance we find ourselves in, in order to accept a prophetic word that applies to that circumstance. We do not need to find a proof text for every subjective word we receive, but the word must not be inconsistent with what God has said about that subject in the Bible. There is no substitute for knowing the Bible.

> **Our subjective perceptions of what we think God is saying are subject to error.**

### 3. Sound Judgment, Common Sense, and Clear Thinking

Once we know the general will of God from His Word we are in a position to use the left side of our brains to apply His truth to the circumstances of our lives. Each of us is wonderfully unique. We are a unique package of personality type, temperament, natural talents, skills, training, life experiences, spiritual gifts, faith experiences and spiritual maturity. We have the ability to look at ourselves with sober judgment and look at the circumstances we are in and the opportunities available to us and make a logical decision. Such a logical decision considers the following factors:

a. Our gifts, abilities, temperaments, passions, & energies

It is highly unlikely that it is God's will for the first violinist from the Dallas symphony orchestra to start a Bible study specifically for the football players from the Dallas Cowboys. A young man with severe plant allergies should not plan on being a missionary in the Amazon jungle. These things are only possible by way of supernatural intervention which is always possible, but more often God takes our gifts, abilities, temperaments, passions and energies into account when He designs ministry for us. We are to use logic when and until He decides to override it with something beyond our logic.

**Using our minds well is not a lack of faith**. The Bible is full of people doing what seemed right and wise according to their best reasoning, e.g. Moses' father-in-law giving him the advice that he could not act alone as Israel's judge and that he must delegate the job. He took his sound common sense advice and the problem was solved, e.g. the appointing of deacons to do the food distribution so that the apostles could stick to prayer and teaching.

b. Our circumstances

Our circumstances often allow or prevent certain ministries that we may be involved in. When we were pastors we were able to study and prepare a message every week. We loved this aspect of the work. Now we are doing different jobs and we don't get to preach like we used to. This does not mean that we are missing out on God's will for ourselves. We have different responsibilities and so different spiritual gifts have been re-awakened in us [prophecy, writing, etc]. It is very exciting, because it means we are growing. Our circumstances are in the control of God. He is able to "open doors", but he can also "close doors."

As Christians, we are not to be governed by our circumstances, but we are to look at them with good human reasoning to see if God is using them to guide us. A word of caution – **just because circumstances line up does not mean that this is God's direction for our lives.** By way of example: David, God's choice of King for Israel, was hiding in a cave from King Saul who was hunting him in order to kill him. King Saul entered the cave alone and defenseless to relieve himself. David was presented with the perfect circumstance in which to kill Saul, end his flight from danger, and take the throne for himself. The circumstances argued in favor of killing Saul, but David would not do it because he had pledged his allegiance to King Saul.

One of the tests of a genuinely prophetic word is that it fits the circumstances in which we find ourselves. By this we mean that it answers a question we have been trying to answer or it may direct us to one of several alternatives. It might free us from a lie that we have been laboring under or it may make sense of a circumstance which seems pointless or destructive.

Often, we find ourselves in a difficult circumstance with no apparent escape. We often view it as meaningless suffering because we cannot see God's hand in any of it. We see it only as a work of the enemy. When we have been in such circumstances we seek a word from God, but the question we ask is very important. We don't ask, "Why is this happening to me?" or "When are you going to do something about this problem?" We ask, "What are you trying to build into my character through this difficult situation?" He has never failed to answer that question and each time He has answered it, we have found the peace that comes from knowing how He is at work in our lives through the present difficulty. It also gives us something to focus on other than the pain – it gives us a purpose beyond the pain.

c. Quality counsel

**One of the biggest problems in determining the will of God for our own lives is that we cannot be objective about our own situations.** When we are head over heels in infatuation with someone, we are not in an easy position to assess whether or not this person will make a good life partner [these are the clamoring desires acting up again].  When we are not enjoying our present job, an offer to go work at a Mission looks like God's answer to our unhappiness, but it rarely is. What is the solution to our subjectivity?

We are part of a body [the church] and God has given it the gifts for us which we lack. We need each other and the gift of good counsel and wisdom is there for our benefit. **"Where there is no guidance, a nation falls, but in an abundance of counselors there is safety. Fools think their own way is right, but the wise listen to advice"** Prov. 12:15.

We have said that prophecy should not be judged by the person delivering the word, but rather by the person receiving the word and those who know them well and who pastor them [their faith community]. This principle is illustrated in Paul's instructions to the Corinthian church regarding the protocol for the public use of prophecy. **"Two or three prophets should speak, and the *others* should weigh carefully what is said"** 1 Cor. 14:29.

This verse seems to be suggesting that the job of judging a prophetic word falls to the other prophets who hear the word. This is not the case; in fact, the opposite is true. The word "others" used here for those who should judge the word actually means, "of a different class or kind." In the context of a worship service this must be referring to those in attendance who are not in the class or kind of those who are identified as prophetic ministers. In other words, the job of weighing or judging the word rests with the congregation. We have experienced this on several occasions. Mark has a good example:

*"It happened that I was not comfortable with a prophetic word that was given at the church I led. Shortly after the word was given I quietly polled many of our leaders. All those polled expressed some significant degree of concern or outright objection to the word. We all had a clear sense that something was "off" about the word. This would be an easy conclusion to reach if the word was clearly unbiblical or heretical, but that was not the case. The word was directional for our church and for some other church it would likely have been a genuine word, but in our calling and circumstances as a church, it was not from God. I say this by way of example to reinforce our understanding that the task of judging a word does not belong to the person speaking it."*

This is very important to keep in mind because immature prophetic ministers have a vested interest in having their words proclaimed as accurate. In their own minds, their worth is tied to our acceptance and approval of their words. This vested interest presents a conflict of interest which should always be considered as a reason to rule out the speaker as part of the process of weighing the word. This is a protocol we believe should be adopted in all circumstances.

d. The desires of your heart

When our general disposition is toward the Lord; that is to say that **when we are normally seeking to know Him and follow Him, the desires of our hearts are often from Him.** Conversely, when we are turning away from the Lord, the desires of our hearts should not be trusted.

The way God leads us is a wonderful example of His reluctance to use His positional authority over us. Lately we have been musing over the means God normally uses to guide us. We have been comparing His guidance through command versus His guidance through influence.

There is little doubt in any Christian's mind that God has the right [as creator of the universe] to issue commands which should be obeyed without question or delay. He has the ultimate positional

225

**God is far more interested in transforming you at the level of your deepest desires than He is in simply getting you to do the right thing.**

authority as King and this is the way we should expect Him to lead us – by command. As Mark was thinking about this, he began to examine all the ways God had led him from the time of his conversion. He was trying to remember any time God led him by command. He could not think of even one.

A short time ago Mark was teaching a conference in San Francisco and doing a training session with the church's senior leadership. There were about twenty in attendance. He asked them to go through their memories to find instances of God leading through a command, e.g. "Do this because I am God and you have to!" None of them had such as example.

As we examine how God has consistently led us we find that it has been largely through influence rather than command. What do we mean by influence? Here is a scripture to help us answer this question:

**"For it is God who is at work in you, enabling you both to will and to work for his good pleasure."** Phil. 2:13

**As we examine how God has consistently led us we find that it has been largely through influence rather than command.**

This verse yields significant insight when we consider the meaning of the words "to will" used to describe the part of our being that God "enables" to do His good pleasure. The word "will" used here refers to the deepest part of our personality where our deepest desires are found. This verse is telling us that God's spirit living at the deepest level of our desires actually influences our desires gently and quietly until we find ourselves desiring what He desires for us. It is often so subtle and gentle that we actually think the desire was our idea.

Mark has a humorous example:

*"Years ago, Shell and I took a sabbatical in San Diego for 5 months of the Canadian winter [clearly God's will!] It was a wonderful time, but I missed my home church, our house, etc. The next year we did it again. About half way through our second winter in San Diego, Shell told me she wanted to move to San Diego permanently. I was dead set against a move. I was actually upset by the idea. I asked her not to speak to me about it again. I further told her to talk to God about it and if He wanted us here He would change my heart without her involvement! Without telling me she set out to do just that. I was happy with my spiritual leadership of the marriage and happily put the matter out of my mind – job done!*

*I remember the moment clearly. About two weeks later we were driving south on the 15 freeway and out of my mouth came the strangest words. I said, "I really want to move here!" My desire was perfectly sincere and genuine. I had expressed my deepest desire and it came as a surprise to me. I had not reasoned out the pros and cons like I usually would. I just knew I wanted to move. The next year we did and we have been happy with our new home ever since."*

One of the things we appreciate most about our Father is that He would rather lead us through His quiet influence within us than through His commands. Perhaps this is because **commands are very effective in the short run, but do not lead to real transformation of the heart.** We have all experienced something like this; your boss [parent, teacher, coach] enters the room and gives you a command. You obey because he is standing watching you, but as soon as he leaves the room, you revert to doing what you really wanted to do.

Simple obedience to commands does not transform the heart. God is far more interested in transforming you at the level of your deepest desires than in simply getting you to do the right thing. He does not simply want your reluctant obedience He wants you to become a person who wants the things that are truly best for you and the rest of His children you are in contact with. Isn't He wonderful?!

e. Supernatural revelation

Everything that we have said about judging a prophetic word thus far has to do with using the reasoning power of our brains, specifically the left side of our brains. Now we will look at what happens on the other side of our brains - the right side. As we have said, this side of the brain is the part of us that is active when we listen to music, look at art, appreciate beauty, and feel emotions. It is also the part of our brains that receives supernatural revelation.

It is the right side of the brain that is active when inspiration and ideas just come to us "out of the blue" and not as a result of "thinking a thing through." Things like prophecy, words of knowledge, spontaneous times of travailing prayer, experiences of God's love, and dreams and visions involve the right side of the brain. We are repeating this because we need to remember that God created both sides of the brain and He expects both of them to be active in our relationship with Him.

There is no question that prophetic words, dreams and visions, and "inner witness" are ways that God uses to guide us in judging or interpreting a prophetic word. A very good example of this is found in the story of Joseph. He finds himself unjustly accused of sexual assault which results in a long prison sentence. Joseph became a model prisoner and so received the favor of the prison warden.

During his time of incarceration, he interpreted the prophetic dream of the cup bearer to the king who was in prison because he had grieved the king. Joseph's interpretation of his dream came true and later the cup bearer told the king about Joseph's supernatural gift of dream interpretation. The king could not find anyone among his magicians who could interpret his troubling dream. Joseph was sent for and the king commanded that Joseph interpret his dream. Joseph responds with nothing but the truth and says, "I cannot do it," Joseph replied to Pharaoh, **"but God will give Pharaoh the answer he desires"** Gen. 41:16.

Joseph admitted that he had no natural ability to interpret dreams. If he receives an interpretation, it is because God has given it to him supernaturally. Joseph hears the dream and immediately receives and gives the interpretation. What is interesting is that Joseph also gives the *application* of the dream. He describes a logical and wise strategy for managing the disaster that God has prophesied to the king.

It is arguable to say that Joseph's wise strategy came as a revelation from the Holy Spirit, but we prefer to believe that Joseph's strategy was the result of his natural administrative ability. We say this because prior to going to prison, he was supremely effective in managing the financial affairs of his master Potiphar, which he did on a routine daily basis. It is hard to believe that every wise daily decision Joseph made was the result of continual supernatural revelation.

Be that as it may, this story illustrates the supernatural gift of the interpretation of prophecy and so we should always ask God to reveal to us the interpretation of an unclear prophetic word prior to applying our reason to the problem. To do so is an expression of faith on our part. Having said this, we wish to give a word of warning.

In our experience those of us who desire most to be guided supernaturally are often those of us who are most lazy about knowing God's word. Such people are not safe to receive supernatural guidance because they lack the Bible knowledge to properly interpret the dream or vision. Even things as clear as prophetic words must be judged by those who receive them. On the other hand, those of us who are highly left brained do not like to give up the security of logic and human reason to trust something that "came to us out of the blue." To such of us we need to repeat that supernatural guidance is biblical and it is for today. We should expect to receive these experiences from time to time and we should take them seriously, but they are safe only when they are in addition to, or an occasional over-riding of, our normal means of determining God's will, which is to know His Word.

A good place to start in learning to hear God's voice in this supernatural way is to ask Him daily if there is anything He specifically wants you to do today. If a thought comes to you and it is not contrary to the Bible, e.g. it is not sin, then go and do it and see if it was Him. By doing this with little decisions we can learn to recognize His leading and apply this form of guidance to larger decisions.

**Those of us who desire most to be guided super-naturally are often those of us who are most lazy about knowing God's word.**

Here is a summary of the steps to discerning God's guidance:

1. Make a decision to obey

2. Know the Bible

3. Use sound judgment, common sense, and clear thinking, in the light of:

    a) your gifts, abilities, temperament, passions, and energy
    b) your circumstances
    c) quality counsel
    d) the desires of your heart
    e) supernatural revelation

## Some questions to consider:

1. What have you learned from this chapter?

2. Why is the interpretation and application of a prophetic word as important as the word itself?

3. With respect to the first three numbered steps to discerning God's guidance which two are most important to you? Why?

4. With respect to the 5 lettered factors in number 3 above which two are most important to you? Why?

5. With respect to all of the steps and factors to consider which do you most often rely upon?

6. Which steps or factors do you need to work on?

# Chapter 22: More on Responding to a Prophetic Word

Before we go on to discuss applying a prophetic word, we need to finish our discussion of guidance and the criteria we use to judge a prophet word. We will finish our list of criteria with the most important – prayer and fasting.

## 4. Prayer and Fasting

Why did we put this aid to guidance at the end when it should be at the beginning? Because every one of the criteria discussed in the last chapter will be more effective when combined with prayer and fasting. We should pray for a knowledge of the Bible, for a will to hear and obey, for a sound mind to reason with, for all of the above to be operating in our lives, and we should pray fervently when we have a major decision to make. Why?

> **Prayer and fasting focus our attention on God and His purposes, which frees us from the loud noise produced by the world around us.**

Prayer and fasting focus our attention on God and His purposes, which frees us from the loud noise produced by the world around us. We say "no" to the loud voice of our own physical comfort so that we can better hear the [often-subtle] voice of God. Prayer and fasting also says "no" to our fears and unmet needs and desires. It is a way that we can put our personal needs and fears and desires on the shelf for a little while in order to focus on His will and His Kingdom. It is the model that Jesus gave us. It was the means that He used to rise above His humanness. If it was necessary for Him to pray and fast how much more is it necessary for us to do so?

**"Now during those days, He went out to the mountain to pray; and He spent the night in prayer to God. And when day came,**

**He called His disciples and chose twelve of them, whom He also named apostles."** Luke 6:12–13

Before we go on to discuss more on how we should respond to a prophetic word, it should be clear that balance is extremely important to the successful application of a prophetic word. Balance is one of the keys to the Christian life in general. Balance applies to almost all the issues of life and so…

A final dangerously redundant word about balance from Mark:

*"The other day Shell asked me for my definition of maturity and something I had never considered popped out of my mouth. One of the dictionary definitions is, "relating to a condition of full development." The definition that popped out of my mouth was, "when all of the faculties and abilities that God has designed into us are operating to their full potential."*

What is interesting is that we have two faculties which God has designed into us that are quite contrary to one another: the ability to recognize revelation and the ability to reason. They are both given by God to provide us with knowledge, but they operate completely differently. **Revelation is guidance we need for successful living that comes directly from God. Reason is guidance that comes from God through processing information which we have available to us naturally**, e.g. principles from the Bible which need only to be read. Charismatics highly value the first and Evangelicals the second, but both are incomplete if they ignore the other.

What this means is that there are many problems that God will not speak about directly to us because He wants us to develop our minds. And for those of us who rely too heavily on the mind, there are problems life presents us which cannot be overcome just by the use of reason and good Biblical principles, e.g. whether to take the job in Seattle or Denver.

Our point is obvious: each of us needs to ask ourselves whether or not we are attempting to rely too much on one or the other.

Balance is the answer on this issue as it is the answer regarding so many issues of Christian living.

## Timing Matters in the Application of a Prophetic Word

Just because a prophetic word does not speak to the present circumstances of our lives does not mean that it is a false word. Prophecy can speak to the present, the near future or the distant future. When Jesus was a baby His mother received amazing words concerning her son's future – ones that would not be fulfilled until the moment of His death and resurrection. The text tells us that she **"treasured up all these things and pondered them in her heart** Luke 2:9. If you have received a word that does not make sense now, just "put it on the shelf" for later.

## Applying a Prophetic Word

Let's assume that you have absorbed all we have said about interpreting a prophetic word. And let's assume that you have arrived at an interpretation of the prophetic word – you know what it means. What do you do next? Again, we turn to the Bible for the answer.

> **Just because a prophetic word does not speak to the present circumstances of our lives does not mean that it is a false word.**

**"In the first year of Darius son of Xerxes (a Mede by descent), who was made ruler over the Babylonian kingdom—in the first year of his reign, I, Daniel, understood from the Scriptures, according to the word of the Lord given to Jeremiah the prophet, that the desolation of Jerusalem would last seventy years. So, I turned to the Lord God and pleaded with him in prayer and petition, in fasting, and in sackcloth and ashes."** Daniel 9:1–3

Here is the back story: Daniel, a Godly man, has discovered from reading God's word that God has set the length of time that his city, Jerusalem, will remain in ruins. He discovers that the time is up. According to God's unalterable word the city is soon to be liberated. God has prophetically proclaimed the exact end of the time of suffering. This should be great news! We would expect a celebration of thanks to God at the very least, but this is not what Daniel does. He puts on sack cloth and ashes and he begins to fast and pray, asking God to do the very thing that God has already promised that He would do. This is very strange; can we take God at His word or not? What is the correct response to a prophetic promise of God?

Here is another similar example:

**"After many days, the word of the LORD came to Elijah, in the third year of the drought, saying, 'Go, present yourself to Ahab; I will send rain on the earth.'"** 1 Kings 18:1

Again, the back story: the nation is being ruled by a corrupt and ungodly leadership [King Ahab] and the country is suffering because of him. Sound familiar?

There has been a drought in the land for three years. God's people are getting desperate. Soon they will be killing their flocks, because they have no water for the animals. Once they kill their flocks, their economy will be ruined and they will be destitute. God decides to rescue His people, not because they are good or are seeking Him [they are not], but because He is good. He sends Elijah to King Ahab to tell him that rain is coming.

Ahab is God's leader over Israel. He should be God's man as well, but he is not. Although he is one of the people of God he is in bed with the world. He has married a woman who is not one of God's people and who is evil. She has been pulling him and Israel away from God. In many ways Ahab is like a portion of the church today; God's in name, but not in heart or action.

God sends His word to Ahab to tell of what He is going to do to help His people:  God is going to send rain! God has sovereignly spoken, rain is coming! So, Elijah says to Ahab, **"Go up, eat and drink; for there is a sound of rushing rain"** 1 Kings 18:41.

Elijah tells Ahab to celebrate because God is going to bring rain. This is what we would expect to do; celebrate because God has promised help. This is not what Daniel did and it is not what Elijah does. **"So, Ahab went up to eat and to drink. Elijah went up to the top of Carmel; there he bowed himself down upon the earth and put his face between his knees".** 1 Kings 18:42

Elijah responds the same way Daniel did. He hears the promise and then he begins to fast and pray fervently. What is the difference between Daniel and Elijah on the one hand and Ahab on the other? All three are Israelites, all three are leaders, and all three are faced with a crisis and a promise. Two pray; the other parties.

Here is the difference; the two who are in relationship with God and are in unity with Him share His heart and enter into His work. They begin to travail in prayer. Because they know God intimately, they know that His promise is an invitation to share His heart and His work and they respond with prayer. The one who did not know his God chose to say, "God has promised to save us, that's wonderful, but I don't have any part in the fulfillment of that promise so I'll just continue to enjoy myself."

Ahab has no real relationship with God and so God's heart means nothing to him and neither does being with God in His work. We need to understand that a prophetic promise is not just a statement of what God is going to do; it is also an invitation to join Him in accomplishing the promise. It is as much an invitation as a future prediction. We need to remember that there is biblical precedent for God to change His mind. He does this when He speaks judgment and then hears a repentant people and gives mercy instead of judgment and vice versa.

At the very least a prophetic word is always a call to pray. As we have said earlier, much prophecy is not given by God to be shared in church, but to be prayed in our prayer closets.

**Our involvement is Key**

**As essential as prayer is, there is more required of us in response to a prophetic word or promise. God expects our involvement in bringing the promise to pass**. It is rare to find an example of God advancing His Kingdom upon the earth that does not involve human action and obedience. He has, for better or worse, decided to work *through* us rather than *around* us. This results in tremendous significance being given to our place in His Kingdom, but it also results in tremendous responsibility upon us. We are His agents upon the earth. Our actions matter.

## The importance of the "middle voice"

The interplay between God's part and our part in advancing His Kingdom on the earth is critical to understand. Most of our lives are lived with God in the "middle voice." The middle voice is a term in the Greek language which describes the degree to which a person is involved in the completion of the activity being described by the verb. There are three common "voices" for Greek verbs. We have no English equivalents. The first voice is called the "active voice." In this voice, the person is solely responsible for completing the action, i.e. it is all up to you! In the "passive voice" the person is not responsible in any way for the completion of the action – it simply happens to you.

The middle voice is the interesting one. In this voice, we neither make the activity happen nor does it simply happen without our involvement. In the middle voice, we cooperate in the activity and have a part to play in its completion. Without our involvement, the activity does not happen, but nor does it happen without God's involvement. Most of the verbs in the Bible dealing with our human action with God are in the middle voice. This is significant as it relates to God's promises.

**Most of the time when God makes a promise, He has a response and/or involvement He is asking of us**. When we fail to do our part, we may not see the result He has "promised." This is particularly true with respect to supernatural ministry. Mark has an interesting example:

*"At one meeting God told me I was going to see a blind person healed. When the person leading the meeting said we were going to*

*pray for healing for blind people, he invited all those with blindness or partial blindness to come up to the left front corner of the room.*

*With all of my heart I wanted to see a blind eye healed. I decided the only way I was going to see this happen was to run up to the front and grab the first person with a blind eye. I did this and saw my first blind eye healed that night! I am certain that if I had stayed in my seat, no one with a blind eye would have sought me out to ask me to pray for them. It rarely works that way."*

**Two mistakes we routinely make:**

> **The best way to apply a prophetic word is to ask yourself and God, "What is the simplest act of obedience I can do immediately [or very soon] which will lead me in the general direction of the fulfillment of the promise?"**

Because the Christian life is a joint venture, there are two mistakes we routinely make in response to God's prophetic promises. The first mistake corresponds to the passive voice. It decides that because God is sovereign and all powerful, there is nothing for me to do but sit passively and wait for the fulfillment of the word. It seems absurd, but can you imagine Bill Bright from Campus Crusade or Loren Cunningham from YWAM sitting back and telling God, "Thanks for the word about my future ministry. I'll just sit here and wait for some leaders to come to ask me to lead them in a world-wide ministry to youth. Go ahead God, knock yourself out!" Of course, we have a role to play in the fulfillment of His promises.

The second mistake is the opposite of the first and it corresponds to the active voice. It decides that God expects me to make the word come true. In this response, I take it upon myself to make the ministry happen. The problem is that if the promise is big enough to require God's power, then it is too big to be accomplished through mere human effort. In this mistake, we often run ahead of God and attempt to do *now* what He intends to

238

do *later*. In this case we suffer from disillusionment and burnout. Obviously, the sweet spot lies in the middle voice.

This was made clear to Mark in an incident that happened years ago.

*"I was in leadership at a church that believed and applied prophetic words. Someone came to me with a dream and interpretation which they wanted the church to finance. In his dream, he saw a very large beautiful house in the country. In it he saw himself and his wife living in the house with all the rooms full of unwed pregnant young women. His interpretation of the dream was that his future ministry would be to run a home for unwed mothers. He also had the application for the dream - our church should give him a million dollars to build the house.*

*I know what you might be thinking, "that dream was not from God!" Actually, I believed it was from God, but my issue was with the application. Our church did not have a million dollars to give, but that did not mean that we had no application for the dream. I asked him if he had a spare room available in his present house. He said yes. I suggested to him that he should make it available to a single expectant mother for the duration of her pregnancy. I suggested that after that experiment they do it again a few times to test the fruit. I told him that if it proved successful as a ministry, then we could discuss funding an addition to his home of another room or two. That proved to be the end of our discussion, but I learned an important lesson. Baby steps are vital to applying many prophetic words."*

The best way to apply a prophetic word is to ask yourself and God, "What is the simplest act of obedience I can do immediately [or very soon] which will lead me in the general direction of the fulfillment of the promise?" As well, we should ask our church's leadership how we might start applying the word in service to the church. We are talking about baby steps. We have found that if we will apply a prophetic word in this way, God will take care of the next step and the one after that, etc, etc. The scripture that comes to mind is "do not despise the day of small beginnings."

## Attitudes Matter

How we successfully apply a prophetic word depends as much on our attitude toward the word as on our actions. **The fact is; our actions are determined by our attitudes. Right thinking makes for right actions**. The Bible is very instructive as to what our attitude should be toward any potentially prophetic word we receive.

**"Do not quench the Spirit. Do not treat prophecies with contempt but test them all; hold on to what is good."** 1 Thess. 5:19–21

Sounds simple enough, yet there is a wealth of teaching about our attitude toward prophetic words contained in these short verses. Paul's admonishment *not* to "quench" the Spirit is only stated because we have a natural tendency *to* quench Him. **Our natural minds, often ruled by pride, do not value what we have not arrived at by our ability to reason and cannot take credit for.** The word "quench" used here can be translated as; "to extinguish a fire" or "to cause a fervent activity to cease." The activity being quenched here is prophecy.

After giving this general warning, Paul goes on to define what attitude is involved in this activity of quenching the Holy Spirit. The attitude Paul is focusing upon is the attitude of contempt. Another translation uses the word "despise." Strong language indeed! The word can be translated as "treat with contempt", "look down upon", "count as nothing" or "reject." The question becomes, why would we look down upon or count as nothing a potential word from God? We believe the answer is that usually a prophetic word falls into one of two categories. Either it is too simple and seemingly insignificant or it is too grandiose to take seriously, both in the judgment of our natural mind.

In the interest of "keeping it real" Mark has a confession to make:

*"I have to admit that I am guilty of devaluing prophetic words for the first reason. I will hear an entry level prophetic word and think "Of course, everyone knows that, so why say it!" You know the kind*

*of word I am referring to. Someone calls out in a meeting, "God says He loves you!" or "God is doing a new thing!" and I think "OK, so...?" The unfortunate thing for me is that right before "God says He loves you" someone might have been thinking "God has never told me He loves me." Sometimes the simplest words are the most profound.*

*I was leading the worship at a conference in San Francisco hosted by a very prophetic church. The conference had gone very well. We had one more worship session to go and it was for the Sunday morning service. The church had a habit of gathering the intercessors and prophetic people together for 30 minutes of pre-service prayer. It turned out to be quite the prayer time. People were packed into a close space and everyone was praying and shouting out praise and prophetic words. I am not a spiritual extrovert and I was not particularly comfortable in this environment.*

*Part way through the prayer/prophecy time a young man shouted out "God says throw away your watch!" Immediately I began treating this word with contempt. "What is that supposed to mean? How silly, how do you apply that? etc, etc," It never crossed my mind that I might be looking down upon a genuine word from God.*

*A few songs into the worship set I paused for a moment. I am not sure why I paused. There was a sweet sense of the presence of the Holy Spirit and I wanted to rest in Him for a moment or two. The moment turned into several minutes. The whole church was standing perfectly still and quiet. The minutes stretched on. I thought of starting another song, but I just didn't want to break out of what was becoming an overwhelming sense of the presence of God. We stood in perfect stillness and quietness for almost 30 minutes. None of the church leadership intervened to "get us back on track." The worship went way overtime, but no one noticed or cared. We had truly "thrown away our watches"."*

**Take the word for a "test drive"**

What Paul is advising us to do is to remain open to any kind of prophetic word no matter how simple. He then goes on to tell us to "test" them all. The word "test" used here could be translated as "examine for genuineness." How do we do that? The word can also translate as "try it out for real" or "use it." The idea is that you should act as if the word is true and try it out in your life in some simple way.

The idea here is much like what happens when you buy a car. Everyone we know takes a short test drive before they buy the car. We believe we can take a prophetic word for a test drive by asking the Lord the question we have already suggested being, "What is the simplest action I can take as soon as possible in obedience to the word?"

Let's suppose that you received a prophetic word telling you that you have the gift of giving financially. Your experience has been that you have never given beyond your tithe. The road test of the word is simple – ask God to show you who He wants you to give money to and go do it. The genuineness of the word is determined by whether you were

> **What is the simplest action I can take as soon as possible in obedience to the word?**

able to do it with love and grace and sincerity. If you experienced His empowering to do it and you experienced His joy in the action, you probably have a positive test result for the word. The next test would be doing it again. If you are blessed and they are blessed, then the word has passed the test.

## Hold on to What is Good

The next step Paul sets out is to "hold on to what is good." This may seem like an unnecessary instruction. After all, who would let go of something good once they have determined its worth? The short answer is everyone. We are a people of fits and starts – we are inconsistent in our commitments. We are easily distracted from following through with our spiritual callings. The words "hold on to" translate to: "don't let it get away", "possess it", and "keep it secure." The command is in the active voice and it is a clear command. The responsibility to protect the word is entirely ours.

## Protect the word

The idea is that once you have determined that the word is genuine you must make every effort to protect it and not lose possession of it. It may provide more motivation to keep the word secure to know that the enemy is committed to separating you from the power the word has to change your life.

There is one thing that needs to be said as a counterpoint to what we have just said about our responsibility to hold onto a word from God. It is a stumbling block that occurs with respect to words that are hard to believe because they are "too good to be true." The usual reaction to a word that is too good to be true is to not believe it. The answer to that problem is to apply the word with small acts of obedience that lead in the general direction of the fulfillment of the word – we have already covered this point.

The less frequent response involves believing the word to such an extent that dissatisfaction and thankless grumbling results because the word has not yet come true. It is possible to hold a grandiose word in such high regard that the present experience of God's blessing in our life or given ministry is held to be insufficient to make us happy or content.

This is not a problem until it results in a bad attitude toward God, specifically grumbling, complaining and thanklessness. There is a fine line to be walked here. We should hold onto the word with enough tenacity to obey everything He has asked of us in order to move toward the fulfillment of the word, but at the same time, not to despise the day of small beginnings. The period of waiting for the fulfillment of a big word from the Lord is not wasted time.

When we learn to wait with a trusting and thankful attitude we are acquiring the kind of character it takes to survive the promotion He intends for us. Big ministries require big character. No one survives a big ministry without a big character to go with it. **Character sustains giftedness, not vice versa.**

## Summary:

1. Prayer and fasting aid in determining the application of a prophetic word.
2. If a prophetic word does not fit the present circumstances of your life, save it and wait and see later.
3. A prophetic word is not just a promise. It is also an invitation to join God in bringing it to pass, which involves intercession.
4. The fulfillment of a prophetic word almost always involves God's part and our part.
5. Our reaction to a prophetic word should be in the "middle voice" - neither entirely passive nor entirely active.
6. Our attitude towards a prophetic word matters – no contempt.
7. We "test" the word by taking baby steps of obedience that move us in the general direction of the fulfillment of the word.

## Some questions to consider:

1. What have you learned from this chapter?

2. Have you received a prophetic word that has not yet come true? If so, what is it?

3. What baby steps have you taken to "test" the word? If not, will you ask God to show you what the next baby step is?

# PART FIVE:

# SAFETY TIPS FOR
# THE PROPHETIC GIFT

# Chapter 23:  Pitfalls of the Prophetic

In the Kingdom of God every strength carries with it a unique weakness. Every spiritual gift has its unique temptation or abuse. Take the gift of teaching for instance. Teachers tend to believe that as long as they teach the Word of God clearly and accurately, people's lives will automatically change for the better. Not true - some will and some won't. For those who do not grow, the teacher is tempted to judge the hearer harshly.

With the gift of mercy comes a tendency to avoid speaking hard truth with the result that sin may go untreated. As we have already mentioned, prophetic people tend to treat their words like precious children, "love me, love my words." Where their word is neglected or not taken seriously they fall prey to judgment just as the teacher does, only often worse. This is because the teacher believes he is teaching *from* the Word of God, but the prophet thinks he is speaking *the very* Word of God. This is why understanding the difference between the prophetic ministry in the Old versus the New Testament is so important.

We would be remiss if we did not discuss the pitfalls that come with prophetic ministry. In the interests of "taking the bull by the horns" we will start with the "Jezebel Spirit."

## The Jezebel Spirit

Much has been made of the Jezebel Spirit. It has become a pejorative label often wrongly used to describe nothing more than a strong-willed woman with a contrary opinion. Despite such misuse, it remains a genuine problem within the church. The Bible associates the Jezebel Spirit [hereinafter referred to as the "JS"] with false prophecy. For this reason, it needs to be understood and opposed. Although the JS is associated with false prophecy, it is actually better discussed under the heading of "counterfeit spiritual authority."

## True and Counterfeit Spiritual Authority

Throughout the Bible we see two kinds of spiritual authority coming into conflict: true godly authority and counterfeit demonic spiritual authority. The second is really no authority at all, but rather an attempt to replace genuine God-delegated authority with rebellion masquerading as authority. We see these two in conflict between David and Saul, Elijah and Jezebel, and John the Baptist and Herodius the wife of Herod.

True godly authority has as its goal the raising up of people into maturity - that is to say into their own mature relationship with Jesus. The goal of true godly authority is to set people free to be all they can be in relationship with God. Counterfeit spiritual authority seeks to acquire power and control over people in order to build oneself up. Its goal is not the maturity and freedom of people, but rather control over them in order to receive attention, power and glory.

The clearest story in the Bible that illustrates this conflict between genuine vs. counterfeit spiritual authority is the story of Elijah and Jezebel. It is such a good representation of this conflict that this particular demonic spirit has been called by many the "Jezebel Spirit." In Rev. 2:20, Jesus rebukes the church in Thyatira for tolerating that "Jezebel" woman. Most commentators do not think the woman's name was really Jezebel, but rather it was being used as a label for a kind of behavior and demonic activity. The name of the spirit is not as important, as what it does.

Jezebel was the ungodly wife of King Ahab, a King of Israel. She was a follower of Baal [a demon]. She brought false religion into Israel. Her husband was the true spiritual authority appointed by God. She had no authority as his wife, but she coveted it. The spirit of witchcraft that operated through her sought to co-opt her husband's authority. This is the first characteristic of this spirit. It craves power and authority not just for the sake of having it, but in order to attack and displace true spiritual authority.

There is always a war going on between the authority of God and demonic spiritual power. Demonic counterfeit authority [which is not real godly authority at all, but rather an attempt to usurp it] will always oppose and attack true spiritual authority. As soon as Jezebel obtained influence with Ahab she had all the prophets of the true God killed. This is because they represented true spiritual authority [they spoke for God]. This remains the same today.

**There is a spiritual force which has as its purpose the displacement and removal of Godly spiritual authority in the church today.** To fail to understand this spiritual reality leaves the church ignorant as to the nature and power of the enemy it faces, a sure recipe for disaster.

The tactics which this spirit uses to undermine and replace godly spiritual authority have not changed and for this reason, we need to identify them. We pick up the story in 1 Kings 21:1. King Ahab wants another man's vineyard. The man will not sell it to him. He knows that he cannot take it by force because this would be a misuse of his God-given authority.

In order to overcome Ahab's reluctance to misuse his godly authority Jezebel comes to him first with flattery in verse 7; **"You are the King of Israel I will get it for you."** She reminds him of his elevated position and importance and she in effect says, "You are special, you are above the law, you deserve to have what you want." She suggests that she will be the means to give him what he deserves.

She then lies to co-opt his authority by forging his name and using his royal seal. [deceit]

Next, she uses false accusations against an innocent man [gossip and slander].

Next, justified by the lies she has used, she has him killed. [murder].

The spiritual power of this spirit is immense. In Ahab's life, it resulted in total emasculation. He became his wife's pawn. It is arguable that Ahab was simply a weak man and that a stronger man would not succumb so easily. Not so!

Even Elijah, a powerful and holy man of God came under the power of the JS. After Jezebel has killed the prophets of God [those who spoke with God's true spiritual authority] Elijah goes after the prophets of Baal. We see the story in 1 Kings 18:19.

This story tells us much about how the JS spirit works. Elijah challenges 400 demonic prophets to a contest of power. Whichever god can ignite the offering without man's help in setting it ablaze is the true god. In verses 25–30 we see the methodology of false spiritual authority. Its methodology is essentially a false but intense religious fervor; shouting, dancing, cutting themselves with knives and spears, and frantic prophesying. This activity results in a religious fervor that lasts for hours.

**The activity of the JS is associated with a religious behavior that looks very spiritual and intense, but it is actually soulish and un-godly.**

The activity of this spirit is associated with a religious behavior that looks very spiritual and intense, but it is actually soulish and un-godly. This behavior is consistent with that produced by a false religious spirit. There is a belief that God can only be moved to act if they do everything right and get their rituals down pat. It relies on self-generated religious fervor. It also helps if they suffer for their faith, so they cut themselves. It is in every way the opposite of simple trust in God which comes by grace.

Now we see in Elijah's prayer what true faith and true spiritual authority look like:

**"At the time of the offering of the oblation, the prophet Elijah came near and said, '... O LORD, God of Abraham, Isaac, and Israel, let it be known this day that you are God in Israel, that I am your servant, and that I have done all these things at your bidding. Answer me, O LORD, answer me, so that this**

people may know that you, O LORD, are God, and that you have turned their hearts back.'" 1 Kings 18:36–37

Then the fire of the LORD fell and consumed the burnt offering. **True spiritual authority is not religious**. It does not make a show of prayer. It trusts in the character of God and quietly and without religious ritual, asks God to be God. **It operates from the foundation of a relationship with God rather than a foundation of legalistic religion.**

After this incredible victory, we would expect Elijah to be full of faith to finish his righteous task by going after Jezebel, the source of the problem. Instead he becomes intimidated by her. She finds out about what he has done to her false prophets and she threatens to kill him. Rather than stand and fight, he runs in fear. He is so full of fear and despair that he actually prays to die: "... I have had enough Lord ... take my life ..." 1 Kings 19:4

It is hard to imagine that a man as powerfully used by God could be so fully intimidated and discouraged – such is the power of the JS.

> For the prophetic gift, a significant weakness is a vulnerability to the Jezebel spirit.

**Two of the principle weapons of the JS are fear and discouragement**. There is no rational reason for this reaction in Elijah, yet he is overwhelmed by fear and discouragement. I [Mark] have known this experience. It is real. The fear and discouragement may be irrational, but it is real because it is coming from a powerful evil spirit. Its goal is to discourage God-ordained leaders until they have had enough and want to quit [which is to die spiritually]. In addition, its other common weapons are flattery, [and when that does not work] false accusations, intimidation, criticism and gossip - all against leaders who have been ordained by God [genuine spiritual authority].

What does all this have to do with the prophetic ministry? As has already been stated every spiritual gift has its own unique weakness or temptation, which the enemy can use to destroy it or turn it in an ungodly direction. For the prophetic gift, a significant weakness is a vulnerability to the Jezebel spirit.

Allow us to summarize what we have learned thus far. The JS has been active throughout church history. It continues to be active today. Its goal is to remove and replace those who have been delegated genuine spiritual authority from God. It does this by flattery, slander, gossip, discouragement, and intimidation. It is usually associated with a false religious spirit evidenced by a lot of religious talk and super-spiritual activity. It is often aligned with a misused or counterfeit gift of prophecy. It seeks control either by gaining influence or control over God's ordained leader or removing his authority from him. The effect of this spirit upon the leader is irrational fear and despair.

In the story of Jezebel (1 Kings 21:19) and in Jesus' words to the church in Rev. 2:20, the consequence for God's chosen leaders of tolerating this spirit is bearing responsibility for its sins. **"Nevertheless, I have this against you: You tolerate that woman Jezebel, who calls herself a prophetess"**. Rev. 2:20

**The response we are to take with this spirit is one of absolute zero tolerance**. The solution God ordained for the problem of Jezebel was her death! God sent Jehu, a warrior King, to deal with Jezebel. The circumstances of her death are significant. When Jehu rides up to Jezebel's home she has put on her makeup [probably in the hope of luring him under her influence] and greets him from her second story window. Jehu is more than capable of killing her himself, yet he calls for her eunuchs to throw her out her window. [2 Kings 30-33]

The symbolism is compelling. Jehu calls upon those emasculated men who have been enslaved by Jezebel to rise up in their manhood and throw her out of the home they live in. God's answer for those who have been under the influence of the JS is to rise up and deal with it by throwing it out of the house [church]. Negotiation is not an option.

## The Jezebel Spirit works Through Human Weakness

This does not mean treating the person [who is under its influence] unlovingly. **We need to understand that although this spirit is exceedingly evil, most of those who come under its control are not.** It is a deceiving spirit and most of those under its control or influence, do not even know it. How can this be? It is because this spirit attacks us in [the places of] our human weaknesses.

**"The acts of the flesh are obvious: sexual immorality, impurity and debauchery; idolatry and witchcraft; hatred, discord, jealousy, fits of rage, selfish ambition, dissensions, factions and envy; drunkenness, orgies, and the like ..."** Gal. 5:19–21

The point is that you don't have to be intent on evil to be used by an evil spirit; you merely have to be human. We are all subject to weakness in our human nature. And all of us have weakness in our lives due to being hurt.

**Often those who have been hurt by a person in spiritual authority [or any form of authority] will be open to the lies of this spirit.** It will tell them that they cannot trust their leadership and that they will be hurt again. So, when this spirit tells them that their present leader is untrustworthy, their default position is to believe it. As well, people who are spiritually gifted, but whom godly leadership [for whatever reason] has overlooked, are vulnerable. This spirit will tell them that their leaders are not godly because they have failed to discern the presence of valuable gifts in the church, specifically themselves.

Frequently, the reason they have been overlooked is not a lack of giftedness, but the presence of a character flaw, which may be a tendency to see everything through the lens of rejection. Or it may not be their time for visibility. Sometimes, especially in charismatic circles, the person has been prophesied over in another church or at a conference and has been told that they have some great gift or budding ministry. Then they return to their home church and their leaders don't see it or don't give them the recognition they now expect. They become jealous of those who do have the giftedness they have been told they have and so they begin to despise their leaders who have failed to recognize their new gifting. The godly answer to their situation is of course humility and patience.

## Rebellion is an open door to the Jezebel Spirit

One-character flaw that we all have to some degree or another is rebelliousness. Samuel told Saul that **"rebellion is as the sin of witchcraft"** 1 Sam. 15:23. What he is saying is that rebellion leads to being influenced by the JS of counterfeit spiritual authority because rebellion is always opposed to true spiritual authority. When you are rebellious you are playing into the hands of the JS. Once you are in rebellion, you are only one step away from coming under its control. Rebellion is a very common response to genuine spiritual authority, especially for those of us who grew up during the 60's and thereafter. Rebellion is also a common response for those who have been hurt in the past and so do not trust their leaders.

> **When you are rebellious you are playing into the hands of the Jezebel Spirit.**

## Pride

The last character flaw, which provides a fertile ground for this spirit, is pride. Pride is at the root of bitterness because pride seeks recognition and **when our giftedness is overlooked pride rises up with anger, jealously and rebellion; thus, allowing the Jezebel spirit a clear path to our hearts.**

All these very human "works of the flesh" have their roots in us - in our fallen nature. It is our own sin and brokenness that make us vulnerable to this spirit. The truly sad thing is that often there is no intention or awareness that one is co-operating with this spirit. This is because the JS will provide its victim with plenty of counterfeit spiritual experiences, which further convince the victim that he or she is drawing closer to God. False prophecy is one of the most effective.

As well. the JS will provide ecstatic spiritual experiences that mimic the experiences of the Holy Spirit. The person appears to be very spiritual and in fact they are – but it is the wrong spirit animating their spirituality.

One of the most frustrating aspects of this evil spirit's work in its victims is that often immature and impressionable Christians are taken in by the hyper-spiritual behavior of the victim. The JS seeks to alienate God's flock from those leaders God has endorsed and a hyper-spiritual-Jezebel Spirit-empowered person is the perfect choice for this job. False prophecy provides just the kind of "proof" immature Christians need to be convinced to follow their new "really spiritual" leader. The final irony is that once the JS has a following, it will attack God's ordained leadership with the accusation that they themselves are the ones in rebellion to God's will.

### How do we Protect Ourselves?

Since our own sinful human nature and past traumas make us vulnerable to this spirit, how can we protect ourselves from it? The first and most important thing is to recognize its ways and means. **It uses flattery and when that fails, it uses criticism, gossip, slander and false accusation against leadership.** It usually does this through those close to leadership. They are often very "spiritual" people in appearance. Lots of "God talk." Maybe they are self-proclaimed prophets or "prayer warriors", but their message and prayers seem to focus on what is wrong with leadership and the local church. They seem to have a consistently negative message.

When you recognize this kind of behavior and attitude, you should be on your guard. If what they are saying is slander, it is not redeemed by putting it in the form of a prophecy or a prayer, no matter how heartfelt.  Maybe you notice that after being with certain people, you find yourself critical of your leaders or your church and you don't even know why. If you see a pattern to this effect, you need to take action, start praying for that person and pray for yourself when and after you are around them.

**Bitterness and Unforgiveness**

> **The way you humble yourself is by submitting to your God-appointed leaders. This is the opposite of rebellion and frees you from it.**

If you are coping with critical thoughts for which there is no genuine foundation in fact, then maybe you are being attacked by this spirit. If this is the case, try praying against it and ask the Holy Spirit to protect your thought life. If you have bitterness against some past authority figure who you have not forgiven, then forgive them, and ask God for the trust you need in your present leaders. **We have found that we need to remind ourselves occasionally that when we put our trust in our leaders, we are really putting our trust in God working *through* our leaders**. If you are rebellious by nature, then repent of it and find ways to submit to your leaders. If you struggle with pride, then repent of it and ask others for prayer against it in your life.

**Lack of Trust in God**

Often the root of vulnerability to this spirit is a lack of trust in God - a lack of trust that He will recognize your giftedness. It is a fear that He will overlook you and you will not have a place in the church. This fear motivates you to "take control" and make something happen. It may be a lack of trust that God can really accomplish His will in His church through the leaders He has chosen. You see how human they are and you don't believe He could really get His job done through them.

Maybe they are actually not as gifted as you and you can't believe that you should have to submit to someone who is not as good at your spiritual gift as you are. The result is that you don't trust

God's choice or timing and so you believe that you have a good reason for rebellion.

**Humility is the Cure**

In answer to all of this lack of trust, fear, past hurt or pride is this one truth: **"Humble yourselves, therefore, under the mighty hand of God, that He may exalt you at the proper time"** 1 Peter 5:6. And **"God opposes the proud but gives grace to the humble"** James 4:6.

The Lord has promised that if you choose to humble yourself, He will take on the job of exalting you. You have nothing to fear from your leaders whether they are great or poor. Your ministry is not up to them, but up to God. God is your protection. If you choose to humble yourself, God will give you all you need of His empowering presence in your life.

The way you humble yourself is by submitting to your God-appointed leaders. This is the opposite of rebellion and frees you from it. It also protects you from the Jezebel Spirit and the spirit of rebellion. When you submit to your leaders, you are not submitting to a man or woman, but to God. As you submit, God will lift you up irrespective of whether they are good leaders or not. This is because when you submit to and trust them, you are really trusting and submitting to God *in them*. When you do this, God undertakes to lift you up and He will do this whether it is through them or otherwise.

**Most significantly, submitting to your leaders and trusting God in them is a direct blow to your pride, which is our human nature's most diabolical trait.** There are so few ways to humble ourselves, so why miss the opportunity?

Finally, if you believe that someone you know has a problem with the spirit of rebellion or the JS, your attitude should be love. Be firm in resisting this influence, but continue to love. As soon as we respond with a spirit of vengeance or anger, this spirit has already won. Our enemy is not flesh and blood, but the spirit behind the behavior. Pray for each other with love, but be wise.

For those caught in the lies of the JS freedom only comes from repentance and humility. Zero tolerance to the JS means calling anyone under its influence to repentance, but it also means providing the counseling and prayer necessary to heal those areas of vulnerability which we have already discussed. Whenever a person agrees to a process of repentance and healing, we should pursue it with patience and grace. Where repentance and openness to counsel and healing does not exist, we should exercise church discipline and expel the person. Allowing such a person to remain in the church only allows the JS to infect others and ultimately further damage the church.

## Some questions to consider:

1. How can you tell the difference between godly spiritual authority and counterfeit demonic spiritual authority?

2. Why do you think the Jezebel Spirit is so closely aligned with false prophecy?

3. Even very godly leaders make mistakes and hurt us occasionally. These unresolved hurts make us vulnerable to the work of the Jezebel Spirit. Do you have any past hurts from leaders in your life that you have not dealt with? If so, have you forgiven them and made a choice to trust God through your present leaders?

4. Are you presently submitted to your spiritual leaders?

5. What is the danger of deciding you don't need spiritual leaders in your life?

6. Do you have hyper-critical people in your life? If so, how are they influencing you?

# Chapter 24:  More Potential Prophetic Problems

## Prophecy and Leadership in the Local Church

Our discussion of the Jezebel Spirit brings into focus a potential conflict between the gift of prophecy and church leadership. The issue of the Jezebel Spirit is essentially demonic - the high jacking of the prophetic ministry by an evil spirit. This is clearly the worst-case scenario facing church leadership in its interaction with the prophetic gift, but it is not the only potential problem. There is an important question to be answered with respect to the interaction between the spiritual gift of prophecy and the spiritual gift of leadership. Paul identifies the spiritual gift of leadership as a gift separate and distinct from the gift of prophecy. (Rom. 12:6–8)

> **The issue of the Jezebel Spirit is essentially demonic - the high jacking of the prophetic ministry by an evil spirit.**

At the very least this suggests that the gift of prophecy is not a replacement for the gift of leadership, which begs the question as to how these two gifts are designed by God to interact. The answer lies in our discussion of the three aspects of applying prophetic words. We made the case that the successful use of prophecy depends upon the correct raw data being received, interpreted and then applied. Effective prophecy is a three-legged stool. Remove any one of the legs and prophecy is no longer useful. Generally, highly prophetic people are very good at receiving the raw data [the uninterpreted word] from the Holy Spirit. In fact, in many cases they receive far too much raw information to use.

By way of analogy, the intelligence services of the United States regularly tap all of the cell phone calls within the country and many outside of it. Super computers are used to record literally billions of words spoken daily. The problem of course, is making use of the messages recorded. Key words are flagged, which may or may not alert the government to a potential terrorist threat. Out of the thousands of daily messages that may be of interest someone has to read them and decide which ones' result in actionable intelligence, that is to say, which will be applied by taking some counterterrorist action. In all cases the experts involved in the recording process are never the experts involved in the analytical process of deciding what to do with a potentially important message.

The same principle applies to the actionable use of prophetic words. The gift necessary for receiving the message from God is not the same gift as is necessary for interpreting the message; likewise, they are rarely the same gift necessary for applying the word to the life of the local church or to an individual. Receiving a prophet word is entirely a right brain function. Applying a prophetic word is usually a left brain, analytical function. Usually prophets are high on receiving the word and leaders are high on applying the word. We say "usually", because prophets may have the gift of leadership and leaders may have prophetic gifts, but most of the time leading a church is a matter of planning, strategy, teaching, administration and pastoral [people] gifts.

Because those with the gifts of leadership are ultimately responsible for the application of prophetic words they occupy a position of leadership above that of prophet and this is not easy for some prophetic people to accept. There is nothing more difficult than to be certain you have heard from God and have your word rejected [not applied] by those who lead your church. In Mark's words;

**The spiritual gift necessary for receiving a message from God is not the same gift as is necessary for interpreting the message.**

*"I know this because I have been in that position several times. Situations like this precede many church splits and prophetic exits, but they don't have to. As a prophetic minister to our local church I have come to accept*

259

**There is nothing better for a "prophet's" pride than being a part of a local church where he or she is just another well-loved saint trying his best to love Jesus.**

*that my prophetic function is to be a resource to those who have the responsibility to lead the local church. What they choose to do with a word I give is not my responsibility. My responsibility is to support them whether or not they find my word helpful.*

*One often unrecognized benefit of accepting my prophetic role as one of submission to my leadership is the opportunity to develop humility as a prophetic minister. Pride is a very real problem for those who carry the label of "prophet." Although they shouldn't, people put prophets on a pedestal. They think more highly of them than they should. When I travel I am often invited because of my prophetic gifting. I am welcomed as a "prophet" and generally accorded a very high measure of respect. I think this is good for those showing the respect, but not so good for me. I don't need to be told I am wonderful or special, I hear that often enough from the enemy by way of temptation."*

There is nothing better for a "prophet's" pride than being a part of a local church where he or she is just another well-loved saint trying his best to love Jesus. And this effort benefits from being under the spiritual authority of the gift of leadership. For all of us, pride is our worst enemy and for those of us whose gifts are largely supernatural we have an increased susceptibility to the spirit of pride. Leadership is a gift of humility to us, if we will see it as such.

There exists a "sweet spot" between the prophetic gift and the leadership gift where the two gifts meet to make the prophetic gift most effective in blessing the local church. The same blessing applies for any group or individual who is seeking the best possible application of a prophetic word. The following graphs illustrate that sweet spot.

In the first graph, we see that prophetic types are high on receiving raw data and lower on interpretation and application. In the second graph, we see that the leadership types are lower on receiving the raw data, but higher on interpreting and applying it.

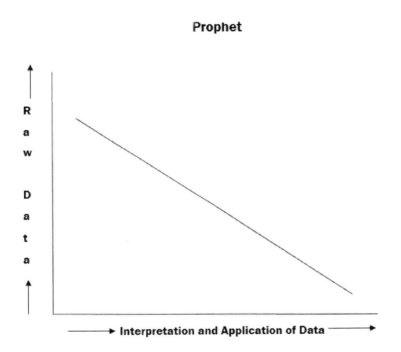

**Prophet**

## Leader

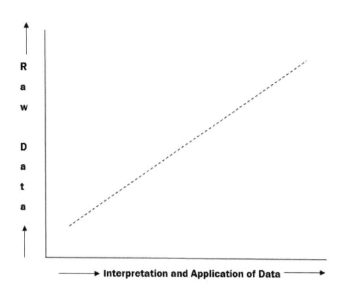

## Prophet and Leader

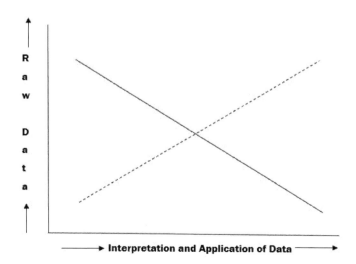

The third graph illustrates the sweet spot where prophetic revelation meets reason and wisdom to result in a valid interpretation and a helpful application. The key to finding this sweet spot is good communication between the prophetic people and the leadership. If the prophetic types do not believe they have the ear of the leadership they will be vulnerable to feelings of rejection and disrespect. This may result in mistrust and create an opening for the Jezebel Spirit.

In a small church, with fewer prophetic ministers and a small staff, communication is easy, but as a church grows the potential for a disconnect increases. **The norm is the larger the church the greater the need for an intentional means of prophet – leader interaction.** This can take whatever form is practical, but it should be a regular occurrence and a high priority.

In Mark's church in San Diego the prophets and intercessors together with the senior pastor and part of the senior leadership team met on Wednesday nights. In Mark's words:

*"It was not unusual for the Sunday message to be shaped or changed by what was received prophetically in those meetings. Prophecies spoken in those meetings were often read to the church on Sunday mornings. Similarly, the intercessors and prophetic types meet before the Sunday service to pray for the service. Prophetic words received in that meeting often confirm the message to be taught without any prior knowledge of what the sermon will be. Such prophetic confirmation of the Sunday message brings a sense of divine guidance to the meeting and is, in itself, a "demonstration of the supernatural power" of God to guide the meeting as He wills.*

*In one large church that I work with they have established a prophetic group that meets regularly to listen to the Lord and share what they are hearing. The group is led by one of the staff which ensures that applicable words are heard by the senior leadership. The existence of such a group communicates to the prophetic types that they are valued by the senior leadership. This builds trust and minimizes the possibility of division. It also provides pastoral care to those who are learning how to manage their growing prophetic gifting.*

*Whenever I visit that church I always spend time training and teaching the budding prophets. The existence of such a group also provides accountability for those who seek to grow into recognized prophetic ministers. Merely being a member of such a group provides an exercise in learning to be submitted to the church's senior leadership.*

*Before leaving the discussion of the interaction between the prophetic gift and the leadership gift we offer one tragic example of what can go wrong when prophecy presumes the role of leadership. I am aware of what was a very healthy and growing church that welcomed a well-recognized prophet to hold meetings at the church. During one of the meetings the prophet prophesied drastic changes in the leadership of the church. A new senior pastor was identified as well as a new worship leader together with a few other radical changes. Believing this prophet to be infallible the leadership made the changes.*

*A short time later the church was destroyed. It simply shrank and died. None of the prophetic choices were good ones. This sad story is illustrative of two serious mistakes. The first is that of confusing New Testament and Old Testament prophetic ministry, specifically believing that New Testament prophecy is guaranteed to be accurate when delivered by a nationally recognized prophet. New Testament prophecy must be judged by "others." Others in this case being the leadership of the church.*

*The second mistake is to fail to understand that the role of the leadership in the church is above that of prophet, no matter how famous or well respected he might be. My practice when visiting a church in my prophetic capacity is to serve the church through submission to its leadership. If I receive a word for the church which is directional or corrective I will speak it first to the leadership for them to decide whether or not the word should be given. My goal is always to leave the application of a prophetic word in the hands of those who must apply and live with it."*

## The Gift of Prophecy and the Gift of Teaching

Not only is prophecy not equivalent to the gift of leadership, neither is it equivalent to the gift of teaching. **Prophets cannot presume to have the gift of teaching simply because they hear from God.** That these two gifts are distinct should be obvious from reading Paul's list of spiritual gifts in 1 Corinthians 12:29–30. **"... Are all prophets? Are all teachers?"** These gifts are distinct because they involve different abilities and skills. Teaching is a largely left brained activity whereas prophecy is entirely right brained. Teaching requires not only the inspiration and guidance of the Holy Spirit, but also the analytical, organizational and logical skills of the teacher.

Sadly, prophets frequently presume to be teachers when they are not, with often tragic results. Unbiblical teaching is usually fairly easy to spot by simply examining the teaching through the lens of the Bible. A good knowledge of the Bible is the prophylactic preventing most heresy from entering the bloodstream of the local church. Unfortunately, bad teaching coming through a prophet is in another category entirely.

The problem arises because people tend to extend the credibility they give to accurate prophetic words to bad teaching. This is because the bad teaching often follows supernaturally accurate prophetic words. It is an easy mistake to make. Imagine that you have just been called out of a crowd of 1000 people and told the secrets of your heart. You have no doubt whatsoever that the words are accurate and came from God. After the prophetic session ends the prophet begins to teach an End Times message that announces the coming of the "End of Days" sometime within the next few years.

> **People tend to extend the credibility they give to accurate prophetic words to bad teaching. This is because the bad teaching often follows supernaturally accurate prophetic words.**

This may sound like an exaggeration, but these kinds of things happen. In Mark's words:

*"I was in a pastors' meeting many years ago in which a nationally recognized prophet gave a series of ridiculously accurate prophet words to several pastors in the room. I was in awe and so was our staff. He then gave a word to the whole group, in excess of 1000 pastors. He told us that God had told him that he would stand before a group of pastors who would usher in the end times by doing miracles on par with those of Jesus [which I have no theological issue with] and that these pastors would present to Jesus at His return a spotless, holy and sinless church [which I have a theological issue with]. He concluded his End Times prophecy with the statement that we, sitting before him that night, were that group of leaders. Encouraging words indeed, if they are true.*

*I have to be honest with you, when he told us that we were to be this group of church leaders, unlike any in church history, I had my doubts. I looked at the guys on both sides of me and then I took a good look at myself. This short exercise increased my doubts. Then I began to consider the "proof text" that he offered for his statement that we would present a sinless, perfect church to Jesus upon his return. His proof text was Ephesians 5:25–28, "**Husbands, love your wives, just as Christ loved the church and gave himself up for her to make her holy, cleansing her by the washing with water through the word, and to present her to himself as a radiant church, without stain or wrinkle or any other blemish, but holy and blameless. In this same way husbands ought to love their wives ...**"*

*The esteemed prophet was offering this text as a proof text for his prophecy that our group of pastors would live to present the world-wide church to Christ [at his second coming] as a group of sinless, perfected Christians. Most competent Bible teachers will agree that this passage is being*

**Because prophecy and teaching are different gifts they are to be judged and received differently. Quality in one does not equal quality in the other.**

*offered by Paul as an illustration of how a husband should love his wife. The context is marriage, not the End Times church. As end times theology, it breaks down further when we consider that Jesus will return for a blameless church, not because of any human action by ourselves or our leaders, but because Jesus has already made us blameless in God's eyes. This occurred at the moment of His death on the cross.*

*This passage cannot be correctly interpreted as an End Times pronouncement. This passage is limited to telling us that just as Christ laid his life down for his church, a husband should sacrifice himself to express God's love through him to his wife. It goes no further than an instruction for sacrificial living on the part of husbands.*

*To summarize; accurate prophecy does not guarantee accurate theology. This should have been clear to each and every leader in the room when this grandiose word was given, but it was not. Serious debate followed for months about whether or not to enroll our teenagers in college, etc."*

At the risk of redundancy, the only reason this theologically unsound word was taken seriously was because of the amazingly accurate personal prophetic words that preceded it. Mistakenly the hearers were taking the credit they applied to the accurate personal prophetic words and lending it to the unsound "Bible teaching" being offered - always a mistake.

Having come down hard on prophets who presume to be teachers we are not saying that the prophetic gift and the teaching gift cannot co-exist in the same person – they can and often do. They do in Mark's case. Our point is that because prophecy and teaching are different gifts they are to be judged and received differently. Quality in one does not equal quality in the other.

### The Confusion of Power with Holiness

One of the standard responses we hear in answer to our argument for more of the church to embrace a supernatural lifestyle is the fact that many of those who have led the way in moving in the supernatural gifts have been moral failures. The objection goes like this; "These [insert label here] supposed Christians who believe in the supernatural gifts are moral failures. I value the fruits of the spirit rather than the gifts. Getting caught up in the supernatural gifts just takes our eyes off of Christian character. Look at the messes these leaders have left behind! Forget about the gifts, just focus on the fruit!"

The fact is; this is an accurate criticism as far as the moral failure is concerned. No one can dispute the moral car wrecks on the highway of supernatural gifts. The problem with the criticism is that it sets up a totally unnecessary and false choice. **God did not give us the supernatural gifts so that we could display our moral superiority by rejecting them.** He gave us these gifts in order for us to demonstrate His power and His love for broken people. Throwing the baby out with the bath water is not the solution. It is possible to hold both power and character as goals for the Christian life – at the same time.

The moral failures we are all aware of did not come because leaders embraced the supernatural gifts; they came because of a confusion between power and holiness. This confusion has plagued charismatic circles for generations and it continues today. We believe this confusion is founded upon a lie sown by the enemy. The lie tells us this; "You are moving in great Holy Spirit power! God is using you mightily! He must be very pleased with you! All those little sins you cling to [and even those big ones] must not be important to Him because He continues to use you. You are special to Him! You know you are special, just look at His power flowing through you. Because you are special you are in a different category than ordinary Christians. This must be the case, just look at all those you are helping."

The lie sounds very foolish when expressed so crudely, but some version of this lie comes to everyone who moves in the power of the Holy Spirit. The real problem comes when those who surround our powerfully gifted leaders turn a blind eye to their sin thereby reinforcing the lie. Very simply the lie says, "You must be holy because a holy God is moving through you." Holiness and

> **The greatest reward we will receive in heaven is the enjoyment of the character we developed here on earth. Our character is the polishing of the mirror that will reflect His beauty in eternity.**

power become equated in the mind of the person and those who put them on a pedestal.

Let's put an end to the lie.

**Power and holiness are two completely different things. Power concerns what God does through you and holiness is what God does to [or within] you.** Both require your cooperation. The power gifts are given through you to benefit others. Their purpose is not to bless you or change you, but rather to bless and change others. **To think that you are special because you are the conduit that delivers a gift of power is as absurd as a UPS driver who expects to be thanked as if he were the one who picked out the gift and paid for it before it was shipped**. We have received many wonderful packages from UPS drivers, but we cannot remember any of the drivers – we do however remember the gifts.

Holiness is about character and power is about action. If we had to choose between the two [and we don't] we would choose character over giftedness. This is because our character will last forever and our giftedness will not. The greatest reward we will receive in heaven is the enjoyment of the character we developed here on earth.

The more of Jesus' character we develop here the more we will reflect of His beauty there. Our character is the polishing of the mirror that will reflect His beauty in eternity. We really believe this! Fortunately, we do not have to choose between power and holiness – God is at work for both here and now.

A moment ago, we said that both power and holiness require our cooperation. Neither comes through or to us without our choice.

Developing a ministry of power is easy – obey His promptings and take risks. Read this book and try it!

Holiness on the other hand is not so easy. Holiness is fundamentally about your relationship with the Father, Jesus and the Holy Spirit. Holiness means to be "set apart." He has made us holy through the forgiveness of our sin and now He calls us to a holy lifestyle. The power to live a holy lifestyle does not come from our will power; it is His power living within us and this power comes through faith. We are saved by faith, filled with the Holy Spirit by faith and we are sanctified [made holy] by faith. Although He is the source and empowering of our holiness it does not come without meaningful choices on our part and these choices we make by faith.

The principle choice we must make is one that must be made daily – it is the choice to spend time in intimacy with Him. Holiness has a relational source. **Holiness is the influence He exerts upon your personality as you spend time with Him. It is a slow transformation brought about by the gentle yet steady influence of His goodness living within you.** It is not forced and it is not rule based. It does not come through a focused attention to laws and religious rituals. It is rather, entirely relational. It is the influence of a perfectly good person upon a not so good person. It happens almost without notice. All that is required is time spent in the presence of the better person. As this happens you come to know him more intimately and accurately. Knowing Him more and more begins to affect your behavior. How could it not?

**Time spent with God is time spent with the best, most influential personality that has ever existed.**

It is like osmosis ["**and we all, who with unveiled faces contemplate the Lord's glory are being transformed into His image ...**" 2 Cor. 3:18].

Back in the day we used to do science experiments in elementary school. Do you remember the one with the potato and the colored water? You cut a potato in half and put it, cut side down, into a dish of colored water. The next day you come back to school and low and behold the potato is one quarter blue. The next day it is half blue. The next day it is all blue. You are the potato and God's spirit is the water!

A holy lifestyle [holiness in action] is simply leaving your quiet time with the Lord and doing what comes naturally after being influenced by Him. It is merely acting more and more like the new person that you are becoming. It is not a life of striving to be good. If that actually succeeded your righteousness would be to your own credit and it would lead to "self" righteousness. True holiness is the byproduct of His influence. It is a life of being good because you are being changed by His influence into a better and better person.

**The pursuit of holiness must involve the Bible.**

**The Bible is our only source for accurately knowing what God is like. It expresses his character, goals, methods, preferences, holiness, etc.** It is the plumb line by which we judge all that we think He is saying to us in our moments of intimacy. It is also the plumb line we use to judge our spiritual experiences. Without it we are prey for religious evil spirits attempting to provide counterfeit spiritual/religious experience for the purpose of separating us from Him.

> **A holy lifestyle [holiness in action] is simply leaving your quiet time with the Lord and doing what comes naturally after being influenced by Him.**

True holiness, although an inner work of the Holy Spirit, ultimately results in holy actions. Actions follow attitudes. True holiness involves both the inner relational life with God and the outer life of actions on His behalf in the world.

Holiness is both what Jesus has made us, and at the same time, what we are becoming. As we have already said, the word means "to be set apart." When Jesus died for our sins He purchased us out from under the rule of Satan and set us apart for life with God and His purposes. We did not have the power over our own selfishness to completely set ourselves apart for God. He did this for us, but once He set us apart we have the choice of living a "set apart for God" lifestyle.

A simple way of thinking of holiness is to add a "W" to the word. Holiness = Wholeness. Holiness is really a wholehearted commitment to our Father God, Jesus and the Holy Spirit. It is being sold out for Him, "all in" as my poker playing friends say.

Another way to understand growing in holiness is to examine how God interacts with the three principle realms of our humanity; the mind, the emotions and the will. Holiness can be defined as knowing him more intimately [affecting the mind], loving him more deeply [affecting the emotions] and serving him more faithfully [affecting the will]. All Holy Spirit experience, whether through us or to us, has these three goals. Holiness is like a three-legged stool. Growth in holiness must mean growth in all three areas of the person.

What this means is that although a spiritual experience may affect only one of these goals, it must ultimately advance all three of these goals to result in true holiness, otherwise it is just an interesting memory and without lasting effect. Anything less means the stool is no longer a stool.

To return to the distinction between power and holiness, power *through* you is not the same as His influence within you. It is not uncommon for a Christian to have a powerful experience of the Holy Spirit either through them [for someone else] or to them [for their own benefit] and have it result in no growth in holiness. Two incidents in the Bible reveal this truth. The first involves King Saul and the second involves Saul who becomes Paul.

## King Saul

The story is found in 1 Sam. 19:18–24. Because of jealousy King Saul is out to kill his faithful servant David. He sends his soldiers to capture David, but when they come to arrest David they run into Samuel and a group of prophets prophesying. The Holy Spirit comes upon the soldiers in great power and they end up prophesying. As a result, they fail to arrest David. Saul sends more soldiers and this happens again. Finally, he decides "If you want something done right, do it yourself" so he goes to where David and Samuel are. He fully intends to take David and kill him. Here is Saul's Holy Spirit power encounter:

**"So, Saul went to Naioth at Ramah. But the Spirit of God came even on him, and he walked along prophesying until he came to Naioth. He stripped off his garments, and he too prophesied in Samuel's presence. He lay naked all that day and all that night. This is why people say, 'Is Saul also among the prophets?'"** 1 Sam. 19:23–24

Saul had a Holy Spirit spiritual experience of prophesying which was overwhelmingly real and powerful, but it did not lead to growth in holiness. When the Holy Spirit left him, he got up and went back to being the murderous rat he was before the experience. The experience was not transformational. It was merely something that happened to affect his actions apart from his choice. The experience was not integrated into any lifestyle of holiness.

We find this story very frustrating because we regularly witness something very much like it at church. It is not unusual for a new person to visit our churches and experience an overwhelming encounter of the love of God. They will come forward after the service and tell us, through genuine tears of joy, "I have never experienced anything like this before. I have never experienced God's love for me like this! This is amazing! I will be back next week. I can't wait to come back!!" And we never see them again.

For decades, we have asked ourselves how they could experience a real touch of God's love and not want to come back for more. Or at least not want to come back and learn more about the Holy Spirit who touched them so deeply.

The more we think about it the more we believe they did not value the experience more highly because they were not really committed wholeheartedly to the pursuit of God. The experience was wonderful in the way that a trip to the mountains is wonderful – a fine vacation, but not someplace I would like to live – too far away, too hard to get to, inconvenient, remote, too radical a move, etc.

## Saul Who Became Paul

On the other hand, let's look at Saul/Paul in the New Testament. Saul is committed to killing Christians, which he wrongly believes is serving God. He is walking down the road and suddenly he has the most powerful spiritual experience of his life. He is knocked to the ground and hears the audible voice of Jesus. This intimate powerful experience of knowing Jesus leads to a deep love for Jesus BECAUSE he is already committed to serving God faithfully. Paul is already committed to holiness as he understands it, but now he experiences the God he has been serving. This happens through coming to know the living Jesus. This experience empowers him to love Jesus and continue his service to God which is now service to Jesus as well.

This experience was not wasted because it was integrated into a life already wholly committed to knowing, loving and serving God. What was added by this experience is the knowledge of Jesus' divinity and a personal experience of Him. Paul now knows God in a newer and truer way – God in the person of Jesus. Now Paul is not just radically committed as he previously was; now he is serving a God he actually knows. The Holy Spirit has given him an experience *of* God. This experience leads to greater commitment by Paul because Paul has come to know God in a fuller way. Truth received and applied leads to greater holiness.

For both of the Saul's, their experiences of the power of God were very similar. Both were overcome by the power of God apart from any choice on their behalf. Both ended up incapacitated on the ground. Both heard from God. King Saul's experience lasted throughout the day and night. Saul's experience left him blind for several days.

Despite the similarities, King Saul's experience left him essentially unchanged. Saul's experience led to a transformation so significant that his name was changed to Paul, indicating a transformation at the heart of his identity – he became a "Christian."

**Prophecy is often used as a justification for doing what would be considered foolish and irresponsible in the absence of the magic phrase "God told me to."**

In summary, we can conclude that we must never confuse power with holiness and, as we seek to live a supernatural lifestyle, we must value the fruits of the Spirit as much or more than the supernatural gifts of the Spirit.

## Lazy Minds

Mark's parents had an expression they used when he was young that has stuck with him. They would occasionally describe a person as being "so heavenly minded they are no earthly good." We think we now know the type of Christian they are describing. **For some people "faith" and "hearing God's voice" have replaced common sense and reason.** As pastors, we see this all too often. Being a pastor means being in the business of giving advice and wise counsel. For us this means that too many counseling sessions have ended with the sentence "I don't care what you are telling me, God told me to do it!" "It" usually involves something very unwise or unbiblical - things like, leaving my wife for the woman I met at the office [because my wife doesn't understand me] or quitting my job with no replacement job to go to or buying the brand-new car even though I cannot make the payments. As crazy as it sounds we have been told that we are weak in our faiths because we will not endorse this kind of decision making.

Prophecy is often used as a justification for doing what would be considered foolish and irresponsible in the absence of the magic phrase "God told me to." This phrase is a definite discussion ender. There is nothing like "Invoking the Deity" by playing the trump card of "God told me" when you are losing an argument or find a discussion too intellectually demanding. To be fair, there are times when a genuine word from the Lord will oppose what appears to be wise counsel but, such times are very rare and should never exclude a loving discussion regarding what is the right decision to make.

In our pastoral experience, the phrase "God told me" is often religious code for "I am losing this argument so I am going to leave now" or "I don't like the advice you are giving me so I am going to do whatever I want" or "The questions you are asking me are hard to answer and they are making me uncomfortable so I'm leaving."

We believe that underneath the hyper-spirituality of using this trump card we will usually find spiritual and intellectual laziness. Christian decision-making is hard work. It requires a good working knowledge of what God has said regarding successful relationships, work habits, submission to authority, the right use of time, energy and money, to name a few. Knowing the Bible takes time and many Christians don't want to take the time to know God's Word. A "revelation" is so much easier to come by.

The problem is that, once we set up a subjective word [God told me] against the counsel of scripture and the wisdom of our brothers, sisters and leaders we exclude from ourselves from the very sources God gave us with which to judge our subjective words. In the absence of these objective sources of correction we often interpret our own desires as God's desires for us. It is called rationalization and it occurs whenever we want something badly enough to hunt for all the reasons why God would want it for us and ignore all of the reasons why He might not.

> **A successful Christian life is one lived in a balance between revelation and reason.**

**What is happening at a deep level is that we make up our minds as to what we want and then create reasons why God would want it too.** The easiest such reason is "God told me so." Once we use this magic trump card all further thought and listening to counsel is rendered superfluous.

Allow Mark this opportunity to "vent":

*"Perhaps I am just venting here, but I have been tempted many times to give up my prophetic ministry – just ask my wife. I have given prophetic words that are incapable of misinterpretation only to have the recipient tell me a few weeks later that they really appreciated the word and it confirmed their proposed decision perfectly, which was the polar opposite of what God said through me! Seriously! Let me give you an idea of what I am referring to. My word to her is "God says don't make the decision now, you need to wait. Don't rush ahead with your plans. This is not the time to act!!" One week later she tells me my word was the confirmation she was looking for and that she has said yes to marrying the non-Christian she has been dating! That faint sound in the distance is me banging my head against a wall."*

A successful Christian life is one lived in a balance between revelation and reason; between what God tells us directly and what He tells us through His Word - between the right and left side of the brain. Since He gave us both, He must intend that we use both, hence balance.

## Manipulation

The "God told me" trump card facilitates another serious pitfall found within prophetic ministry and that is the sin of manipulation. Good Biblical leadership involves facilitation. As leaders, we are to facilitate opportunities for the people we lead to establish their own mature relationships with God. We must

277

never take God's place in their lives. When they are immature in their faith we can be quite directive in our leadership over them, but our ultimate goal must be to bring them to the place where they no longer need our advice. We essentially work ourselves out of the job of directing them. At this point we lead by influence not by command.

The problem inherent in prophetic ministry is that when it is genuine it speaks for God. This leaves it very open to the sin of manipulation. Extremely accurate prophecy creates its own credibility. **It is very hard to question the leadership of someone who hears from God accurately.** It takes a very strong mind and personality to differ with the instructions of a strong leader who moves in the supernatural gifts, even when the instructions are unbiblical or even sinful. A strongly charismatic leader is like a very sharp knife – the blade can cut in both directions – for good or for evil.

Because of the persuasive ability that comes with the prophetic gift it is safest when operating as a part of a team exercising shared spiritual authority. In Mark's younger years as a senior pastor he chaffed at sharing his authority with a team. It seemed to slow everything down. The truth is; it does. Moving more slowly becomes far more attractive after a few big miscalls. We have discovered the value of shared spiritual authority. Today neither of us would ever want to lead apart from a strong team. These days the car moves more slowly, but the wrecks are far less frequent.

## Some questions to consider:

1. What are the keys to the successful interaction between the prophetic and leadership gifts in the local church?

2. How are the spiritual gifts of prophecy and teaching different?

3. What happens when you confuse holiness with power?

4. We have said that the Christian life is a balance between revelation and reason. Discuss the problems that arise when we tend to focus on either to the exclusion of the other. Where are you on the continuum of the two?

5. Have you ever had a discussion end with someone telling you, "I don't care what you say, God told me to do it"? What was the effect on the relationship? How did their decision turn out?

6. What makes us easily manipulated by people who move in supernatural spiritual power?

# Chapter 25: The False Prophet Syndrome

There's been a huge trend in the last twenty years in regard to the movie industry. Comic book superheroes have been a source for films and television for a long time, but now more than ever this pantheon of mega gifted champions have had major movies made about them. Typically, there have been stars like Spider Man, Superman or Batman, but now with the release of Dr. Strange as a major motion picture a new dimension is being added to the genre of superhero. Dr. Strange and others like him not only have super powers, but also have tapped into the supernatural using sorcery, witchcraft and other occult influences to fight for their cause. One has to wonder what this will do to the worldview of those who idolize these heroes.

The scriptures are clear on the occult and the improper tapping into the realm of the supernatural through sorcery and witchcraft. Now through this new influence it will potentially be legitimized more than ever. With this legitimization will come a great fascination with the occult and as a result a whole new generation of people will be introduced to, indoctrinated into and potentially start to seek such powers. Where superheroes like Superman either have come from another planet or have gained their ability through some freak of nature, men like Dr. Strange have gained their powers through training from other sorcerers and mentors. The message is clear - a typical human can gain great power, supernatural power, if trained in the occult. This adds a whole new angle to the current and increasing trend to glamorize demonic power.

This trend has been a long time coming and it is a part of what could be called the False Prophet Syndrome. God's legitimate prophets of old warned against wizards, sorcerers, witches and false prophets that could perform false miracles and other feats of power. (Deut. 18:10; Isa. 8:19) Today, year by year, these sorts of demonic oracles, false prophets and workers of magic are growing in their influence. In the 20th Century people like Jean Dixon and Uri Geller fascinated the public with their visions, prophecies and supposed supernatural abilities to see the future or manipulate matter. No doubt a new group will arrive on the scene to respond to this hunger for alternative spiritual power.

The growing flood of Science Fiction, Fantasy and Witchcraft books and movies that blend science and sorcery are also part of this craze to legitimatize the demonic forces as something that those who seek answers, hope and promises from the realm of the supernatural should pursue.

Is it possible, as this current movement grows in influence, that the church will face a new confrontation with the occult the way the apostles of the first century did? And if so, what will be the outcome? Articles and warnings from church leaders announce that demonic possession is on the rise. Exorcists are being called on more and more, even as science claims that things such as demonic possession are a fantasy from the dark ages. In the third world, sorcery and dealings with demons are common. Now it appears that the first world is being set up to invite this view of the supernatural into our culture.

What will be the church's response? I believe that we have a firm pattern from the scriptures that point the way. Here's a list of just some of the ways God's prophets and apostles dealt with the false prophet syndrome in their time.

Moses was confronted by Pharaoh's magicians, but in each instance the power of God overcame their sorceries. In the end Pharaoh's false wonder workers had to admit that what Moses represented was the very finger of God. (Ex. 8:19; 9:11)

Elijah faced the prophets of Baal who were powerless against the fire of God from heaven. (1 Kings 18:36–39)

Daniel lived in a day when the kingdom of Babylon was filled with magicians yet the Bible tells us that Daniel and his colleagues were ten times better than all the enchanters that sought to influence the king.

In the New Testament, we read accounts of Paul and Barnabas facing the sorcerer Elymas on the Island of Crete. As this false prophet attempted to lead the governor astray, Paul, full of the Holy Spirit, rebuked the sorcerer and commanded him to go blind. This display of God's power brought the governor of the island to a place of faith in God. (Acts 13:7–12)

It is this link between the preaching of the gospel and the display of God's power over demonic forces that is likely to emerge here in the first world, very soon. If we are correct in this prediction we trust that the church is instructed in the principles of these sorts of cosmic clashes and are filled with faith in the power of God.

One of Bob's heroes was Missionary Sam Sasser, who in the 1960's traveled to the Islands of Micronesia and preached the gospel to the natives there. He often faced demonic forces and the power of witchcraft. Routinely the power of God triumphed. One striking story involved the display of God's power in breaking up a demonic miracle. On one island a group of islanders, through the use of demonic power, had levitated men into the air – a particularly impressive feat. Through praise and worship to God Sam broke the strength of these forces in a dramatic display of God's power that left the natives clearly amazed at God's work. By the end of Sam's work on the Islands more than 90% had become Christians!

Missionaries have told many other stories like this as they've recounted the intervention of angels and God's kingdom when confronted with demonic forces. It should come as no surprise if these same sorts of encounters start to occur here in the first world with increasing frequency. We trust that the teachings in this book will help to prepare believers for such confrontations. It's clear from scripture that the gospel is fully preached when accompanied with a display of God's supernatural power. The current fascination with the demonic supernatural, as horrible as that may be, has also set the stage for a display of God's power as supreme. (Rom. 15:19)

## Some questions to consider:

1. Have you noticed the rapid growth of the occult in our entertainment industry?

2. What is the subliminal message being presented by this "entertainment"?

3. How is our Western world view being changed?

4. What opportunities does this change bring for the Christian church?

# Chapter 26:  Recognizing False Prophets

Wouldn't it be convenient if the Bible made our job of cataloguing the pitfalls to prophetic ministry easier by simply listing most of them? Well, we have good news. The Apostle Peter has done the job for us.  In his second letter Peter deals with the characteristics of false teachers in the church age [our age]. Although he is dealing with the teaching gift, the sins associated with that gift apply equally or with even greater force to the gift of prophecy. Let's go through his list scripture by scripture: 2 Peter 2:1–22

## 1. The "secret introduction of destructive heresies." (2 Peter 2:1)

We have already discussed the problem of prophets presuming to be theologians. Good prophecy does not equate to good theology. Accurate prophecy must not be used to contradict the clear teachings of the Bible. We believe that when Peter uses the word "secret" to describe the introduction of destructive heresy he is referring to heresy that comes in a hidden manner. Bad theology can come hidden within the Trojan horse of otherwise accurate prophecy. The End Times prophecy Mark has already mentioned is a good example. The word promised a band of supernaturally powerful leaders who would usher in the second coming of Christ and present a sinless church to Jesus at His appearance.

Contained within the prophecy is a theological statement about the nature of Christians. It "teaches" that there will be a group of sinless Christians living prior to Jesus' second coming. It suggests that sinless perfection is possible for Christians. Nowhere in the Bible does it say this, in fact, the Bible teaches the opposite. (1 John 1:8–10) All prophecies should be examined for any theological statement inherent in the message.

> **Bad theology can come hidden within the Trojan horse of otherwise accurate prophecy.**

## 2. Greed leading to false accounts of the prophet's exploits. (2:3)

Undoubtedly you have heard of the three pitfalls of church leadership; girls, gold and glory [sex, money and pride]. Peter will deal with sex and pride later in the text, but for now he starts with money. What Peter is driving at is what we popularly refer to today as "marketing." **Marketing is the embellishment of truth to the point of lying in order to sell a product**. The product here is the prophet himself [including his CD's, books, newsletter, T-shirts, bumper stickers, etc.]

We have been in meetings in which self-proclaimed prophets have told stories that Jesus would have trouble topping. In all the years of hearing these stories we have never heard any proof offered. The stories inevitably end with a "love offering" being taken which is then followed by a short [45 minute] product promotion time [books, CD's, etc.]. We know you think we are exaggerating, but we are not.

A Horror Story from Mark:

*"I can remember going to one such meeting because a pastor friend of mine invited me, telling me that the prophet had a word specifically for our city. We were in the middle of a move of unity within the churches of the city and all of us were hungry for any word that would speak to the move of God we were experiencing.*

*I sat through the worship which was fine and then the "man of God" got up to speak. The message turned out to be an introduction to the offering which took almost half an hour! Following the offering the speaker introduced all of his books and CD series' which took another 30 minutes. I have to admit I was getting impatient to hear the specific word for our city.*

*Following the product promotion, men who resembled furniture movers started up the aisles carrying large boxes of books on their shoulders. They sold them left and right until the boxes were empty. Because I was in the middle of the row I became the conduit through which the books went one direction and the cash [only cash] went the other. I personally handled a lot of cash!*

**In Western Christianity, there is a cult of celebrity that has infiltrated the church.**

*Finally, after waiting through more than 1.5 hours of marketing, the prophet came to his word for our city. I have to tell you, I was shocked. It turned out his word for our city was ... yes, you guessed it.... more stories about his worldwide exploits [unsubstantiated] ending with the application of the word which was... that he takes another offering! Really! It was no great surprise a few years later to learn that "he was suspected of "financial mismanagement"."*

*Allow me one more story - it is one of my favorites. Several years ago, our church leadership attended a conference at which several nationally known preachers were invited to speak. On the second night of the conference a pastor of a large church on the Eastern Seaboard got up to speak. He started his message by telling us that he had wanted to arrive the day before so as to be able to make the dinner meeting with the other speakers. Sadly, for him he was not able to get a flight early enough to make the dinner. He reminded us of how important fellowship is and what a shame it was to miss this wonderful time of sharing a meal together with his peers. He then asked us to join him in a prayer of faith. I was wondering what this prayer of faith could possibly be about given his introduction as to the importance of peer fellowship. It turned out we were being asked to join him in intercession for a private jet! Seriously! No, really!!*

*He was completely serious about how much better his fellowship would be if he just had his own private jet! I was shocked, but not as shocked as I was when I heard the response of the congregation. Cheers of Amen rose throughout the large room. People were more than ready to commit to interceding for his new jet. As far as many in the crowd were concerned his request was reasonable. Was it reasonable?*

*Let's take a moment to do the math. A small entry level private jet will start at about the 5 – 7-million-dollar level. The operating costs will run to a few hundred thousand dollars per year. The cost of drilling a water well in Africa, to support a village of approximately 200-300 people, is about $4,000.00. Let's say the jet cost 6 million dollars. That means that we could have drilled 1500 wells and brought a daily practical example of Jesus' love to approximately 375,000 people. The math leaves me wondering, what kind of self-deception makes it possible to even attempt to justify such greed and materialism? I think I know..."*

In Western Christianity, there is a cult of celebrity that has infiltrated the church. Shameless self-promotion seems the norm. It is very hard to reconcile this with the examples seen in the early church. The self-promotion of our celebrity teachers, pastors, evangelists, healers and prophets are so close to those of rock stars we even call them "rock star pastors." We cannot imagine any of the early church leaders tolerating being treated that way, let alone seeking out such treatment.

Mark's encounter with the "real deal":

*"Some years ago, I came across a prophet by chance. I had been invited to a small group meeting in which we were told would be a prophet with a world-wide ministry. During the meeting, he asked my wife and I to stand up whereupon he told us in detail the events of the last several years of our lives [which had been very hard]. He then described our characters and personality traits with uncanny accuracy.*

*After the meeting, I found out he led a group of several hundred churches around the world. I told him I was very impressed with his ministry, but that I was confused as to why I had never heard of him before. In a very humble and casual manner he told me that he and his fellow leaders "preferred obscurity." As I grew to know him over many years I was able to affirm the accuracy of that statement. He was the antithesis of the celebrity prophet. He was in fact "the real deal."*

*He was the prophet I mentioned earlier who was offered a large amount of money to prophecy the sale of someone's house in Hong Kong. He turned it down and rebuked those who offered him money in exchange for favorable prophecy. He is one of the finest men I have ever known and you have probably never heard of him. He never owned a big house or a fancy car. He flew coach. He was the real deal..."*

In judging a prophetic word, the character of the prophet is always relevant. Good character does not guarantee an accurate word, but bad character suggests the word be judged very carefully.

## 3. They follow the "corrupt desire of the sinful nature" and despise authority. (2:10)

The phrase used here is first describing a lust for sexual sin. Peter will deal with this later in the passage so here we will discuss the despising of authority. Peter describes these false teachers/prophets as "bold and arrogant". Pride is the issue and it is the natural default position of our human nature. Let us explain by starting with a question.

What defines "being human?" Some say it is our highly developed language skills, others say it is our opposable thumbs that allow us to make tools, and others say it is our highly developed brains that allow abstract reasoning.

As Christians, we think the definition exists at a deeper level. What separates us from all the other animals on earth is our ability to make choices that are contrary to God's will. Your cat never gets up in the morning and says, "Today I will be a dog." All the rest of creation acts in accordance with God given natural laws and instincts. Humans can and do act in ways contrary to God's design for them. This is because humans have been created as beings separate from God. We are capable of acting independently from God. Not only that, we are capable of acting independently from one another. **Another way to define humanness is "self-awareness."**

Each of us is aware of our separateness both from God and from other selves. Because each of us is completely unique and self-aware, we are very aware of our uniqueness. Our self-awareness of our uniqueness defines who we are. Because our uniqueness and separateness defines who we are, most of the choices we make are made in order to protect and accentuate that separate uniqueness. The goal of the "self" is to maintain its identity as a separate being - more than that - to maximize it.

The tendency to maintain our separate identity in independence from God is the root of all sin. In a word, the root of all sin is pride. Pride is the desire to prefer our "self" to all the other "selves" around us, including God. What makes pride so powerful is that it is our inevitable and ultimate temptation because it is a consequence of our God designed separateness [individuality]. This separateness never goes away and so pride is always waiting to destroy our relationship with God and others. Kind of scary, isn't it?

**The tendency to maintain our separate identity in independence from God is the root of all sin.**

What is most distressing, is that pride survives conversion. When we accept Jesus, we don't lose our "selves." Worse, when we become filled with the Holy Spirit we don't lose our "selves" either. It is a strange thing to see, but we have known people who were incredibly prideful before they were filled with the Holy Spirit and afterwards they were just as proud only now their pride was spiritual pride.

Simply becoming a Christian does not remove your pride. Likewise having the Holy Spirit living within you does not immediately remove your pride, but it will tend to reveal it and allow you the opportunity to fight it. The good news is that the Holy Spirit is committed to helping you fight your pride. So, what are the sources of pride?

IN THE WORLD:

- physical beauty
- money and possessions
- talents and abilities
- education & influence
- fame

IN THE CARNAL CHURCH:

- all the above

IN THE EVANGELICAL CHURCH:

- Bible knowledge
- witnessing
- a theology degree
- charitable giving
- a radical conversion testimony

IN THE MAINSTREAM CHURCH:

- good deeds
- giving to the poor/social programs
- having a friend who is a member of any persecuted minority

IN THE CHARISMATIC CHURCH:

- Holy Spirit experiences
- tongues
- visions
- prophetic discernments
- miracles/healings
- unusual spiritual experiences
- being "blessed" with lots of money

Pride is indeed the root problem for all of us, but it flourishes most where any spiritual power is held in high regard. Prophecy, physical healing and miracles attract a fan base like no other spiritual gifts. As we have already discussed, the presence of spiritual power is often taken as a reason to ignore obvious sin. The answer to this weakness within the church is submission to those in leadership over us.

The problem of pride goes unaddressed when the prophet opts out from under spiritual authority. This often means opting out of the local church. Lone Ranger prophets are far too common. Despising authority is a consistent temptation for prophetic ministers and it is at its worst when the prophet is most powerful [accurate].

Being under God's ordained spiritual authority is God's mechanism for protecting prophets [and all of us] from the seductive power of their gift. **Prophets need someone close to them to regularly tell them "You are not as wonderful as your fans say you are."** Any gifted person in public ministry needs someone who can speak these words to them from a position of spiritual authority.

Here are the signs of pride to look for in yourself and when judging the character of a prophet:

- does not receive correction easily (Prov. 12:1; 15:12)

- is easily offended (Rom. 15:1: Eccl. 7:7–9)

- is un-submitted to leadership (Heb. 13:17; 3 John 1:9)

- has a high regard for his own subjective spiritual "discernments" (Gal. 6:4; James 1:26–27)

- states personal opinions as fact (Prov.18:2)

- always talking about himself (James 1:19–20; 4:16)

- interrupting others and failing to listen (Prov. 18:13; James 1:19–20)

- unbending opinions on debatable spiritual matters (Rom. 14:1; 2 Tim. 2:23–26)

- unforgiving (Matt. 6:14–15)

- a lack of interest in fellowship (Heb. 10:25)

- an independent attitude toward other Christians [I don't need you] (John 13:35; Rom. 12:15)

- a low commitment to relationships and/or superficial relationships (Matt. 5:43–46)

Isn't the Bible practical!

## 4. "Their idea of pleasure is to carouse in broad daylight" (2:13)

The essence of what Peter is driving at here is shamelessness. Arrogance reaches its zenith when it is completely shameless about sin. This can take the form of being completely un-teachable or uncorrectable when confronted with obvious sin, but it can also take the form of denying the sinful nature of the act by displaying it as if it were normal. Peter goes on to describe the nature of the shameless sin as being sexual in nature.

## 5. Their eyes are "full of adultery." (2:14)

Now we come to the third of the unholy triumvirate of gold, glory and girls. You cannot be a Christian for long before you hear the story of some well-known Christian leader who has been caught in sexual sin. Again, the confusion between power and holiness is at work. "The Lord is using me so mightily and He continues to pour His power through me despite my problem with lust. He must want me to be happy in my ministry. He knows I need the comfort. I work so hard for Him. Surely, He will forgive my occasional failures. Or maybe they are not failures at all..."

Peter describes this sin as one of "seducing the unstable." When we hear the word "seduce" we usually think of it in sexual terms. The fact is; seduction occurs whenever anyone is deceived, enticed, allured or beguiled into doing something they did not intend to do. When Peter uses the word "seduced" with the word "unstable" [regarding those who are being seduced] he is

292

suggesting that the false teacher/prophet is using his spiritual gift to trap someone who is not steadfast in their moral stance. In other words, the prophet is using his power and position to subvert the will of a weak partner. The partner is half accomplice and half victim.

It is very easy to image how such a seduction can take place. Any spiritual leader occupies an exalted position of spiritual authority and more so for those who move in supernatural spiritual power. A woman who is unsure of her faith can be easily persuaded to believe that intimacy with a powerful man of God might be permitted for the same reason he may believe God will permit it – how can it be wrong when God is pouring His power through the man? Beyond this justification exists the imbalance of authority that exists between any leader and follower. Whether it exists in the workplace or the church, superior positional authority is always hard to say no to.

Bob was a witness to how quickly an anointed leader can spiral out of control. Here is his story:

*"One quality that most of us are attracted to is strong leadership. You find it throughout the Bible, from Moses to David to Debra. These leaders all had charisma, a firm direction and the clear element of the prophetic that drew others to them. In the church, the same is true. Sadly, for all people who wield this sort of influence great temptations come with it. Look at the lives of biblical characters like Samson and David, who caved into temptation and brought disaster on themselves and others.*

*These sorts of failures are just as troubling today. As a young Christian, I was greatly influenced by the dynamic and prophetic ministry of an older but powerful evangelist. He was not only a great preacher, but also a man that moved in the supernatural realms. He had picked me up on the highway when I was a wandering hippie and shared the gospel with me. Three years later, after I'd come to Christ, he held a six-week revival at the small church I was attending. During that season, I saw amazing demonstrations of the power of God under his ministry. People had radical encounters with God and there were powerful manifestations of the Holy Spirit. One evening near the end of one of his messages the glory of God so filled the room that I could see the glow of heaven resting on the place. That night his daughter was healed dramatically as well.*

*Because of his vision and passion for souls he was collecting a following of eager young disciples. Together with a string of churches he formed his own small but effective training and evangelistic ministry. My wife and I considered the possibility of becoming part of his ministry, but felt led to work with our local church instead. In the ensuing years his ministry continued to grow as he sent teams overseas as well. Gradually his control and influence over the lives of his ministry took on an unhealthy aspect. He became more and more controlling. Soon it became apparent that he was taking sexual advantage of some of the women in his group even to the point of being involved with the wives of some of his leaders. As things continued to come to light his ministry spiraled out of control and fell apart."*

This is a tragic story in several ways. First, because it brought great reproach on the Body of Christ. Second, because of the devastation that was visited on those who poured their lives into his work. When a leader has a moral failure like this it often leaves those under him devastated which often results in many turning away from Christ. The fallout from this tragedy continues to this day even though the man has passed away. Our hope and prayer is that those who were so negatively impacted by the events surrounding his life have found a place of restoration.

As we read Peter's description of leaders who "seduce the unstable" and we listen to Bob's story we are shocked at how similar the early church is to our churches today. We tend to idealize the early church because it moved in such supernatural power yet, at the same time, it displayed all the moral problems in leadership that we see today. Little has changed because human nature has not changed. As we reflect on our years of involvement as a part of church leadership we can think of more moral failures than we can easily count. Girls, gold and glory

294

remain the problems. The question is; how can we strengthen our leaders?

In a future book Mark intends to explore the role that honesty plays in the Christian life. The Christian life is largely one of attending to three distinct relationships; your relationship with yourself, your relationship with God and your relationships with others. Why did we place your relationship with yourself ahead of your relationship with God? The truth of the matter is that you can go no deeper with God than you are honest with yourself. The things that you refuse to face in yourself are not available for God to heal. God will not force himself into areas of your life into which you have not invited him – we wish it were otherwise.

Although God will not force his way into uninvited territory, other people will. Those who know us well often feel compelled to "speak into our lives." This usually means they feel the need to confront us about our sin or some character flaw they find annoying. Typically, this usually results in a hurried retreat on our part, but it shouldn't. **Everyone needs those in their life who will lovingly tell them what they are doing wrong.** When we do not have this kind of support we tend to drift into greater and greater self-deception and error. We need people to call us into honesty with ourselves. This is a large part of what it means to be in fellowship with other believers. Leaders are no exception.

**The problem for many itinerant prophets, healers, etc. is that they are not a regular part of a local church fellowship.** They live a largely unaccountable lifestyle. They "blow in, blow up, and blow out." It is sort of like being a rock star on a tour bus. After a few months, deep relationships seem like a fantasy and the shallow relationships seem real. We all need to be a part of a spiritual family that "grounds" us. The local church is that family. Why? Because, just like in a biological family, in the church you do not get to hand-pick your brothers and sisters. God-picked siblings are rarely the ones that we would pick for ourselves. We want the ones that are most "encouraging", the ones that make us most comfortable. This usually means those who will tell us we are doing just fine and have no issues to face - comfortable but dangerous.

Prophets operating outside of a local church lack more than a support group – they also lack personal accountability. They are often true lone rangers who are under no spiritual authority. This is not a lifestyle God has designed for anyone. It is tempting to suggest that prophets can hold each other accountable as peers, but unless they share much time together they do not have the opportunity to observe each other sufficiently to speak from credible observation.

They also have a vested interest in not holding each other accountable. Sadly, a traveling itinerant ministry is based upon maintaining a public image and reputation. Being a whistle blower is bad for business. It is easy to adopt a "don't ask, don't tell" policy with one's peers when to question the integrity of a fellow prophet is bad for the prophetic business in general. This can lead to an unconscious conspiracy of silence. This means that local churches must vet prophets for themselves.

The questions that should be asked of every prophet before welcoming his or her ministry into your church are; "who is your pastor?" and "how much time do you spend together?" followed by "may I call him or her for a reference as to your gift and character?" We find it unusual that many churches insist on background checks for all those who work in their children and youth ministries yet think nothing of having an unvetted prophet come in to "speak the very words of God" into hearts and minds of their adult members.

The character of the prophet is an important criterion to address in judging a prophetic word. Bad character does not guarantee a bad word and good character does not guarantee a good word, but the influence of a prophet goes far beyond the words he speaks. His life also speaks a message and that message matters as much as his words.

## Some questions to consider:

1. When you hear a prophetic word, do you ever ask yourself what theological statement or assumption it may contain? Why or why not?

2. Have you seen examples of slick marketing and greed in a prophet or teacher? What was your reaction?

3. If pride is the problem what do you think is the solution? Do you see the signs of pride in your own life? If so, what are you going to do about it?

4. Do you see a shamelessness about sin in the church today? If so what are we shameless about? Why is it so easy to dismiss sin as unimportant?

5. Have you known a leader who has fallen because of sexual sin? What affect did it have on you or your faith? What can we do to prevent this kind of moral failure?

# Chapter 27:  Character Matters, Even for Prophets

As New Testament believers who choose to move in the prophetic we soon discover that there is a well-worn path to growth in this spiritual gift. Initially we find that prophesying can take place when one is first filled with the Holy Spirit. Such was the case with the believers Paul encountered in Ephesus. Immediately upon being baptized with the Holy Spirit they began to prophesy. (Acts 19:1–7) As we grow in our faith, God calls us to both develop the gifts that He's given us and maintain an exemplary life that will insure that these gifts are not corrupted.

The Apostle Peter addressed the issue of the prophetic in his first letter and encouraged it. (1 Peter 4:11) He challenges those who want to move in this dimension to realize that they have a serious calling. As we have just read he confronts the issue of false prophets and teachers in his day. (2 Peter 2:1–22) After the detailed expose on the dangers of the abuse of these gifts he gives clear instructions that helps us today to avoid these pitfalls. He ends his second epistle with a warning to be on guard against such abuses, but also the exhortation to continue to grow in grace and the knowledge of the Lord. (2 Peter 3:17–18)

Just as we grow in the grace and knowledge of the Lord we also grow in the proper operation and maintenance of the prophetic. God requires diligence from those who desire to move in the spiritual gifts and with it come some prerequisites.

The prophet Jeremiah's life was one lived in a continual state of prophetic growth. From the time, he was a child this call was clearly placed on him. As exalted as his call was, he paid dearly for this gift as he declared God's message. He also sought to live in a way that those who proclaim God's word should live. In the fifteenth chapter of his book we find him recounting his personal path of growth and God's requirements of him to maintain a proper life that would make him an able oracle of the Lord. There are at least four major aspects we can learn from him as we seek to hold forth the word of life in our generation. Each of these four aspects deal with what matters most – our character. Here they are:

## 1. Hunger for God's word

In Jeremiah 15:16 we read the following. **"Your words were found, and I ate them, And Your word was to me the joy and rejoicing of my heart; For I am called by Your name, O LORD God of hosts" (NKJV).** Like Job of old, who considered the words of God's mouth of greater value than his food, Jeremiah had a voracious desire to consume God's Word. (Job 23:12) A good mark of our spiritual maturity is the level of hunger that we have for the scriptures. In our present Christian culture, the amount of Bible knowledge is severely lacking. This can directly be linked to the absence of any sort of consistent time spent reading and meditating in the Bible. Often people find their hunger for entertainment and socialization a serious distraction from the time that might be spent in gaining a deeper knowledge of the scripture. As we have already pointed out surveys and polls done within the Christian community reveal that there is a great absence of consistent Bible reading and study.

What is so striking about Jeremiah's heart is that he delighted in discovering new things in God's Word. He considered it a feast to hear from the Lord. If we want to flow in the prophetic, we need to be constantly feasting on scripture, listening at the door of wisdom so that we might hear what life-giving words God has for others. It's been our experience that those who consistently flow in the prophetic are people who enjoy time searching the scriptures. We've often used what we call the Bible vs. Pizza test when speaking to a group. It goes something like this. You've had a busy day and have come home to discover the following: The

> **A good mark of our spiritual maturity is the level of hunger that we have for the scriptures.**

Bible is open to an important passage of scripture, but also setting nearby is a steaming pizza.

The question is; which will you go for first, the Bible or the Pizza? With a laugh people often say, "I'd eat the pizza while I read the Bible." Great idea, we love pizza and using it in a moment of humor is always helpful in making a point. The point here is to ask, what is the level of hunger for God's word in our lives? If we're going to fully develop the prophetic gift it is crucial to have a serious hunger for the God's Word. God's gives us a wonderful bounty of good things to eat, but this passage in Jeremiah reminds us that God's Word should be our chief desire above all other appetites.

Not only did Jeremiah actively seek to hear from God he also "ate" God's Word. **When we've "eaten" of God's Word we're also full of His Word and therefore have a pool of knowledge from which the Holy Spirit can draw to share with those He desires to speak to.** As we have already said, the use of scripture is one of the ways God communicates a prophetic word to us. The greater the knowledge of scripture, the greater the pool of data the Spirit can draw from.

The prophet Ezekiel tells us how God instructed him to "eat" His Word. In a way, it's very similar to the natural approach to having a meal. First the food is swallowed, then digested and finally absorbed. The World English Bible translates the first three verses of Ezekiel 3 in a way that we believe clearly describes this process. **"He said to me, Son of man, eat that which you find. Eat this scroll, and go, speak to the house of Israel. So, I opened my mouth, and he caused me to eat the scroll. He said to me, Son of man, cause your belly to eat, and fill your bowels with this scroll that I give you. Then I ate it; and it was as sweet as honey in my mouth."**

First, we see that God's Word "tasted" good to the prophet. He delighted in it. Hopefully those desiring to be an oracle for God are first of all those who enjoy the simple pleasure of reading the Bible consistently. Second, God's Word went into his stomach and finally into his bowels. In other words, he absorbed the Word completely. One of the best ways to absorb God's Word is to meditate on it. This sort of meditation is different than some form of New Age exercise. Rather than staring at the proverbial third eye, Bible meditation is more akin to a cow chewing the cud. The process involves the chewing again of the meal. The cow initially bites off a portion of its food, but later retrieves it from one of its four stomachs and crews it again. So, taking time in the scriptures and "chewing" on it over and over allows each word to sink into our heart. This is an important requirement for those who seek to be a mouthpiece for God.

An example from Bob's past:

> "Years ago, when my daughter was young she adopted a hamster. From time to time we would let it out of its cage and it would roam around our home enjoying the hospitality of my family. On one occasion, in an attempt to feed it, I set a small bowl of grain nearby. When I returned to see if the animal was hungry to my shock I found the entire contents of the container gone. My first thought was that the delightful little creature was really hungry. Upon closer examination, I saw that its cheeks were bulging with the complete contents of the dish. It hadn't eaten any of the grain. Instead it had merely used its mouth as a temporary storage place before later depositing it somewhere for future use.
>
> It made me think that sometimes we can be like that hamster. We read God's Word, but don't fully absorb it. That's why the instruction to Ezekiel is so important to us. We need to "fill our spiritual bowels" with God's Word. In other words, meditate on it long enough that it is fully absorbed into our lives before we speak it to others. Those who are truly hungry for God's Word will practice this important daily discipline of Christian living."

## 2. Heartache from brokenness

Jeremiah has been called the weeping prophet. He carried a huge burden for God's glory and wept many tears for a nation that had wandered away from its Lord. He declared to Judah its sins and as a result became a target. In the midst of this time he also wondered if God had abandoned him. We find the account in Jeremiah: **"I did not spend my time in the company of other people, laughing and having a good time. I stayed to myself because I felt obligated to you and because I was filled with anger at what they had done. Why must I continually suffer such painful anguish? Why must I endure the sting of their insults like an incurable wound? Will you let me down when I need you like a brook one goes to for water, but that cannot be relied on?"** Jer. 15:17–18, NET.

Jeremiah paid a heavy price because of his prophetic call. He often stood against the tide of the culture he was in and declared truth to those who were not interested in hearing it. This conflict left him lonely and broken from the ridicule of those who didn't agree with him. In the midst of this crisis he was tempted to doubt that even God had abandoned him. Perhaps most of us will never have to face the sort of rejection and turmoil

> **A broken heart often comes with drawing close to the heart of God. Often to speak for Him you must first experience His sorrow over His people.**

that he faced, but there are lessons to be learned from his journey. A broken heart often comes with drawing close to the heart of God. Often to speak for Him you must first experience His sorrow over His people.

Years ago, a famous minister shared something that has stuck with us. He said something like this, "Don't trust a messenger that doesn't walk with a limp." He implied that as Jacob went through a season of testing and struggling with God that left him with a permanent handicap, so those who have been tested by God and come out with a certain brokenness are people who can be trusted to bring forth a balanced and seasoned word. Too often when God moves through us with a powerful and accurate message the temptation comes to think too highly of ourselves. In some circles, those who move in the prophetic carry with them a subtle but destructive pride. There's no heartache there.

Jeremiah was broken over the sins of God's people. The account in Jeremiah 9:1 records his heartache over what's happened to them as a result of their sin. **"I wish that my head were a well full of water and my eyes were a fountain full of tears! If they were, I could cry day and night for those of my dear people who have been killed."**

Not only was he grieved by their suffering, but he was also upset because of the way God's people had turned away from their Lord. Jeremiah 9:2 records this, **"Oh, that I had in the desert a lodging place for travelers, so that I might leave my people and go away from them; for they are all adulterers, a crowd of unfaithful people"** (NIV). Jeremiah's heart aches because of these things, yet he responds to these issues with genuine concern not in a self-righteous way. **"My sorrow is beyond healing,"** he cries, **"My heart is faint within me!"** The passage in Jer. 8:21 gives this perspective, **"For the brokenness of the daughter of my people I am broken; I mourn, dismay has taken hold of me."**

Here is a man with true compassion for his fellow Jews. This sort of concern should always be at the heart of anyone who brings a word from the Lord. In the world of the New Testament, prophetic words are usually words of encouragement, but sometimes they may include a warning as in the account recorded in Acts 21:10–11. Such messages should always be shared from a place of tenderness and genuine empathy.

Church history is full of examples of men and women of God who brought forth God's Word with tears. Men like George Whitefield are quoted as saying to a gathering "That if you will not weep for your sins then George Whitefield will." He would then throw back his head and pour out his grief in their behalf. D.L. Moody would also cry genuine tears of concern for those he declared the truth to. God has not called us to be gunslingers with Bible verses leaving our mouths like bullets, but rather people who show sincere and humble love for those we bring His message to. **The difference between a prophet and a critic is that the first loves his hearers and the latter does not.**

### 3. Holiness of heart and mind

As Jeremiah went through an inner catharsis over his issues and the Lord's seeming unconcern with his plight, we see God encouraging him with a promise. It appears from the context that Jeremiah's hardships had brought him to a place of doubt concerning God's character. His unbelief has left him in a place of defilement. He allowed his sufferings to cause a spirit of complaint to arise in his heart. The Lord calls him to change his improper mindset and quit his accusations. Even in this great man of God there were things that needed purging, things that kept him impure. So, God instructed him to "clean up his act" so to speak such that he can be used again. This promise also included the caveat that he must remain pure from the polluted lifestyle of his countrymen.

Holiness does not mean living an ascetic life of the denial of pleasure. Serving God in a pure manner will not leave us stiff and miserable people. Holiness creates true happiness of the sort that is evident in the lives and faces of those who walk before God. It's important to note that there are things that are vile and things that are precious. Those of us seeking to be God's messengers need to recognize that we're not to be molded by the vial parts of the culture of the world, but be agents of change within it.

**A prophetic lifestyle is always a counter-culture lifestyle.** Paul in his letter to the church at Corinth called them to live separate lives in the midst of a pagan society. (2 Cor. 6:14–18) They were not called to live in a cloistered community never interacting with unbelievers, but rather through their lifestyle show that they did not indulge in things that were vile. This was something the Apostle Peter encouraged as well. (1 Peter 4:4)

The world today needs a pure prophetic message. Individuals need to hear the truth from those who walk in truth and whose hearts are pure before the Lord. If we're to handle the Word of God then let us make sure our souls are feeding on the precious and not the vile. (Ps. 101:2–4)

In this book, we have shared some of the tragic stories of people who moved powerfully in the prophetic, but in their personal lives they were polluted through a sinful lifestyle. Although they were highly honored, eventually their sin was revealed. Having the ability to speak prophetically does not automatically mean that the person is living a pure life. Nor does living a pure life mean that you will naturally become more successful in developing in the Spirit's gifts. God gave great ability to Samson even though he chose to defile himself not long after his judgeship began. The gifts and calling of God are irrevocable and those who have them sometime fail to live up to them. Such was the case with Samson. He soon was blinded and bound because he failed to keep the vile and the precious separate in his life.

Nothing brings greater reproach and doubt on the prophetic than hypocrisy. The last forty years of church history has been marked by major scandals amongst Christian media personalities and individuals who claim to move in the supernatural. Hopefully such embarrassing humiliations have caused us to expect a higher standard from those who call themselves followers of Christ. As people who seek to hold out God's message to a broken world let us make sure that we allow God to keep us free from the same mistakes that defile our culture. Let's set as a goal not just to speak for a holy God, but behave in a way that properly represents Him. (1 Peter 1:15)

## 4. Helplessly dependent on God

Independence has its virtuous side. Historically it was a rallying cry during the birth of the United States. Yet, when it comes to our relationship with God it is a completely different matter. Throughout scripture God calls on his people to depend on him, lean on him and trust him over and over again. It's no different in the realm of the prophetic. As we've shown earlier in this book, there are times when a word from the Lord becomes as rare as a loaf of bread in the midst of a famine. In fact, the space between the two covenants, Old and New, are separated by four hundred years when God was silent. There were no new, recorded prophetic words until John the Baptist. That very point is important. If God is not speaking let's not assume that He is.

As was mentioned earlier, Jeremiah's message was not very popular in his day. As a result, he faced a lot of resistance, some to the point of physical persecution. Despite his suffering God was with him and as we see, the Lord also promised to defend him. In Jeremiah we read, **"'And I will make you to this people a fortified bronze wall; and they will fight against you, but they shall not prevail against you; For I am with you to save you and deliver you,' says the LORD. 'I will deliver you from the hand of the wicked, and I will redeem you from the grip of the terrible'"** Jer. 15:20–21.

Four times God uses the personal pronoun I. He's trying to make a point. Jeremiah is living in a city besieged by the Babylonian army and is personally besieged by a host of enemies that can't stand to hear what he's prophesying. He desperately needs protection and God promises to give it to him. He's stuck in Jerusalem with no way out and therefore is helpless in his own strength to do anything about his dilemma. In this situation, this is a good thing not a bad thing.

Too often we tend to rely on our own abilities rather than wait for the Holy Spirit. Being a person of the prophetic and the supernatural is, by its very nature, fraught with challenges. We're called to speak for a God that people for the most part can't see or hear. We're not to create some false theatrics like the man behind the curtain in the Wizard of Oz. Instead we're to totally and completely rely on God to speak when He chooses and in the way, He chooses.

The wonderful thing about this issue is that God is speaking today, we just need to listen and speak when He speaks. This of course requires a great degree of patience and confidence. Be assured if we wait with openness He will speak to us so He can speak through us. It's presumptuous to say something when God isn't saying anything. This was His argument with the false prophets of old. They spoke when He wasn't speaking and said what He wasn't saying. Today, as people who live in a New Testament dispensation, we are instructed to carry the supernatural message of God to others. We're also not held to the same standard. If we "miss it", were not going to be stoned. We're to develop in our ability in this realm. Even though there's a great amount of grace in this dimension, we still never want to treat lightly such a wonderful gift.

Jesus told us that it was impossible to accomplish anything of value without him. Yet, He also said that if we depend on Him we can achieve much. (John 15:5) The key here is learning to depend on Him and not run ahead and announce a word as from God when we don't have the assurance that it is. It's so vital that like Jeremiah we are helplessly dependent on God. This is the essence of humility.

We are struck by the amazing patience that men like Evan Roberts, the great revivalist of the Welsh awakening had. Years ago, a wonderful minister that had come to America shared with Bob a story concerning Roberts' ministry that left a lasting impact on him. As the story goes, Roberts had been invited to speak at a great gathering in large meeting place. The host for the meeting was anxiously waiting for Roberts' to appear. There was no sign of the minister as the building filled to capacity.

Finally, the man walked onto the platform and to his surprise he found Evan Roberts' stretched out in prayer on the floor, hidden from sight by a low curtain at the edge of the stage. Relieved he went over to Roberts and said, "Brother Roberts' the building is full now we need to begin the meeting." To which the revivalist replied. "We can't begin yet, God's not here yet." So, the man sat down and Roberts went back to praying. Then after a while the gathering place filled with the awesome presence of God and Roberts' declared, **"We can start now, God's here."**

When he walked to the podium to speak all he needed to do was give an invitation and people streamed from their seats to give their hearts to Christ. God had showed up in power. Evan Roberts knew that this was the key to seeing God move powerfully. We realize this is an anecdotal story, but any that have read the history of the Welsh revival know that awakening was marked by just such moves of the Holy Spirit. That great move of God was also clearly marked by the fact that those who led it acknowledged their total dependence on God's Spirit.

We're called to bring a supernatural declaration in a world that is skeptical and hardened from seeing the failures of those who claimed to speak for God. More than ever we need to depend on God for a clear and powerful word that comes directly from His throne and not from the heart of man. The scriptures clearly encourage us to move in the prophetic gift, but one of the surefire ways of being successful in it is to spend time waiting on God, listening attentively until we hear from Him.

In a day when some cavalierly approach God's prophetic gifts we need to recognize the high calling that accompanies this vocation. These prerequisites that have been mentioned are not laws in themselves, but rather guidelines that we have found that enhance, support and give credence to the life of those who desire to speak for God. Hopefully you'll find them helpful.

## Some questions to consider:

1. In a world of distractions how can we cultivate a hunger for God's word?

2. Jesus tells us that poverty of spirit [a broken heart over the things that grieve God's heart] is a good thing. What about the world today breaks your heart?

3. What is the solution to that Godly pain?

4. How do we cultivate a holy heart and mind? What needs to change in your life to do so?

5. How do we grow in dependence upon God rather than upon our own natural abilities?

# PART SIX:

# FINAL THOUGHTS

# Chapter 28:  What Did We Learn?

A great preacher once said that we need to be reminded far more often than we need to be taught. In that spirit, we want to review the major conclusions that we have reached. Here is our summary of what we have attempted to present:

1. Our Western culture is changing rapidly. We are moving away from a rational scientific worldview toward an inclusion of a spiritual reality of power expressed through ungodly spiritual experience, which includes demons, witches, etc. God has "placed eternity in the heart of man". This means that within each of us, Christian or otherwise, God has created a longing for life to be about more than just our material physical existence.

Although our secular culture is moving in this direction, much of the church remains committed to the Post-Renaissance Western culture created by the union of Humanism and the scientific method. We claim to have a supernatural God, but in practice we define our lives within the framework of the material world. By doing so we miss the opportunity to address our culture's growing fascination with false unchristian spirituality.

2. The Western Church has been significantly influenced by our humanistic culture and remains under the influence of humanistic values together with a materialistic definition of reality. This has resulted in an aversion to the supernatural dimension of our Christian faith. This aversion exists in 4 major areas:

> **a.   Our   historical   humanistic/scientific   tradition.** Humanism has replaced God with man as the object of human study. Science has become the principle means by which reality can be described with the result that phenomena which cannot be scientifically explained are devalued or discarded.

**b. Our theological aversion to the supernatural dimensions of our faith.** Having been influenced against the supernatural, the church developed theologies which rule out a present day supernatural experience. These theologies are of very recent invention and are inconsistent with the teachings of the writer Paul from which they are derived. They do not stand up to good Biblical exegesis.

**c. Our Fear of being deceived by spiritual counterfeits.** The presence of spiritual counterfeits, of which the Bible clearly warns us against, has become a source of fear which has become stronger than our faith in God to lead us to the genuine gifts He has promised. We have effectively "thrown out the baby with the bath water".

**d. Our psychological fear of getting emotionally "carried away".** Consistent with the distrust of experience which cannot be scientifically explained we have tended to distrust or devalue emotional experience. Because God has emotions and because we are created in His image we should expect Him to interact with us emotionally and not just rationally. Despite this fact, we fear being "out of control" and so we avoid any situation which could result in a strong emotional reaction. This tends to rule out experiences of joy, well-being, happiness, passionate worship, etc. The Bible is filled with just such experience, but we also acknowledge that they must be evaluated by God's word applied through reason.

3. Turning to the Bible we examined the phenomena of becoming "born again". We discovered that being born again is a supernatural event. It is not merely a rational decision based on accepting a set of intellectual assumptions. Without the supernatural involvement of the Holy Spirit conversion is impossible.

4. The evidence of the truth of the foregoing is found in the life of Jesus. Jesus' method of evangelism was typically through a supernatural experience. These include words of knowledge, healings, casting out of demons, raising the dead, etc.

5. The same pattern of supernatural evangelism is seen in the life of the early church.

6. The same pattern of supernatural evangelism is seen in the lives of Christians today of which the authors are two.

7. We spend time clarifying and defining the terms commonly used to describe the revelatory gifts of the Holy Spirit; prophecy, words of knowledge, words of wisdom, discerning of spirits, etc.

8. We discovered that the gift of prophecy is the entry level gift into a supernatural lifestyle. It is intended by God to be available and operational in the life of all Christians therefore it is very important.

9. We clarified the difference between Old Testament prophetic ministry and New Testament or "church age" prophetic ministry. This is important because attempting to apply an Old Testament prophetic model to present day church life will prove destructive.

10. Having cleared the garden of the weeds we begin a very practical tutorial in how to recognize God's communication to us. He speaks in many ways which we often fail to recognize. These include: mental images, random unbidden thoughts, unbidden emotions, physical sensations, unbidden Bible scriptures, dreams, and visions and more.

11. Because hearing from God is only half of the work of prophecy we also deal with how and when to present the message we think we have received. A prophetic word improperly delivered is usually rejected and hence a word wasted. We learned how to present a prophetic word in a natural, un-spooky way. We learned how to be natural with the supernatural.

12. Dealing with prophecy is not simply a matter of delivering a word from God, it also matters how we receive a potential prophecy. Our attitudes toward a potential word from God determine our actions with respect to the word which may determine whether or not the word is fulfilled. Important stuff indeed!

13. No discussion of prophetic ministry would be fair or complete without dealing with the abuses to which it is vulnerable. We deal with how to recognize false prophets and false prophesy, which leads us to a discussion of the character prerequisites necessary to maintaining a godly prophetic ministry. Character matters!

14. Finally we conclude with our conclusion: "What did we Learn?"

And here we are, at the very end. We hope and pray that this book will have encouraged you to begin listening to the Holy Spirit in a deeper way. We pray that you will be motivated to risk speaking what you think might be a message from God. We pray that when you are correct you will not give in to the temptation of pride. We also pray that when you are wrong you will not give in to the temptation of discouragement which leads to quitting.

We would love to hear from you with your questions and comments. In this regard, you can reach us through our websites.

Mark and Bob would be happy to connect with you. Just fill out the contact form on the website and they will reply:

*www.Reluctantlysupernatural.com*

Mark Cowper-Smith

   - see Amazon.com & Mark's website for his other books

**www.mark.cowpersmith.org**

Bob Maddux – see Amazon.com for Bob's other books

**www.twilighttrek.com**

# Appendix A

Let's look at the dictionary definitions of the terms and "isms" dealt with in chapter 4.

All definitions are from the Merriam-Webster dictionary

## Humanism

"A doctrine, attitude, or way of life centered on human interests or values; especially: a philosophy that usually rejects supernaturalism and stresses an individual's dignity and worth and capacity for self-realization through reason".

## Scientific Method

"principles and procedures for the systematic pursuit of knowledge involving the recognition and formulation of a problem, the collection of data through observation and experiment, and the formulation and testing of hypotheses".

The scientific method is a method of investigation based on what is termed empirical and measurable evidence. Empirical evidence is only that which can be observed through the five senses. Measurable evidence is that which can be repeatedly quantified in a standardized way.

## The Enlightenment

"A philosophical movement of the 18th century marked by a rejection of traditional social, religious, and political ideas and an emphasis on rationalism".

This movement stressed the belief that science and logic give people more knowledge and understanding than tradition and religion.

## Determinism

"A theory or doctrine that acts of the will, occurrences in nature, or social or psychological phenomena are causally determined by preceding events or natural laws."

 Also defined as:

"The philosophical doctrine that every state of affairs, including every human event, act, and decision, is the inevitable consequence of antecedent states of affairs."

"the doctrine that all events, including human action, are ultimately determined by causes external to the will. Some philosophers have taken determinism to imply that individual human beings have no free will and cannot be held morally responsible for their actions."

## Note from Mark and Bob:

It is worth our time to examine a few of these definitions in greater detail. Determinism tells us that all facts and events [including our human choices, decisions and actions] are the result of natural [think scientific] laws. In other words, humans are nothing more than a collection of cells which interact according to immutable laws of cause and effect such that our feelings and sense of free will is really just a matter of chemical reactions.

The second definition makes the foregoing even clearer. "Every human event, act and decision is the inevitable consequence of a chain of causation that preceded it." To put it another way, you are nothing more than a series of chemical reactions determined thousands of years ago. You are a prisoner of your DNA and your conditioning. To be truly contemporary, you are nothing more than a very sophisticated organic computer.

Although these conclusions seem contrary to our sense of self, individuality and freedom of choice, they are completely consistent logically with Humanism and the scientific method. If

316

all we can be certain of are those "facts" which can be scientifically demonstrated and explained, then we can only be understood by investigating our humanity as the interplay of natural physical cause and effect. Crazy as it may seem, our culture has embraced many of the conclusions that come from seeing ourselves as nothing more than blips in the chain of cause and effect. Logically, these beliefs bring us to our next "ism", being Hedonism.

## Hedonism

"The doctrine that pleasure or happiness is the sole or chief good in life. A way of life based on or suggesting the principles of hedonism."

As well defined as: "the pursuit of pleasure; sensual self-indulgence."

"synonyms: self-indulgence, pleasure-seeking, self-gratification, lotus-eating, sybaritism;"

"the ethical theory that pleasure (in the sense of the satisfaction of desires) is the highest good and proper aim of human life."

## Materialism

1. a) theory that physical matter is the only or fundamental reality and that all being and processes and phenomena can be explained as manifestations or results of matter - scientific materialism.
    b) doctrine that the only or the highest values or objectives lie in material well-being and in the furtherance of material progress
    c) doctrine that economic or social change is materially caused

2. preoccupation with or stress upon material rather than intellectual or spiritual things

# Appendix B

American Bible Society Survey 2016 by Barna Group Research. Frequency of Bible reading by Adults

"One News Now" article August 28, 2016 by Michael Haverluck, quoting a Barna group research study of teenage Bible reading frequency.

Statista – The Statistics Portal – January 2015 - study of the duration of Bible reading per incident of reading.

http://www.cnn.com/2016/06/30/health/americans-screen-time-nielsen/

# Footnotes:

[1] Hamilton Camp, *Paths of Victory*, 1964.
[2] Ibid.
[3] Gordon D. Fee, The First Epistle to The Corinthians (The New International Commentary on the New Testament) (Grand Rapids: Eerdmans, 1987), 651–652.

[4] C.S. Lewis, Letters to Malcolm: Chiefly on Prayer (San Diego: Harvest, 1964), 92–93.

[5] CS Lewis, Mere Christianity, [Zondervan, 2001], 136

[6] Peter Wagner, Your Church Can Grow (Regal Books, 1976), 75–76. See also, Peter Wagner, Your Spiritual Gifts Can Help Your Church Grow (Regal Books, 1976),90-92

[7] Mark Cowper, Is God Religious? If not, why are we? [2014, Available at Amazon.com]

# ABOUT THE AUTHORS

Mark Cowper-Smith was a lawyer in Canada for many years. As a result of a radical conversion to Christ, he began to teach the Bible wherever and whenever he was asked. In 1988 a group of people requested Mark to plant a church. The church experienced very rapid growth as well as severe trials. Mark and his wife Shell have traveled and ministered at churches in 11 countries. They have a heart to see the Church powerfully filled with the love of the Father and released to minister that love in power. Mark's principle gifts are teaching and prophecy. Mark and Shell are currently on staff at a local church.

Bob Maddux, has been in full-time ministry since 1968. He is the founding pastor of Trinity San Diego, formerly The Connection and Christian Life Assembly in Poway, California a suburb of San Diego, where he has served as senior pastor from 1988 to 2015. Under his leadership the church has had local and international impact through its various outreaches. One example is Project Compassion, (www.projectcompassion.org), which he co-founded in 1992. Besides his Pastoral work he has ministered on five continents training national pastors and doing evangelistic outreaches. In 1976, he founded Pleasant Valley School of Ministry which became Capital Bible College in Sacramento and served as its president for nine years. In 1979, he founded and directed Jesus West Coast, a large annual mission festival attended yearly by thousands and credited with recruiting many into missions. Bob has authored the Angel award winning book Fantasy Explosion, and has produced and directed various films and documentaries including the award winning Mzungu. He's written 4 other books. He and his wife, Claudia, have been married since 1969. They have 3 married children and 6 grand-children.

## Connect:

Mark and Bob would be happy to connect with you. Just fill out the contact form on the website and they will reply:

*www.Reluctantlysupernatural.com*

Mark Cowper-Smith

www.mark.cowpersmith.org

Bob Maddux

www.twilighttrek.com

## Help spread the word for *Reluctantly Supernatural:*

1. Give a review of the book on Amazon.

2. Follow Reluctantly Supernatural Facebook page and YouTube channel.

3. Book a workshop or Q&A time for your church or group.